SOLVE YOUR CHILD'S SCHOOL-RELATED PROBLEMS

Solve Your Child's School-Related Problems

National Association of School Psychologists

EDITED BY MICHAEL MARTIN
AND CYNTHIA WALTMAN-GREENWOOD,
WITH PAMELA PATRICK NOVOTNY
PRODUCED BY THE PHILIP LIEF GROUP, INC.

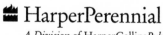 HarperPerennial

A Division of HarperCollins*Publishers*

Children's behaviors vary from individual to individual and from situation to situation. This book is not intended as a substitute for the professional advice of your school psychologist, educator or other appropriate professional, particularly because new research and strategies are constantly being developed. The reader should consult with one of these specialists in matters relating to your concerns about your child.

HarperCollins books may be purchased for educational, business, or sales promotional use. For information, please write: Special Markets Department, HarperCollins Publishers, Inc., 10 East 53rd Street, New York, NY 10022.

FIRST EDITION

Library of Congress Cataloging-in-Publication Data

Solve your child's school-related problems / National Association of School Psychologists : edited by
    Michael Martin and Cynthia Waltman-Greenwood, with Pamela Patrick Novotny : produced by the
        Philip Lief Group, Inc.
            p.   cm.
        Includes bibliographical references.
        ISBN 0-06-273366-4 (pb : alk. paper)
        1. Learning, Psychology of.   2. Home and school—United States.   3. Education—Parent
    participation—United States.   4. Behavior modification.   I. Martin, Michael, 1994–   .
    II. Waltman-Greenwood, Cynthia.   III. Novonty, Pamela Patrick.   IV. National Association of School
    Psychologists.   V. Philip Lief Group.
    LB1060.S676   1995
    370.15'23—dc20   95-20286

95 96 97 98 99 ❖/RRD 10 9 8 7 6 5 4 3 2 1

CONTENTS

PART II—YOUR CHILD'S SCHOOL BEHAVIORS

FOREWORD

Over the past ten years, the National Association of School Psychologists has published many books full of extremely valuable information to help practicing school psychologists help children, teachers, and families to adjust to school and to learn well.

While the information was vital to school psychologists, it wasn't written in language accessible to parents, nor did it offer parents hands-on strategies that could show them how to help their own children.

Solve Your Child's School-Related Problems presents our effort to take this material, select the topics we believe parents would most like to know about, and present it in an accessible, user-friendly style.

The NASP books, from which the material for this book was obtained, are listed below. Hundreds of authors contributed to them, and their work represents the most current research and thinking about how to most effectively serve the needs of children.

If you find that one of the topics in *Solve Your Child's School-Related Problems* is of particular interest to you and you'd like more information, please contact the school psychologist at your child's school; he or she will be happy to discuss these issues in more detail with you.

PREFACE

The National Association of School Psychologists has been helping children succeed, both academically and personally, for over 25 years. We recognize that if children are to do their best, educators and parents must work as a team. This link between home and school is essential if students are to grow up to be productive, caring, and responsible citizens.

Research shows that you really can make a difference in your child's education. Parental involvement leads to more positive attitudes and behavior, long-term achievement gains, better attendance, higher grades, and better test scores. Indeed, parental involvement in a child's education has been proven to have a greater impact than income or family background.

This is why I am so excited about *Solve Your Child's School-Related Problems*, the first book ever written expressly for the use of parents. It contains the very latest in research-based thinking on how you can help your child succeed in his or her most important career—that of student.

Susan Safranski
1994–1995 NASP President

ACKNOWLEDGMENTS

We wish to acknowledge the contributions of the many individuals who were so helpful and supportive during the preparation of this book: first, our graduate students who spent so much time assisting us with additional research for this book: Paula Pawlowski, Michelle Stallworth, and Walter Young; and we thank our secretary, Tanya Jones, for all her assistance.

The following individuals provided us with valuable information and advice: Peg Dawson, David C. Arnold, Frank Stuart, Paul W. Cascella, and Ralph Suffolk. We particularly want to thank C. Paul Mendez, Director of Communications for NASP, and Leslie Hale, chair of the NASP Publications Board, for their unfailing support.

And finally, we want to express our deep appreciation to our writer, Pam Novotny, who so effectively translated all our notes and material into the warm and readable document that this has become.

MICHAEL MARTIN, PH.D., NCSP

CYNTHIA WALTMAN-GREENWOOD, PH.D., NCSP

SOUTHERN CONNECTICUT STATE UNIVERSITY

OCTOBER 1994

INTRODUCTION:
HERE'S THE FIRST STEP...

"Every evening it's the same story: Matthew says he'll do his homework, but then he procrastinates until it's bedtime, and we have a big fight. I've run out of ideas; what can I do to help him develop the responsibility to get his homework done?"

"Eva came home from the first day of fourth grade in tears. She says she hates her teacher. I've tried talking with Eva but it's no use; she really is unhappy with this teacher. I've never been one to meddle in my children's school lives, and I'm afraid if I talk to someone at school about this, I'll be labeled a troublemaker. On the other hand, I can't stand to see Eva so unhappy either. I just don't know what to do."

WHO NEEDS HELP WITH THEIR CHILD'S SCHOOL BEHAVIOR?

Even the most involved, caring parent is sometimes stymied about how to handle their child's school problems: a son who fights you tooth and nail over every math problem on his homework assignments, a daughter who hates her teacher. And that's not all: there's the bully on the playground, the fleeting motivation of your middle schooler, the drug culture confronting your high schooler, and on and on.

No parent instantly knows what to do about every problem that comes up for every child, and those moments of helplessness can feel terrible. Add to that a sometimes daunting school hierarchy, and even the most competent parent can feel at a loss as to how to both help her child and navigate unfamiliar bureaucratic waters. For all your commitment to guide and assist your child, there's not much you can do unless you have the proper tools.

The NASP Handbook provides those tools. For the past 25 years, the National Association of School Psychologists, the largest organized body in the world representing school psychology, has been instrumental in setting professional and ethical standards for school psychologists throughout the United States. When you pick up tips from the NASP Handbook, you can feel confident you are tapping in to the most current thinking from the most prominent school psychologists in the field.

UNDERSTANDING EXPECTATIONS AND REALITY

Expert thinking isn't all the NASP Handbook offers. The focus is on you, too—on how you see yourself, how you perceive the world of education, and how you see your child.

Have you ever reassured your child that just doing her best is all you can expect, then found yourself focusing on the misspelled word instead of the 95 percent she got on her spelling test? Do you find yourself feeling outraged that your child's first-grade teacher doesn't recognize your child as gifted when you are sure he is? Or do you assume your child will have a hard time with math because it wasn't your favorite subject in school, and find yourself subtly steering her away from math-oriented careers or subjects?

Issues like these all have to do with the

expectations we have for our children, and how sometimes, those expectations don't line up with who our children really are or what they are really capable of. Winding like a golden thread through *Solve Your Child's School-Related Problems* is one of the most important things you can learn about your child's school behavior: before helping your children to learn better or to be happier at school, you, the parent, must be able to see your child for who she is. It's the key to keeping expectations in line with reality. That may sound easy, but it can be extremely difficult to abandon a cherished vision of your child as a chemistry whiz, class president, or even as a better reader than she really can be.

On a smaller scale, keeping our expectations in their place means remembering that just like grown-ups, no child has a perfectly smooth school life. Children have good days and bad, easy months and tough ones, school terms that breeze by and others that seem never-ending, constantly stirred up with one small crisis after another. While it's good to be reasonably vigilant about how school is going for your child, try to remember that bad days are just part of the mix for everyone. So are tough school years when your child has to work with that teacher he doesn't particularly like.

Keep in mind too, that some school children find certain developmental stages more difficult than others. Remember when your child was teething and you talked to other parents about the process? For some infants, every new tooth was an exercise in torture for them and their parents. Others had teeth that appeared like pearly surprises, without a whimper. And plenty of other babies fell somewhere in between, crying all night for that incisor, and then surprising everyone with a hefty, apparently painlessly-acquired molar. You probably learned then that no matter what your expectations, your child would react in her unique way.

And so it may be for your child in school when you look at how he or she deals with situations individually. Just when your expectation is that your child will lose his temper and his confidence because he got that stern fifth-grade teacher you were hoping he wouldn't, your child tells you he likes her because she has clear rules. Just when your expectation was that second grade would be smooth sailing because first grade was such a snap for your child, she tells you she hates math, can't do it, and doesn't want to try any more.

Then there are your expectations for your child compared to other children. Keep in mind that in any classroom there is at least a one-year, and sometimes as much as two years', difference in age between children. Take into account your child's age if you—or she—compares her work to that of others in her class, particularly in the early grades when the most basic things, like motor development or social maturity, for example, may simply not be as far along for a younger child or may appear vastly advanced for a child as much as two years older.

And take into account that everyone learns differently: some children flourish in an open environment with plenty of freedom to move from one activity or topic to another at their own pace, and some need the structure and direction that a traditional classroom offers. Some children learn to read quickly and painlessly using a method called Whole Language Learning, and for others, nothing makes sense until they learn to sound out words using phonics. If you don't know how your child learns best, go back to that golden thread: see her for who she is and observe how she reacts to different teaching methods and environments.

Just as learning styles differ, so abilities differ from child to child. That is the key issue teachers address every day in the classroom, and it is the key issue we address in this book: The more clearly you see your child and his or her abilities, the more real help you'll be able to offer.

You may find that *Solve Your Child's School-Related Problems* not only gives you ideas and activities to help your child through some tough times, but it may also challenge you to think more deeply and clearly than you have about your expectations, how you see the educational process, and how you see your child.

HOW TO USE THIS BOOK

Solve Your Child's School-Related Problems is divided into two parts:

Part I demystifies the working of the school system and offers a crash course in understanding and coping with the common, yet far-reaching issues every parent faces at least once in their child's life: from whether an incident or issue will appear permanently on a child's school records, to handling parent-teacher conflicts, to dealing with a child who needs special education. No matter whether your child attends a small neighborhood elementary school down the block, or a large regional high school across town, once those doors close behind him, it's easy to feel that your child is in a foreign land, where you neither speak the language nor know the rules.

Part I of *Solve Your Child's School-Related Problems* opens those doors and lets you in on how you can work within the school system to help your child. We describe systems as they exist in most public schools; many private schools have similar hierarchies, although they are not necessarily subject to the same state and federal regulations. But no matter whether your child attends public or private school, in Part I we focus on the big issues in a broad way that we think will be easily translated between the two. This broad view also prepares you to deal with the individual problems and concerns discussed in Part II.

Part II topics apply to all students, no matter what kind of school they attend. Topics are arranged alphabetically, and recurring subheads used in each topic put information at your fingertips. For example, in each topic the subheads will guide you through:

What We Know Now—A summary of the best studies, research, and conclusions reached by school psychologists.

When Should I Be Concerned?—A clear listing and explanation of red flags in your child's behavior that may alert you to more serious behavior issues and the possibility that you or your child may need help from a professional.

What Can I Do to Help?—Solutions and approaches you can use at home, or in collaboration with your child's teacher or school psychologist, to make a difference in your child's behavior.

What Will a Professional Do?—Details of what the school psychologist, and in some cases, other school personnel such as reading or speech-language pathologists will do for your child and why.

Last, the Appendices tie everything together by offering parents the next step in information. Appendix A lists privileges to offer and take away, which we call motivators, and how to use them to help change your child's behaviors. Appendix B offers a comprehensive listing of parent-oriented groups and organizations. Appendix C provides information on helping children through crises, and Appendix D gives the names and purposes of typical tests used by school psychologists, including some representative questions."

How do you know when to jump in to your child's school life with both feet? When do you offer words of guidance and then step back to let your child figure out a few things for himself? When and how can you work effectively with school personnel for your child's benefit? *Solve Your Child's School-Related Problems* puts the tools in your hands to do all this and more. Page through the book and see how easily accessible, useful information can take the guesswork out of shepherding your child through school.

1

YOUR CHILD'S SCHOOL

CHAPTER 1

Know Your School's Personnel

WHO THEY ARE AND HOW YOU CAN WORK WITH THEM TO SOLVE PROBLEMS AND PREVENT CRISES

Understanding who is responsible for what in your child's school system is key to knowing where to go for help when you need it.

Ever since the first statewide school system was established in Pennsylvania in 1834, school districts have been set up and run in pretty much the same fashion: a centralized administration stands in the middle between government courts and agencies which allocate funds to, rule on, and in some cases set policy for education on the one hand; and the teachers, parents, and students of individual schools on the other.

EDUCATIONAL HIERARCHY

❏ Federal Courts
❏ Congress
❏ Federal Department of Education
❏ State Courts
❏ State Legislatures
❏ State Department of Education
❏ Local School Boards
❏ Superintendent/Assistant Superintendents
❏ Principals/Assistant Principals/Directors of Special Education or Pupil Services
❏ Teachers and Support Professionals
❏ Parents and Community Residents and Students

School districts are defined differently in different areas; they can be set up as urban, suburban, rural, community, countywide, or regional districts. And while the names of the departments and administrators within them may vary from one district to another, the hierarchy is the same.

The list above shows that what happens at your neighborhood school is colored by what happens at the highest levels, beginning with the federal courts, and what happens at the bottom levels, meaning parent, student, and community influence. Here is what each of them does for education:

❏ *Federal Courts, Congress, and the Federal Department of Education:* Traditionally, the courts (U.S. district courts, courts of appeal, and the Supreme Court) do not set education policy, but they do rule on the legality—or the illegality—of existing policies that concern the constitutional and civil rights of children, parents, or school personnel. Congress and the Federal Department of Education try to be responsive to pressure for change in education with legislation and programs or incentives that help guarantee the right of all children to equal educational opportunities. They leave most of the power to enact broad school policy to the states, their courts, and legislatures.

❏ *State Departments of Education:* Most states have a department that is the education policy-making body for the state. State legislatures usually consult with this body, which conducts the day-to-day business of education for the state's schools, including such operations as budgeting and accounting, personnel and labor relations, equal education services, and curriculum and research. In larger states, these jobs may be divided up regionally. Most states mandate curriculum guidelines describing what must be taught in each grade, but they vary as to how much flexibility they give local boards of education in carrying those out—in choosing textbooks and teaching methods, for example.

State education departments also certify teachers and other school personnel, define the age parameters for compulsory school attendance, set high school graduation requirements, and decide the length of the school year.

At the center of the hierarchy is your local administration. Even though efforts beginning in the 1980s toward decentralization of school administrations have brought about change in some districts, most local districts will look much like the actual suburban Connecticut school district described in the chart below.

Positions noted on the flow chart most likely to be included in most districts are:

School board or committee: School boards are almost always made up of elected citizens whose job it is to oversee the school administrators for the schools in their district. Usually these members are unpaid, and terms of office are usually two or four years.

Most importantly, the school board serves as the district's policy-setter and goal-setter, within state guidelines. The board can decide how money is raised and allocated for schools and programs, and can decide whether new schools are needed or old schools should be closed. It works with the superintendent, both giving him direction and using him as a con-

Sample Chart of Organization

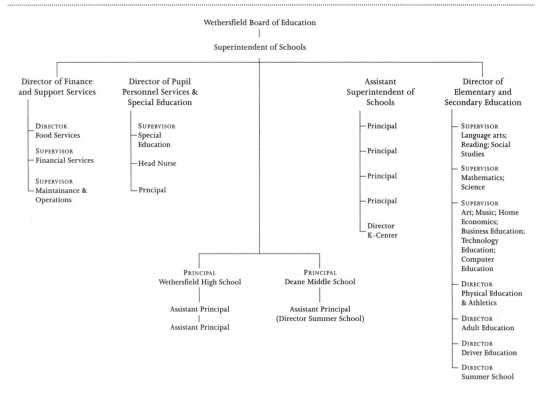

sultant in decision making. The school board is also charged with responding to questions and concerns raised by parents, students, and teachers.

❒ *Superintendent and assistant superintendents:* Most school superintendents are hired by the local board of education. He or she is the plant manager for the school district, and is charged with hiring school staff and overseeing the district's daily operations, from business decisions and program management to curriculum planning. All personnel in the school district are ultimately answerable to the superintendent.

The superintendent is also responsible for seeing that the district meets goals set for it by the state and by the school board.

❒ *Directors of Special Education or Pupil Personnel Services:* They oversee professionals providing special education and related services. School psychologists, social workers, and coordinators of gifted programs, for example, all report to this director.

❒ *Directors of Curriculum:* If you live in a large school district, there may be one or several directors of curriculum. They are responsible for making sure the state and local curriculum guidelines are being met by working with teachers on selecting appropriate curricula and evaluating new curriculum ideas.

❒ *Principals:* These are the administrators with whom you, as parents, are likely to have the most contact. Because they are in charge of their own schools, they define those schools through their personality and educational philosophy, although they are also responsible for carrying out school board policies. Many have been, and sometimes still are, teachers themselves, so they are likely to have a good understanding of classroom issues. In most districts, the principal makes teaching assignments, evaluates teachers, recruits and hires other

classroom help, and directs and oversees the implementation of the school's curriculum. The principal is also responsible for school-building maintenance and security, and for financial and accounting issues along with preparing and submitting school budgets. Usually, principals are hired and assigned by the superintendent and the board of education.

In large schools, a principal may have one or more assistants assigned to specific areas, such as educational services (which might include assigning classroom space, scheduling classes, overseeing registration, and directing home study programs), student services (which might include overseeing personnel in specialized areas like special education, along with the school psychologist, school counselors, social worker, and school nurse), or administrative services (which might include coordinating student teachers, writing the faculty handbook, supervising bookkeeping and school expenditures, and submitting reports to state agencies on school goals and student achievement).

❒ *Teachers—Regular and Special Education:* These are the people who create the day-to-day educational experience for your child. In most schools teachers operate fairly independently in their own classrooms, although they always have to follow the curriculum guidelines of their district as well as observe the philosophy of their principal. Special education teachers always have to follow the Individualized Education Program developed for children in their classes. While the principal is the administrator to whom you're likely to have greatest access, the teacher should always be the first resource you turn to, the first educator you contact for help with your child.

❒ *Support professionals:* These are a specialized

group whose members will vary from school to school. In smaller districts, one professional may work in several schools. These positions usually fall under a Director of Special Education or of Pupil Personnel Services. In a small school system, they would be under an assistant superintendent. The most common support professionals you're likely to find are:

■ School Psychologist: These psychologists help teachers, parents, and students to understand, prevent, and solve problems, and promote mental health and effective environments for learning. They are called on to:

1 work with people from preschool age through adolescence and with teachers, parents, and their families;

2 consult with educators, parents, and families about learning, social, and behavior problems;

3 help others better understand child development and how it relates to learning and behavior;

4 assess with others on a team a child's learning aptitudes, academic skill, social skills, personality, and emotional development;

5 help assess whether a child qualifies for special education;

6 solve conflicts and problems related to learning;

7 provide individual and group counseling, social skills training, crisis intervention, behavior management, and other interventions;

8 conduct research to evaluate the effectiveness of academic programs, behavior management procedures, and other services provided in the school;

9 and to act as a liason with outside psychological resources and agencies.

■ School Counselor: Usually found in middle and secondary schools more often than in elementary schools, school counselors focus on the academic and social development of your child. School counselors provide students with appropriate information about educational and career opportunities after high school, and monitor each student's achievement with reference to that student's ability. She also assists with college decisions and compiles and interprets data from standardized tests. She also provides activities and direction for students in learning how to make decisions in both academic and personal matters.

■ School Nurse: In a large district, there may be a head nurse who supervises nurses at individual schools. The nursing office in general is responsible for coordinating your school's vision, hearing, and—in some districts—scoliosis (curvature of the spine) screening programs, and for following up to be sure students in specified grades have had the required physical examinations. She will also work on prevention and control of communicable diseases, follow-up on health-related absences, and maintain first aid facilities in each school. Of course, the school nurse also deals with day-to-day medical concerns of students and is responsible for administering medication to your child during the school day.

■ Reading Consultant: The consultant oversees reading programs in the system, organizes remedial services and classroom programming, and provides guidelines for reading curricula.

■ Speech-Language Pathologist: This person

identifies speech and language disorders through screening and diagnostic evaluations, provides clinical and educational services to those students who need them, to help them with both academics and interpersonal communication. The speech-language pathologist also consults with parents and teachers of students with speech and language disorders so as to develop and plan activities to meet classroom goals and so as to develop communication skills of all children in the classroom. She may also propose to modify or add to the curriculum to improve student performance, and, in the early grades (K–2), she may visit classrooms to work with the whole class on language development. You don't have to wait until your child is in school to contact the school's speech-language pathologist.

■ School Social Worker: This person may act as a liason between school, family, and other community agencies in nurturing a child's normal growth and development. Social workers may also plan and implement counseling for referred students and parents when appropriate and provide support and consulting services to teachers and other staff.

WHOM DO YOU ASK?

When your child is having a problem, the last thing you want to do is struggle to figure out whom to contact first. The individual behaviors in Part II should go a long way toward letting you know where to find help in specific situations. You can also use the position descriptions above and the list below as further guides. Of course, some schools will have different names for some positions, or slightly different duties for them. Some schools may not have a suggested position, such as assistant principal. In any case, it shouldn't be difficult for you to make the necessary adjustments (for example, contacting the principal if your school doesn't have an assistant principal) to the following list to get you pointed in the right direction.

If your question is about:	Contact:
Absences	teacher, asst. principal, principal
Academic credit requirements	school counselor, asst. principal
Activities—student	the sponsor, a teacher
Admissions	school counselor, registrar, asst. principal
Advanced Placement	school counselor, teacher
Behavior issues	teacher, school counselor, school psychologist
Board of Education	board member, principal
Calendar	office secretary, principal
Changing class schedule	school counselor, asst. principal
Classroom issues	teacher, school psychologist
Clubs	the sponsor, a teacher
College Planning	school counselor, asst. principal

If your question is about: (cont.)

	Contact:
Community Programs	school psychologist, social worker
Counseling, academic	school counselor, teacher
Counseling, personal	school counselor, school psychologist, social worker
Curriculum	teacher, principal
Deficiency or Demerit Notes	asst. principal, principal
[a] Department	chairperson, teacher
Discipline/Detention	teacher, asst. principal, principal
Drop-out Prevention	school counselor, social worker
Drug Education	school counselor, social worker
Emergency Response Info	principal and crisis intervention team
Exams (semester)	teacher
Exams (regular tests)	teacher
Field Trips	teacher, principal
Grading Guidelines	teacher, principal
Graduation Requirements	school counselor, asst. principal
Grievances	teacher, principal
Honor Roll	teacher, asst. principal
Immunization Forms	school nurse
Make-Up Work	teacher
Parent Committees	PTO/PTA, principal
Parent Conferences	teacher, principal
Parent-Teacher Organization	PTO/PTA, teacher
Peer Counseling	school counselor, school psychologist, social worker
Philosophy of School	teacher, principal
Report Cards	teacher, principal
Retention	teacher, school counselor, school psychologist, principal
Special Education	teacher, school counselor, principal
Standardized Testing	school counselor, principal

CHAPTER 2

A Parent's Primer

FACTS ABOUT KEY ISSUES

As a parent, there are not many things you can predict, but we can bet that before your child is out of school, you will be faced with questions you don't know the answer to, such as:

❏ Will tracking harm or help my child?
❏ How can I best deal with a difficult teacher?
❏ Can I be sure my child will get the special education he needs?

The issues that can affect your child are as many and as diverse as there are children. Of course, no one could lay out all the perfect answers for you ahead of time. But it will help for you to have some fundamental facts about the most basic of these issues, so that if they do apply to you and your child at some time, you'll at least know where to start as you make important decisions for your child.

In this section you'll find overviews of six basic issues:

❏ Parent/Teacher Communication
❏ Tracking
❏ Standardized Group Tests
❏ Special Education
❏ School Records and Your Access to Them
❏ School Entry Decisions

PARENT/TEACHER COMMUNICATION

In survey after survey, parents and teachers agree that communication between home and school is a good thing for the children. Research bears this out. Studies have shown that when parents are involved in their child's education, many good things happen. Among them:

❏ Student achievement is higher; students earn higher grades, do better on tests, and have better long-term academic achievement. This is particularly true when parents become involved while their children are young.
❏ Student attendance, attitudes about school, maturation, self-concept, and behavior all improve when parents are involved with school.
❏ Educational programs and schools themselves become more effective when parents are involved.

While almost no one would question the value of parent involvement, almost everyone would define it differently. In some schools, parent involvement means baking cookies for class parties. In others it means weekly tutoring in the classroom, correcting papers for the teacher, and driving on field trips. On the other hand, if you ask most teachers, parent involvement means attending conferences; if you ask many parents, it means offering input on curriculum decisions.

And therein lies the problem: involvement which is welcomed by teachers is not always what the parent is willing or able to offer. There are no hard and fast rules about how to live with that or how to change that. But through effective communication, you can learn how to make your school's practices and policies about parent involvement work for you and your child year by year with each new teacher.

Experience has shown us that there are three key steps you can take toward establishing a relationship with your child's teacher.

1 The first step is for you to see your role clearly as the primary and the strongest advocate for your child and her right to an education. Some parents shy away from speaking up to teachers and administrators because they fear they will be labeled as troublemakers. No one can make promises about labels, but when your child's welfare is at stake, whatever label you may be given needs to be relegated to the bottom of the list of important issues. That is not to say that you should be obnoxious or overbearing in your demands, or that you should blindly defend your child's inappropriate behavior no matter what the consequences. It is to say that you should think carefully about your rightful role as your child's advocate and be clear about discerning her needs, presenting them to educators as you see them, and balancing those with the realities of school life.

2 The next step is to think about what that term, "parent involvement" means to you. Research suggests that the most effective parent involvement is an attitude, not a particular activity, and that it occurs when parents and teachers share common goals and responsibilities, when they see themselves as equals, and when they both contribute to the child's education. The box below shows what parents and professionals in one study agreed were some of the most important factors that make up this attitude.

The ability to seek a partnership with your child's teacher grows out of what you do with

A Strong Parent–Teacher Partnership Depends On . . .

- ❏ Trust
- ❏ Mutual Respect
- ❏ Open Communication
- ❏ Honesty
- ❏ Active Listening
- ❏ Openness
- ❏ Flexibility
- ❏ Caring
- ❏ Understanding
- ❏ Shared Responsibility
- ❏ Full Disclosure of Information

your child at home that tells her school and learning are important. To have a strong home curriculum you should:

❏ have conversations with your child about everyday events,

❏ encourage and discuss leisure reading,

❏ monitor television watching and analyze with your child programs you do watch,

❏ express affection,

❏ have an interest in your child's academic and personal growth,

❏ and delay immediate gratification sometimes in favor of long-term goals. This, after all, is what is often required of children in the classroom. Even though a child must wait many weeks or even months for a reward, such as a final grade in a class, she must nevertheless continue to work towards the goal.

3 And the third step is to nurture in yourself a feeling of personal responsibility for helping your child gain knowledge and literacy skills, for communicating regularly with school personnel, and for being involved in school functions. It's this kind of on-the-ground follow-up that will push you to sit down with your child and have her review her homework assignments with you, instead of asking her at bedtime if her homework is done. It's this kind of follow-up that will ensure that you do have a solid base of communication with your child's teacher and that you are as involved as your life allows in your child's school, and ultimately, in your child's success at school.

HOW TO TALK TO A TEACHER

Perhaps the best thing you can do to start off in a positive way with your child's teacher is to contact her before your child has a problem. Experience has shown that when there is little or no communication between teacher and parent, each party is likely to misinterpret the others' silence as either a lack of concern for the child or as a sign that everything is just fine. Then, when the first parent-teacher contact comes, whoever gets the call may feel they are in an adversarial position.

It doesn't have to be that way. Early in the school year, perhaps during the first few weeks of school (after some of the newness has worn off and you and your child have settled into a comfortable routine), contact the teacher and make an appointment to see her for a short, maybe a 15-minute after-school meeting. Even if you are already well into the school year, you can still ask for a get-to-know-you meeting.

During this meeting you can:

❏ tell the teacher a little about yourself and ways in which you are able to help out—even if it is simply making sure your child has a study area and homework help at home.
❏ ask the teacher about her approach to this grade level and her expectations and goals for the class as a whole. It may be too early for her to have clear goals for individual children.
❏ talk to her about specific goals you may have for your child this school year. While you need to be open and honest with her, you will want to be judicious about not overemphasizing or labeling your child because of difficulties he may have had—and resolved—last year.

As your time allows, you can also get to know the teacher better, and let her get to know you, by volunteering to help with class projects or class trips, and by becoming an active member in the school PTA.

Perhaps you're already concerned about your child's behavior, and you know you need to call the teacher, but don't know quite what to say or how to handle the conversation in a positive, constructive manner. No matter who makes the first call, parent or teacher, there are some typical responses you can be prepared to hear—or to try not to make. They are:

❏ anger: It's not uncommon for the surprise of a negative phone call to make the recipient angry.
❏ defensiveness: It's normal for most people to want to protect their role. The teacher may feel defensive about her teaching abilities or the way she handles the class; the parent may feel defensive about his parenting abilities.
❏ denial: Some people automatically want to deny the fact that problems may exist, or construct a less threatening scenario: "Maybe he's just bored," or "We never see that behavior at home."
❏ blaming: Trying to shift the responsibility, suggesting a solution—or a cause—too quickly, saying things like, "My husband and I are separated," or "I was just like that when I was a kid."

❏ disbelief or doubting: Sometimes when the issue raised is too overwhelming for the person to accept, she will say she doesn't perceive the problem as valid, with comments like, "Isn't this a phase all children go through?" or "She couldn't have been referring to anything that happened in my class."

The box (opposite) gives you some ideas for how to handle these responses in a more constructive way.

The bottom line in developing a working partnership with the teacher is that you must be able to talk openly enough to know that you agree on your child's basic nature. If you are "seeing" the same child, you can work together for your child's good. If, despite your best efforts, the child the teacher describes is nothing like the child you know, then it's time to contact a third party—perhaps the school psychologist—to help you figure out what to do next.

PLANNING YOUR PARENT-TEACHER CONFERENCE

Whether you are scheduled to see the teacher because of a problem you or she called about, or you know you'll be there for the regularly scheduled parent-teacher conference, it's a good idea to plan for what you need to know and want to say during the meeting.

First, you should review the material you have at home, and if you are missing some of the items on the following list, do your best to get them together before your meeting:

❏ Go through the school file you have at home for your child. If you don't have one, it will help you to be organized about dealing with school issues if you start one before you attend the conference. It should contain all previous report cards, immunization records, and tests or homework papers you want to save, along with any correspondence you have with teachers or the principal.

❏ Review whatever correspondence you have from the school.

❏ Go over the student handbook, especially if you are seeing the teacher about a behavior problem.

Once you have set up or reviewed the file, use it to help you make a list of questions. When you attend the conference, bring materials from the file (homework papers, tests, correspondence) you'd like to talk about, and a pencil and paper or notebook for taking notes.

Here's a sample list of questions to ask at a conference:

❏ Is my child performing at grade level in math? reading? writing? other courses?

❏ Has my child taken achievement, intelligence, or aptitude tests in the past year?

❏ What do the scores mean?

❏ Does my child have strengths and weaknesses in major subject areas that I don't know about?

❏ How would you describe my child's learning style?

❏ Does my child need special help in any subject? in social adjustment? in learning skills?

❏ Would you recommend referral to school specialists such as school psychologist, speech-language pathologist, or social worker?

❏ Has my child regularly completed classwork?

❏ Has my child regularly completed assigned homework?

❏ Has my child regularly attended classes?

❏ Does my child get along well with teachers and students?

❏ What can we be doing at home to better support my child's learning?

What to Say Instead . . .

TEACHER SAYS . . .

"I'm sorry to have to call, but Jimmy's behavior is causing a lot of trouble in class. He won't listen to me. We have to talk."

WHAT NOT TO SAY . . .

(Angry response): "Well, he said you've been treating him pretty badly too."

INSTEAD, SAY . . .

"I'll be happy to come in; what time would be good for you?" (You don't need to solve the problem or escalate the teacher's anger and frustration over the telephone.)

WHAT NOT TO SAY . . .

(Defensive response): "I'm getting sick and tired of you people calling all the time and making Jimmy sound like the bad guy."

INSTEAD, SAY . . .

"We have heard these complaints before; I'm disappointed that this behavior of Jimmy's is continuing, but I'm sure there are some things that can be tried to make it better."

WHAT NOT TO SAY . . .

(Denial): "He never complains about following the rules at school. I can't believe he's a problem."

INSTEAD, SAY . . .

"I find it hard to accept that he could be like that, but at this point, I will take your word. Jimmy does tell a very different version of this at home. We do need to meet. I need to talk to you so I know how to handle this at home."

WHAT NOT TO SAY . . .

(Blaming): "Do you think you've really tried hard with him at school?"

INSTEAD, SAY . . .

"I'm at my wit's end over this. I'm having such a hard time accepting that he's like this in school."

WHAT NOT TO SAY . . .

(Disbelief): "Surely you can't know Jimmy this well this quickly?"

INSTEAD, SAY . . .

"I don't want to believe that this is my child you're describing, but I'll take your word for it. I want to know more, particularly about when this happens and why you think it happens. I'd like to meet with you to talk about it."

As you are talking with the teacher, keep two things in mind:

❐ Try to be as open-minded as possible. You may not like all that you're hearing about your child, and while the teacher may not be blameless, you need to hear how another adult is reacting to your child, as well as realize that your child may need to share some of the blame for classroom difficulties.

❐ Try to give the teacher positive feedback as well as saying the negative things you may feel you need to say. Realize that if you go in simply to attack the teacher in defense of your child, it's only natural the teacher will defend herself, and neither of you will be likely to come any closer to helping your child. If you have a more balanced approach, you leave room for the teacher to work with you.

While most parents would agree that trying to keep these kinds of principles in mind is a good idea, it still can be hard to know exactly how to say what you need to say and still remain constructive and positive. Here are some examples of how to talk to your child's teacher:

❐ "I have some concerns about Alyssa's writing skills that I want to discuss with you. I see that her grades are good, but her work looks so poor to me. I need to understand this better."

❐ "I really want to meet with you. Erin has been more upset about going to school than ever before. I think that working together we can help her."

❐ "I'd like to meet and talk with you about Tiffany's homework. She seems to be putting in so much effort, yet her grades are really poor. Perhaps if we better understood what is being expected of her, we might be able to help her better."

❐ "I can tell that you really want Kevin to do well, but he's not a child that has ever been motivated by using homework as punishment."

❐ "Brianna says that she feels more comfortable in your class than in any other because you are so strict. She knows that there won't be any trouble while you're in charge."

❐ "I'm sorry that we don't agree on this grading issue. I can tell that you want every child to achieve to their utmost potential, and you really push them to do that."

❐ "I now see what Sherise is reacting to. What she describes as lack of organization on your part is really great, creative teaching. Unfortunately, Sherise is so organized, controlled, and perfectionistic, that she doesn't learn well unless there is a lot of structure. We face the same problem at home."

TRACKING

Tracking has been a hot topic in education circles for about 150 years, ever since the 1840s when Boston-area schools made the first move away from the mixed age and ability groups of "one room" schools. They were the first to try grouping children by age so that those coming to school for the first time were called "first graders," second year students were "second graders," and so on.

When you think about it, the Boston schools' move was not unreasonable. Any time you get a number of children together, they will be grouped, or will form groups themselves, on the basis of something. It could be age, where they live, ability, religion, or any number of things. In school terms, there are more than 40 identified types of grouping possible, ranging from the obvious such as age and overall ability, to groups based on more subtle characteristics such as learning styles and social maturity.

The rationale for tracking seems reasonable too: Because students differ widely in ability, maturity and skills, placing them with others like themselves will theoretically make for more effective teaching and learning, with children able to proceed at their own rate because the material will be geared to their own ability and achievement level.

But for the last 60 years or so, there have been considerable debates about how effectively grouping or tracking works, and at what cost.

Tracking can be an emotional issue, and whether you are on the "pro" side or the "con" side, you can probably find research to support your view. Many studies on rigid tracking fail to show either positive or negative effects on academic achievement. Some studies show that a special track for high-achieving students does enhance their achievement. But many studies also show that tracking stifles those in the lower tracks, which brings up another point of criticism: that of the studies that have been done on tracking. Critics say the studies only look at achievement measured against the track and have ignored such other important variables as the quality of the teachers assigned to the tracks and the resources made available. It may be that those qualities make the difference in achievement between high track students and lower track students, not the track itself. That's what has been shown in programs like Head Start, where children who would be described as at-risk or likely to be in lower tracks are given extra help and resources, boosting their achievement.

In most schools today, long-term grouping by anything other than grade is rare in elementary schools. By middle school, tracking or grouping becomes more prevalent, and it's the norm in high schools.

On the elementary level, there may be some grouping in the classroom, breaking into different groups for math or spelling or reading, and sometimes with special programs (mostly in reading) for children at both ends of the achievement spectrum.

Middle school is when tracking usually begins, based on a combination of ability and achievement measures, grades, and—most of all—teacher recommendation to place children in faster or slower classes. Within the last 20 years, it has been customary to "cross-track" students so that, rather than being placed in a faster or slower group for all classes, students can be in placed in classes according to their own particular strengths and weaknesses.

In high school, tracking occurs either as:

❏ classes offered in different levels (Level 1 or A, to Level 4 or Remedial, for example),
❏ special classes, like advanced placement or electives not open to everyone.

This is where tracking is most ingrained, with an elaborate structure for deciding class rank, selecting the valedictorian, getting into college, and the like. For students who want to be top ranked, the pressure can be enormous: not only do you have to do well, you have to do it in the top tracks, as in advanced placement classes.

On the positive side, many secondary students favor tracking in part because they have the opportunity to "be smart" and not be embarrassed or teased about their intellectual skills.

The main concern many people have about tracking centers around some problems it hasn't solved, and a few that it has created:

❏ Once it's in place, those benefiting from it

most (usually the advanced students) are very resistant to changing it.

❏ Tracking becomes a political issue rather than an education issue for the school administration and school board because of parental pressure one way or the other.

❏ Tracking inadvertently also often tracks kids on other variables not intended at first: race, socioeconomic status, and level of motivation, for example.

❏ Everyone hates the lower tracks. Teachers may dread teaching them. Students hate the implications of being in them. Parents are legitimately concerned about the effectiveness of education children get there.

❏ But the so-called middle and lower tracks actually still have an enormous variability among the students. Usually only the very highest and the very lowest (which might mean special education) tracks are relatively homogeneous. In the others, you are likely to find students with excellent intellectual potential, decent academic skills, and no academic motivation mixed in with students with much less ability, erratic skills, but better motivation.

Right now, tracking is being looked at more critically than in the past, but although most educators are familiar with the pitfalls of tracking, there really isn't a great alternative to put in its place.

One alternative might be what many school districts are doing: abandoning their rigid tracking systems in favor of more cooperative learning groups where the brightest kids help those less so, making them responsible for making sure that everyone in the group understands the material. Rather than holding back the bright students, research is indicating that it makes them understand the material even better.

As you formulate your opinions about tracking and how it works, or doesn't work, for your child, and how your school uses it, here are some conclusions we have reached about tracking that you might want to keep in mind:

1 No scheme for grouping children for instruction can erase individual differences. Individual differences are so pervasive there is no way to match them all in any group.

2 No plan for grouping can eliminate the need for adapting instruction to these individual differences.

3 A school's grouping plan should be related positively to the goals of the instructional program and the educational system. This is a tough one to satisfy. Tracking does a fair job of helping schools reach some instructional objectives, such as achieving specific skills in math. But the overall philosophy of most school districts usually has to do with the more subjective goals of "producing good, productive citizens," and "using good judgment and reasoning." Tracking probably sets that back because it teaches a subtle lesson that it's all right to segregate or get away from problems in order to accomplish a personal mission most effectively. The concern is that when these students become adults, will that lesson be translated to thinking that someone else should solve problems we don't want to deal with directly, such as homelessness or welfare issues?

4 Groups should be based on what we know about children's development. We know that children learn in very different ways and at different rates, and however we group children, we need to accommodate those developmental differences.

5 Grouping practices should result in placing each child in instructional situations in which maximum attention can be given to the many factors that influence learning, for instance, your child's abilities, her motivation for learning that subject, and what you and the teacher know about which teaching strategies are most effective for your child.

STANDARDIZED GROUP TESTS

Standardized group tests have been used in schools since the turn of the century. They were first widely used by the Army during World War I to screen out recruits who had significant language problems or whose basic skills were so poor they wouldn't be able to understand orders.

And that's in a sense what standardized group tests are meant to do today: screen large groups of students on specific skills or aptitudes. Almost every child will take a standardized test at one time or another, and the test will be administered to an entire school, all the children in certain grades, or everyone in the district, depending on the test and your district. The information you receive from those compares your child's score to that of other children in the same group (grade or age) nationally, regionally, by state, and by cities or towns in that state, and by schools within a town.

Although standardized group testing has come under fire in recent years for being biased or being relied on too heavily, it still is an effective method for screening large numbers of students and comparing their skills or aptitudes to those of other students in other groups. At the same time, most educators recognize that while standardized tests can give very accurate comparative data about groups of students, they may not be as reliable when it comes to giving accurate individual student profiles. That's because on group tests, there's no way of measuring if one child could understand or read the questions or the instructions on the test as there is on the kinds of individualized tests described in Testing and Evaluation.

There are three primary types of standardized tests:

1 *Achievement tests:* measure achievement in basic skills or the subject areas of language (including reading, comprehension, usage, grammar and mechanics), math, science, social studies, and study skills.

Some examples of the many types of group achievement tests are:

❏ California Achievement Test (CAT)
❏ Comprehensive Tests of Basic Skills (CTBS)
❏ Iowa Tests of Basic Skills (ITBS)
❏ Metropolitan Achievement Test (MAT)
❏ Stanford Achievement Test (SAT)
❏ Sequential Test of Education Progress (STEP)

The key to making these tests more meaningful is for the district to choose a test that most closely taps the same knowledge base presented in their system's curriculum. Without a close match, children will be tested over subjects, terminology, or skills they've never been taught, or asked to approach subjects in ways they're unfamiliar with.

Teachers may use test results to get an idea of which students are mastering the curriculum and who needs help. Changes in scoring have helped make these tests a little more useful for teachers. Historically, scores were only "normative," in other words they only measured how an individual placed compared to other children in all areas of the test. Now, most tests also give individual strengths and weaknesses on separate subjects as well, called "criterion" comparisons. While even this is not comprehensive enough to pinpoint academic problems, it can be a guide for parents and teachers.

2 *Intelligence tests:* assess the child's overall level of intellectual functioning. Usually has both verbal and non-verbal parts. Less achievement or skill oriented than reasoning and memory oriented. Some examples:

❏ Kuhlman-Anderson Test (KAT)
❏ Cognitive Abilities Test (COGAT)

3 *Special aptitude tests:* assess a child's aptitude in specific areas like foreign language, art, creativity, music, etc. They are not often used in schools, but these types of tests might be used, for example, by a school counselor to assess a child's vocational interests, or to determine if a child new to the school is ready for a particular level of music or foreign language.

WHAT DO THOSE SCORES MEAN?

Understanding how standardized tests are scored is also key to their usefulness. Most tests offer several types of scores. It's important to remember that none of the scores is a perfect representation of your child's achievement or ability; each scoring method has its advantages and its disadvantages. The four most commonly used scoring types are:

1 *Standard scores:* The best scoring method and the most accurate, it's the one used for the SATs and the PSATs. Because of its accuracy, more and more group tests are giving this as the primary score. It simply measures in equal intervals how far each child falls from the mean, or the group's average, score.

2 *Percentile scores:* These place a child's score along a continuum from 1 to 99. The higher the number, the more children's scores your child surpassed. For example, if out of 100 children, your child scored in the 75th percentile, your child did better than 75 of the other 99 children. The difficulty with interpreting percentile scores is that they are not evenly distributed along the continuum. If you made a mark along a line for each score, you'd see that most of the scores would be grouped between about the 25th through the 75th percentile, with a few scores falling lower and a few higher, just like the bell grading curve you may remember from school. What that means when you interpret your child's score is that the 30th percentile, for example, while it sounds so low, is not bad at all; it's still within the average range. It's not the same as getting 30 percent on a test.

3 *Stanines:* This is an abbreviation for STAndard NINE. This method takes a distribution of scores and breaks it into nine groups; the average is 5, the highest is 9. That means your child's score represents a range rather than a single number which, in some cases, can give a truer representation, because single number scores imply a precision that tests just can't deliver. The table below shows how stanines work.

4 *Grade Equivalents.* Even though they are probably the poorest representation of how your child did, unfortunately grade equivalents are still included on most tests. These divide the school year into 10 months and present the score as a grade level followed by the decimal equivalent of a month, with September being 1. So a child doing typical work in November of his third-grade year would have a grade equivalent of 3.3. Grade equivalents of test scores aren't accurate representations of ability or skills because they assume that learning progresses at a perfectly even pace, and that every school everywhere is studying the same thing in the same month.

Stanine	Percentile	Percent of children obtaining this score
1	1–4	4
2	5–11	7
3	12–23	12
4	24–40	17
5	41–60	20
6	61–77	17
7	78–89	12
8	90–96	7
9	97–99	4

Another problem with these equivalents is that if your child does very well or very poorly, the scores are even more misleading. For example, if your second grader scores high on the math portion of an achievement test and it's expressed as 4.1, it does not mean she is actually doing fourth-grade work, or that she could walk into a fourth-grade math class and do fine. All it means is that she got the same raw score as the typical child with a class placement of 4.1. It doesn't even depend on the specific items your child got right or wrong. The grade equivalent score is merely a projection along a scale that assumes a perfectly predictable world.

SPECIAL EDUCATION

No matter what your child's abilities are, federal law guarantees that she is entitled to a free, appropriate public education in surroundings as close to that of a standard classroom as possible. But while the law guarantees an education for your child, it will be up to you, as the spokesperson for your child, to work with your school's personnel to be sure they meet your child's needs.

That can be a tall order, whether you have just been told your child has a disability or whether you have been living with your child's more obvious disabilities for years. Digging through paperwork and federal regulations is the last thing you may want to do when you've been knocked off-balance by a new diagnosis, or when you're feeling overwhelmed just knowing your child's education is at stake. Even so, you can be a more effective spokesperson for your child if you understand what your rights are and how your school handles special education. (See also box below, Parent's Rights.)

You can start by talking with your school psychologist about how your school evaluates and develops individualized education programs for a potential student who needs special education. While federal law mandates that every child gets an education, federal funding usually covers only a part of the cost of special education; it's up to state boards of education and school districts to make up the rest. For example, even though your child may have already been receiving special education services at one school, if a job transfer takes you to another state, your child will not necessarily receive exactly the same services in her new school.

Despite differences in how federal requirements are carried out, there are some milestones in the process that you should expect to see, no matter where you live. (See also box below, Special Education Referrals—How They Happen.) Those steps have been determined by two federal laws whose titles you may hear discussed. They are:

- The Education for all Handicapped Children Act, now known as the Individuals with Disabilities Education Act, which requires all

Special Education Referrals: How They Happen

This chart should give you an idea of what happens when you or your child's teacher expresses concern about your child.

TEACHER CONTACTS PARENT, OR PARENT CONTACTS TEACHER.

Teacher and parent meet.

Teacher consults with team at school.   Teacher comes up with her own plan.

Teacher checks with parent.

Teacher implements plan.

Teacher and parent stay in touch.

After about 30 days, teacher and consultants report to principal and parents.

Problems alleviated,   Problems still there,
mission accomplished.   refer for team meeting and evaluation.

EVALUATION

Team, parents, teacher review evaluation results.

Team develops IEP.   Team recommends other
                                        non-special education interventions.

Parent gives written consent.   If parent does not consent,
                                        team decides which other
                                        strategies might be helpful.

Parent and teacher continue to stay in touch.

public schools to provide every child with a disability an appropriate education and related services, and

- Section 504 of the Rehabilitation Act of 1973, a civil rights amendment that prohibits discrimination against persons with handicapping conditions.

When a team of specialists at your school evaluates your child, the diagnosis the team (which includes you) reaches must fit the descriptions of disabilities covered by these laws in order for your child to receive the kind of special help they provide for. Legally, children between birth and age 21 or high school graduation, are eligible for services under these laws if they have hearing, speech, or vision disabilities; learning disabilities; chronic or long-term health problems; emotional problems; mental retardation and/or physical impairments. Services offered at no cost to you may include speech and language, physical or occupational therapy; social work, psychological, or school health services; transportation; vocational education; and parent counseling and training.

The special education evaluation process is similar to the steps followed for psychological evaluations in the section called Tests and Evaluations. It can be initiated by you or by a teacher, usually after several different approaches to your child's problems have been tried and have not worked. It may feel frustrating to you if you feel efforts to help your child are inching along when you want sweeping change. But it might help to know that schools are legally required to try to solve a child's academic problems within the regular classroom first. So your child's teacher will probably try several different teaching strategies and consult with such specialists as the reading consultant, the speech-language pathologist, or the special education teacher before she recommends a special education evaluation.

The steps you should expect to see if you do choose to begin the referral process start with the teacher or the principal letting you know that a multidisciplinary team meeting has been scheduled to discuss how best to help your child, and inviting you to attend. Your school may have a different name for this group, but usually it is made up of five or six professionals, including your child's teacher, a special education teacher, a reading consultant, the school psychologist, a speech-language pathologist, and the principal.

Bring a written list of your questions and observations about your child to the meeting, along with the kind of home file described in the Parent-Teacher Communication section under Preparing for the Conference. Bring, too, a trusted friend for moral support, or a friend who is a teacher who can help you discuss the issues concerning your child and ask pertinent questions.

It is at this meeting that an evaluation may be suggested and planned. If it is, make sure that the reasons for the evaluation are clearly defined. If an evaluation is not recommended, and you want an evaluation for your child, you can request a second meeting of the team, and bring more evidence of your own or from outside specialists to make a case for why you believe your child should be evaluated. Or you can contact your school's equivalent of the special education supervisor or director of pupil services to discuss the team meeting's decision further.

If an evaluation is recommended but you don't want your child evaluated, you might speak with the school psychologist to clarify exactly what the evaluation process will be. (See Chapter 3, Evaluation and Testing.) If you still feel uncomfortable with it, you can check with an outside specialist to get a second opinion about the need for an evaluation for your child.

Once an evaluation is complete, the team will share their results with you, and in some cases, with your child. At this meeting, you'll know if your child is eligible for special education or related services, what exactly your child needs and how those needs will be met, and how long your child is likely to need special services.

On the basis of all of this, the team will develop what is called an Individualized Education Program, or IEP, for your child. Keep in mind that the plan should be defined by your child's needs, not by which services are available at your school. You are entitled to help formulate the plan, and your input can be key to being sure your child's needs are met. The plan should be reviewed yearly to be sure it still fits your child's needs. And, your child should be re-evaluated every three years. These evaluations can include some testing and observation, but are often less formal than initial evaluations, with you and a team of professionals meeting to review whether your child is making progress and whether she still needs extra help.

Your Child's Individualized Education Program (IEP)

You can use this checklist to help ensure your child receives the special services she needs. Be sure your school provides:

❏ not less than five days notification to you of multidisciplinary team meetings.

❏ a mutually convenient meeting place and time.

❏ a team that includes appropriate school specialists, your child's teacher, the principal, and you.

❏ an IEP that includes a statement of your child's present level of performance, a statement of the type of services she will receive, who will provide them, when the services will begin, clearly stated goals and objectives, methods of evaluating the goals, and criteria your child must meet in order to end the services.

❏ an IEP that is implemented as soon as possible after it is written and approved.

❏ an IEP that is in effect at the beginning of each school year.

❏ a copy of the IEP for you, along with copies of written evaluations and minutes from the team meetings.

❏ a yearly review of your child's progress toward the goals of the IEP.

❏ a re-evaluation of your child every three years.

Once you have an IEP for your child, unless she requires some other arrangement, she must be educated in the school she would attend if she didn't have a problem, unless doing that would be harmful to your child or the services she would receive were not of high quality. Your child could be placed in:

❏ a regular classroom with no basic change in teaching procedure.

❏ a regular classroom with modifications made by the classroom teacher and additional aides or special instructional materials if needed.

❏ a regular classroom with specialists available for consultation with the teacher or parent as needed.

❏ a regular classroom with specialists who provide services directly to your child.

❏ a resource room for as much as two hours a day, that is, a regular classroom with a special education teacher providing extra instruction.

❏ a part-time special class in which a student is enrolled in a special class for a portion of the day, going back to the regular classroom for other subjects.

❏ a full-time special class in which students are assigned to a self-contained special class for half or more of the school day.

❏ an out-placement program, in which students are placed on homebound instruction, in a residential school, hospital program, or a treatment center because he cannot be reasonably educated within the context of regular or special education.

The bottom line for any of these placements is that the law requires your child be placed in the least restrictive environment, in other words, in the environment most like a regular classroom that your child can handle.

SCHOOL RECORDS

Formalized record keeping in schools is only about 50 years old. Even so, until 1974, when Congress passed the Family Educational Rights and Privacy Act, also called the Buckley Amendment, record keeping and who got to see the records was fairly hit-or-miss. School records were often handed out to police or prospective employers (and less often available to parents), and they could contain inaccurate information.

With the passage of the Buckley Amendment, which applies to all schools and colleges (including private institutions) receiving state or federal funds, parents' rights as to records access, and school's responsibilities as to record keeping, were both better defined.

Under the Buckley Amendment:

❏ School districts are required to establish a written policy regarding student's records and to inform parents of the policy each year.

❏ Parents can examine all their child's records.

❏ Schools have to establish procedures for challenging the accuracy of all records and for having erroneous information removed. Schools may, but are not required to, change information when there is a difference of opinion between you and the school or the specialist who evaluated your child.

❏ Parents can include their own comments, disagreements, opinions of another specialist, or the results of a private evaluation if they cannot get the unfavorable material removed.

❏ Parents must give permission for access to the records to those who wouldn't automatically have access. The only people who can see the records without the written consent of the parents are those who have "a legitimate interest in the child," which usually means the cur-

rent teacher, principal, and school specialist, if that applies. Records cannot be shown to other school officials, other community groups, or used for employment, financial aid, or other school applications without your written consent.

❏ All of these parents' rights become your child's rights when she turns 18.

The school should also keep a list, available to you, of all those who have examined parts or all of your child's records of dealings with school specialists (see item 3, below), the date they saw them, and the reason. Although in most states schools are required to keep a child's file for many years after the child has left the school (75 years in some states), you should be notified if the school intends to destroy any of your child's old records, and you should be able to keep those files yourself if you want them.

All of which means it's a good idea to examine your child's school records once a year. Make an appointment at the office where most of the student files are kept, which is often the principal's office. You may have to check in other offices too, because, in most schools, records consist of more than one file, each maintained by a different school official and kept in a different place. The reason for this is not really to make it harder for you to find all the files. It's mostly for the convenience of the school personnel using the records, but separation of the records also controls access to them. Although schools vary in their policies, there are generally three kinds of school records:

1 *General School File.* This one contains the most basic information, and most people are not as concerned about the confidentiality of this as they may be of others. This is what most parents and schools consider to be the main school record on your child, and it contains information like:

- ❐ grades, year by year
- ❐ teacher's comments and evaluations, year by year
- ❐ attendance records
- ❐ standardized test scores
- ❐ transcripts from other schools

2 *Health and Counseling Records.* These are maintained by the school nurse and by the school counselor and are almost always kept separate from the main file. Access to these files is controlled by the nurse or counselor. These records most often contain:

- ❐ health records, including vision, hearing, immunizations, and medications. This follows your child throughout her school career.
- ❐ teachers' recommendations for class placement
- ❐ teachers' and school counselors' career or college recommendations

3 *Specialists' Reports.* This is the most controlled type of record, and it contains information from school psychologists, social workers, or other school specialists who may have had contact with your child. It also contains any records of meetings regarding referrals of your child for possible special education programs or services, such as those done by a multidisciplinary team. This file might contain:

- ❐ school psychologist and social worker reports and reports from any other specialist who may have tested your child, as well as reports from welfare and social services agencies (if applicable).

- ❐ your child's Individualized Educational Plan (see Special Education, Part I), and the records of any multidisciplinary team meetings held about your child.

School specialists, like psychologists, usually also keep their own file of private working notes. These are not considered official school records, so they are usually not available to parents, and definitely not to anyone else. Reports in your child's file are the summaries of those notes; but if you have further questions, the specialists would be glad to meet with you to discuss any concerns you have about your child.

In addition, the school principal or assistant principal may also maintain a private file including administrative notations and reports made when children are referred to them because of bad conduct. These are her way of documenting for you the exact nature, date, and frequency of behavior concerns about your child which were brought to her attention. Typically, these notes are not passed on to the next school.

SCHOOL ENTRY DECISIONS

Deciding when your child is ready to begin school can be a confusing business. Chronological age, not individual readiness, is the measure school districts across the country use to decide if children are ready for school. However, there isn't much agreement on just what that age is: there are 14 different age cutoff dates in the United States, with some states allowing children as young as 4 years, 8 months to enter kindergarten, and most agreeing that a child should be at least 5. That's probably because there isn't compelling evidence showing that any particular age is better than any other for entering school.

Parents' Rights

These are your rights under the law regarding evaluations and special education. You should be given a booklet at your team meeting describing these in more detail.

YOU HAVE THE RIGHT TO:

❏ Refuse to permit the evaluation.

❏ Review all records related to your child.

❏ Review all procedures involved in team meetings.

❏ Attend and participate in all multidisciplinary team meetings related to your child's needs.

❏ Know that your child's educational program will not be drastically changed without your knowledge.

❏ Be informed of and give written permission for an individual evaluation of your child.

❏ Bring a friend or a professional with you to all team meetings.

❏ Know the results of all individual evaluations of your child, including psychological and educational evaluations.

❏ Get an outside evaluation for your child from an independent, qualified examiner if you disagree with the findings of the school's evaluation team. You can do this any time at your own expense. If you want the school to pay for it, you can request that of your local board of education. If they refuse, you can request an administrative review of the matter by your local board or a hearing with the state board of education.

❏ Be told when a referral is made for special education and/or related services. Initial placement or services will be provided only with your written consent.

But there are a few rules of thumb to follow in judging if your child is ready. As you decide, talk with your child's preschool teacher and with the kingergarten teacher your child would have to gather as much information as you can about your child's readiness. Some facts to consider:

❏ The majority of children, no matter their age at entry, do fine in school. For a variety of reasons, most differences caused by age tend to even out by about third grade.

❏ Studies show that because of many factors—including, among others, social expecta-

tions—boys and African Americans who are relatively young for their grade are at risk for retention, referral to special education services, and eventual dropout from school.

❏ Studies also show that socioeconomic status is a more powerful and accurate predictor of academic success than chronological age, presumably because parents at higher economic levels have the resources to better prepare their child for school tasks.

❏ Children who have had preschool experience do better in school, both academically and socially.

❏ Contrary to what some might assume, children who have been identified or suspected of having learning problems or other kinds of disabilities before school age benefit by beginning school as soon as possible because at school they can receive the special help they need.

If your child's school conducts screenings to see if potential kindergartners are ready for school, you can request your child be screened. Talk first with the teacher, or whoever is to conduct the screening, to be sure these factors are addressed:

❐ Are the results of the screening to be used to exclude some children from kindergarten, or to identify special needs which will be addressed in kindergarten?

❐ Is more than one specialist involved in administering and evaluating the readiness tests? Are they familiar with the school's surrounding community and available resources?

❐ Do they gather information from more than one source, including parents, preschool teachers, the child and the test material?

❐ Is the screening conducted in such a way that information can be gathered from your child on more than one day? Preschool childrens' mood and attention can fluctuate dramatically from day to day, or even from hour to hour. Having your child participate in the screening at more than one sitting is the best way to get a reasonable picture of her abilities.

❐ What does the screening test measure? Good screening programs consider skills (like the ability to hold a pencil, to count, or to name letters), as well as perceptual and motor abilities, language development, and social skills.

C H A P T E R 3

Evaluation and Testing

A PARENT'S CRASH COURSE IN THE TOOLS PSYCHOLOGISTS USE

If your child is scheduled to be evaluated by the school psychologist, or if you'll be talking with her about a problem your child has, it can help smooth your way if you know how the testing and evaluation process works. Keep in mind that a psychological evaluation is an attempt to better understand your child's academic and behavioral functioning, nothing more; nothing less. In addition, a good evaluation uses several methods to get the broadest, most accurate picture of your child possible.

PARENTAL PERMISSION

The first thing to understand about the testing and evaluation process is that, legally, initial evaluations cannot happen without your written permission. (Once your child has been evaluated and is receiving special education services, the school is only required by law to notify you of follow-up evaluations. However, most schools ask for written permission as a courtesy.) Before the initial evaluation, you should be given a document to sign that explains the reasons for the evaluation and the types of tests that might be used during the evaluation, such as intelligence, achievement, or personality tests.

If your child is scheduled for an evaluation, you should have already seen this document, and you should have already spoken with several school specialists, such as the school psy-

chologist and other members of your school's version of a multidisciplinary team (see Special Education, Part I), at a meeting at which it was decided that an evaluation might help determine which steps to take in helping your child. You may have asked questions during that meeting, but if you think of other questions, or more concerns occur to you before your child's evaluation, you should contact the school psychologist again. It will help your child, and ultimately the professionals working with her, if you and your child feel comfortable about the evaluation. While the psychologist will answer questions about the testing, she is ethically bound not to tell you specific questions on the test, in the interest of keeping the testing of your child as pure as possible.

If you are frightened at the thought of having your child evaluated, or feel unwilling to go ahead with the evaluation without knowing specifically what will be asked on the tests, it might be best for you to talk further with the school psychologist, or even with a private psychologist, to ease your own fears about the evaluation before having your child tested. You and your child will benefit most if you wholeheartedly trust and support both the evaluation process and the psychologist administering the tests.

Your fears about evaluations may take many forms. Some possible fears are:

❏ A fear that your child will, in fact, be found to have a problem. Parents often worry not only about their child, but about what their role may have been in their child's developing the problem. Discussing this worry with the school psychologist, a private psychologist, or with your family physician would be helpful.

❏ A fear of your child being labeled as a result of testing. If your fear is of your child being ridiculed by others for being tested, you can take some comfort from knowing that this is a confidential process, and no one outside the immediate school personnel who work with her need know unless you tell them. And if your child is having enough difficulty to warrant even the consideration of testing in the first place, of course those school personnel closest to her already know your child is having some kind of difficulty.

On the other hand, if your child is tested and as a result you and the multidisciplinary team agree that your child fits into a specific category, for example, because she has a learning disability or she is gifted, then the "label" is the first step toward getting the kind of help your child needs. Children cannot be placed in federally funded or state funded programs unless they fit the diagnostic criteria for those programs. While most school psychologists would prefer to work without having to label children, in most schools specific programs—whether they are for special education or gifted classes—are available only to those children who have been tested, evaluated, and explicitly "labeled" as qualifying for those programs.

Finally, even if the whole multidisciplinary team agrees that the evaluation shows your child fits a certain category, a special education program for your child cannot be implemented without your consent.

A BROAD-BASED, FUN APPROACH

A good psychological evaluation never relies on just one form of testing because it's too easy to misinterpret results if you only have one approach. Instead, most evaluations rely on several sources of information:

❏ test data itself (see What Kinds of Tests? below)

❏ observations the pscyhologist makes of your child while she takes the test

❏ observations the psychologist makes of your child in a variety of settings, as in the classroom and on the playground

❏ information the psychologist gathers from you, your child's teacher, and other important adults in her life

❏ existing records on your child, including the results of any previous testing, report cards, health records, etc.

The strength of this kind of evaluation is that it is individualized. The psychologist who sees a child pay close attention to the test, focus, and think before answering gets a very different picture than she would from watching another child daydream, wring her hands, or stare out the window during the test. Because observing the child's test-taking behavior is so crucial, in some cases the actual score of the test may not be as important as how the child seemed to feel and how she acted during the test. It's also important to know that other than on tests of reading itself, these tests generally rely very little on reading ability, so the psychologist can make a distinction between academic performance and other problems—emotional, behavioral, physical, etc. For example, most tests are administered verbally and involve such tasks as answering questions, drawing pictures, or pointing to objects. Because these tests are so individualized and they are administered one-on-one by the psychologist, if your child is having a hard time understanding a word, a question, or any aspect of the test, she can ask for help; if she is distracted or not motivated to complete the test, the psychologist can stop or switch to a different test.

Some parents are surprised to find that their children love to be tested this way. When you think about it, it's not hard to see why. The tasks are made to be novel, interesting, and challenging, and the child has the undivided attention of an adult who keeps encouraging her and telling her what a fine job she's doing. More than a few children in our experience have wanted to come back and be tested again.

While most children are fine once they meet with the school psychologist, your support can help your child approach testing in a positive fashion. You can explain the need for testing by simply saying something like this: "You know how we've been talking about your difficulties in spelling? Ms. Jones is going to work with you for a while tomorrow afternoon to find out what will help you to learn spelling better." A positive attitude towards using the evaluation as a way to find solutions to problems is all you and your child need. If you need more help figuring out how to explain the need for the evaluation to your child, ask your school psychologist for the right words.

WHAT KINDS OF TESTS DO SCHOOL PSYCHOLOGISTS USE?

There are many categories of tests commonly used by school psychologists and several types within each category. While there are probably too many categories to completely discuss

them all here, understanding a few key categories can help you gain a clearer understanding of your child's evaluation.

Four key categories are:

1 *Screening vs. Diagnostic Tests:* Screenings are usually briefer tests, quicker to administer. They are fairly accurate in gaining a quick overall picture of a trait such as intelligence; math, reading, or spelling abilities; or overall self esteem. The disadvantage is that they give no in-depth information about the trait, just how your child places with respect to others or to a criterion (see Criterion-Referenced Tests below).

Diagnostic tests are much longer and break down the trait being measured into many parts. For example, a diagnostic math test would break math down into component skills such as addition, subtraction, multiplication, division, carrying, fractions, etc. Each area would be scored separately so the profile from this test would reveal more exactly where your child was having a problem.

2 *Norm-Referenced vs. Criterion-Referenced Tests:* Norm-referenced tests compare your child to other children, usually either on a national or regional basis. This is the classic way tests are scored, and it shows how far above or below the norm a child scores, compared to others.

Criterion referenced tests compare your child to a specific level of mastery of a skill. These tests are constructed around learning themes, such as multiplication tables, correct use of punctuation, knowledge of state capitals, etc. They show how much of the skill your child has mastered, but not how she compares to others.

3 *Standardized vs. Classroom-developed Tests:* Standardized tests are developed by commercial test publishers. They choose a representative group to become the standardization sample in order to set a norm. Once the test is published, all children are compared to this group. The choice of the norm group is, of course, critical to how good the test is. Good tests take into account factors such as the region of the country where a child lives, gender, age, economic status, and race and are sensitive to all ranges of childrens' abilities, including children with disabilities. The better the norms, the more applicable the test results.

Classroom-developed tests are developed by teachers based on instruction and the curriculum presented. They can offer a good measure of how a child has mastered what has been presented in school, but they may lack the breadth of the knowledge base that can be tapped by standardized tests.

4 *Level of Inference Needed:* Unlike the other three test categories listed here, this one is not an either-or situation, but a continuum. Some tests—spelling tests, for example—are highly objective and require little or no interpretation. Others are more subjective—projective personality tests, for example—and require training and skill to interpret correctly.

In addition to these categories, there are four types of tests psychologists often use. They are each described below, and you can also check the section on standardized testing for more information about how many of these tests are likely to be scored. Four types of tests are:

1 *Intelligence Tests:* There are a number of different intelligence tests available, and different psychologists prefer different tests. One test is not necessarily better than another, but each does differ slightly in emphasis so that a psychologist would choose a particular test to fit a particular child's needs, which would vary depending on why the child is being referred for testing.

Even though they have small differences, all intelligence tests are fairly extensive; most take over an hour to administer. They all measure many traits, all thought to be a part of intellectual functioning. And they all result in one overall score, or general IQ, along with several other scores representing the components of intelligence based on the theory behind the particular test. (See descriptions of tests in Appendix D.)

There is a lot of controversy in psychology about the use of intelligence measures like these. While IQ is obviously related to achievement, we know that IQ scores are not finite limits on what a child can accomplish. Motivation, attitude, previous school experiences, parental support and expectations, and perseverance are as important or even more important in determining a person's success.

Try to take any results of any IQ test with a sense of balance, knowing that other factors are critical as well.

2 *Achievement Tests:* These measure scholastic accomplishment and mastery of a subject. For a psychological evaluation, the focus is on the underlying skills rather than on the specific subject areas. So the emphasis will be on screening and diagnostic tests in reading, spelling, and math, for example. These tests are usually administered by the school psychologist or by a learning specialist or special education teacher and are straightforward "pencil and paper" types of tests. Some of them are the Wide-Range Achievement Test, Kaufman Test of Educational Achievement, Key Math Test, Wechsler Individual Achievement Test, and the Gray Oral Reading Test. (All of these, as well as all the other tests listed in this section, are described in Appendix D).

3 *Learning Ability Tests:* These try to evaluate the psychological processes critical to learning: memory, attention, problem solving, perception, and motor skills. Usually they involve your child's completing fairly complex tasks such as serial learning, which is learning lists of words in order, or paired associate learning, which is memorizing things like the capitals of all the states. Examples of these are the Woodcock-Johnson Tests of Cognitive Ability, the Detroit Tests of Learning Aptitude, and the Bloomer Learning Test.

4 *Personality Tests:* These are the tests parents are usually the most wary of, but they are far less mysterious than you may think, nor do they dig as deep, in a psychological sense, as many parents are afraid they might. For the most part, these tests involve direct questions requiring simple answers like, "Does Sally have many fears?" The school psychologist pairs results of these tests with information she gleans from interviewing your child and others around her before she draws any conclusions. Some of the tests are more objective than others, and the trend is toward using these rather than the more subjective variety that require a great deal of interpretation on the part of the psychologist. (See Level of Inference Needed, above.)

Some types of personality tests many school psychologists use are:

■ *Self-Report Inventories:* In which a child answers questions related to herself, usually as True/False, Like me/Unlike me, Yes/No, or on a scale from Always to Never. While this is a direct way to get information, it may not always be accurate because the child can control what she wants to reveal. Other reasons this may not be the most effective choice for some children are:

❐ The child may not be willing to face or deal with a problem, so she purposefully gives answers reflecting what she wishes were the case, which is not necessarily true. The child may not understand herself very well and may answer in what she considers a truthful manner, but because she lacks insight, the results are still different from what others may see in the child. Two self-report inventories are the Piers-Harris Children's Self Concept Scale and the Junior/Senior High School Personality Questionnaire.

■ *Rating Scales:* These are filled out by someone who knows the child, usually parents and teachers, making them potentially very helpful to the psychologist. They can show how a problem is perceived in different settings and can serve as a basis for how and where to begin to address the problem. However, they can have the same down side as self-report inventories if a parent or a teacher really cannot or will not face a problem. Two examples of these tests are the Child Behavior Checklist and the Conners Parent Rating Scale.

■ *Projectives:* All of these tests are characterized by less structured situations that require a more lengthy response from the child. They also require a great deal of interpretation by the psychologist. These tests are based on the assumption that when presented with an open-ended and ambiguous situation, a person will naturally come up with answers that reflect her inner thoughts, feelings, and perceptions. Some typical projective tests used with children are:

■ *Drawings.* These can be used as ice-breakers at the beginning of a session, and are to be interpreted only in the broadest sense. A child could be asked to draw a house, a tree, and a person in sequence; she could be asked to draw her family with each person doing something (called a Kinetic Family Drawing); or she could be asked to draw a scene from school with everyone doing something (called a Kinetic School Drawing). These should be used only to get an idea of what's on a child's mind.

The point to remember is that these drawings take a lot of skill and training to interpret; interpretations of them are speculations, not statements of fact, and must be compared to what the psychologist gathers from interviews with the child and her parents and teacher, from observations, test data, and—most important—what is already known about the child.

■ *Sentence Completion.* Several varieties of these are available, some developed and distributed nationally (for example, the Rotter Incomplete Sentence Blank), and some developed locally. In these tests, a child is asked to complete a sentence. For a younger child, the psychologist will read the beginning of the sentence and write down what the child says to finish. Older children will write in their own answers. Once again, the psychologist is looking here for general themes. If a theme is clear, the psychologist might follow up with other tests and interviews to see if the theme is a valid one. For example, a child may have several answers that center around anxiety: *When I was at the party* . . . "I felt scared."; *No one knows* . . . "I worry a lot." The psychologist might then follow up to find out if the child really feels as anxious as she sounds, and why.

■ *Story Telling.* In these tests, a child is shown a picture or a drawing and asked to make up a story about it to see if any themes emerge. Most currently used tests (such as the Thematic Apperception Test and the Roberts Apperception Test for Children) picture chil-

dren in common situations, but their role is somewhat vague in the picture in order to allow the child to project herself (her ideas, thoughts, feelings, and concerns) into the picture. For example, one picture might be of a child looking into a room where the parents appear to be arguing.

■ *Diagnostic Interview.* An interview is not only a great way for the psychologist and child to get to know each other, but a rich source of information from the child, not only in the things she says, but the things she chooses or refuses to talk about. It's not so much facts that the school psychologist is looking for in these kinds of interviews, as it is the child's perception of the facts. That's why this is the most extensively used of these techniques. The same goes for interviews with parents.

Questions range from very simple (like "What's your address?" for a young child, to see if she knows this by a certain age), to their perceptions of roles, responsibilities and relationships at home. Questions may also be open-ended, like "If you had three wishes, what would they be?"

■ *Rorschach.* Everyone's heard of the famous inkblot test. This is the least structured of the projective tests, and its interpretation is guided by two assumptions:

1 The manner in which the child responds to this test represents how the child sees and responds to other experiences she may have. That is, interpreting the inkblot is a problem-solving task, and children try to solve it using the same cognitive, perceptual, and personality traits they would use when faced with decisions they have to make in school or outside life every day.

2 If we can understand those psychological

traits used most often to make the kinds of decisions described above, then we can know more about the disposition, attitude, and emotions the child uses; all of which can help explain why the child has behaved the way she has, and can help predict how she might act in certain situations.

HOW AN ASSESSMENT TAKES PLACE

For most people, the unknown is usually less appealing than the known. Whether you're in the midst of an assessment process or just contemplating finding out more about your child's behavior, it may help you to anticipate all the steps involved.

Assessments can be requested by a teacher or by a parent or by both, jointly. Either way,

❐ Parents must always be informed about the need or request for an initial assessment
❐ Parents must give their written consent for the assessment
❐ Parents must be invited to a school meeting to discuss the concerns they or the school have.

Before an assessment takes place, the school psychologist must decide whether or not an evaluation will answer the questions a parent or a teacher has about a child. In some cases, it won't. For example, a frustrated teacher who refers a child for evaluation reveals during a pre-assessment interview with the psychologist that her real concern is whether the mother is emotionally capable of caring for the child. While the kind of parenting a child gets can certainly affect her school work, an evaluation of the child will not determine anything about the child's mother. Or take the case of a child referred by a parent for evaluation because she doesn't do well in

math, and the child says she hates math. The evaluation may simply show that the child is bright and capable, that she has a normal personality, but that she just doesn't like math. In a sense, an evaluation in this case won't show much more than everyone already knew.

Whether it's you or the teacher who has requested that your child be evaluated, you should ask the psychologist how, specifically, an evaluation will be helpful for your child. Simply to better understand your child's functioning, or to update an old evaluation are NOT good enough reasons to do an assessment. But if you are satisfied that the evaluation will be helpful, be sure you insist that the evaluation be designed to answer a clear question. Some examples are:

❐ Does my child have a learning disability?
❐ Is he capable of doing math at a fourth grade level?
❐ Is my child's reading difficulty related to her poor memory?
❐ Is my child eligible for special education services as a child with a language disability?
❐ Why has the behavior modification program being used with my child not been more successful?
❐ Is the curriculum being provided for my child the appropriate one?

In most schools, these questions are developed during a Multidisciplinary Team meeting (see Special Education). Then:

❐ The school will expect you to tell your child about the evaluation, help her understand its importance, be sure she will be cooperative, ease some of her concerns, and give permission to your child to share family information. If you feel uncertain about exactly how to do this, ask the psychologist for some ideas for how to say these things to your child.

❏ It's a good idea to schedule a joint pre-assessment meeting between you, your child, and the school psychologist to answer any further questions or concerns you or your child may have.

❏ The school psychologist will observe your child in the classroom, the playground, or other school settings.

❏ Your child will be seen by the school psychologist during the school day, when she will either go to the classroom to pick her up (in elementary school), or send a pass to your child's homeroom teacher (middle and high school).

❏ Be sure the teacher is in agreement with you about the importance of your child having the assessment done, even though it means your child will miss some class time.

Assessments usually take place over several meetings, the number depending on the questions you're trying to answer about your child. Early meetings will probably focus on interviews, drawings, and other school-like activities like academic achievement tests. Personality testing usually comes later, when a rapport has developed between your child and the psychologist. Recently, the trend has been towards understanding the child in her whole environment, so that part of the assessment process will be to have you and the teacher complete some tests and interviews similar to those your child will be doing.

When the psychologist has collected all the information, she will meet with you or with you and your child, depending on your child's age, to share the results. For the youngest children, results are presented very briefly in a manner appropriate to their age and level of understanding. For older children, a more detailed presentation is usually made.

Then, you will be asked to come to another meeting with the Multidisciplinary Team. This is the meeting at which results of all tests are shared with all the specialists, and decisions will be made about what to do, given the results of the evaluation and the resources your child's school has.

Keep in mind that no matter what the results of your child's assessment, and no matter what the plan developed at these meetings, nothing is implemented without your permission. If you are uncomfortable with any aspect of a plan, or with the results of the evaluation, you should talk with the members of the multidisciplinary team and the school psychologist until you are satisfied.

2

YOUR CHILD'S
SCHOOL BEHAVIORS

C H A P T E R 4

ADHD
Attention Deficit Hyperactivity Disorder

"John's teacher keeps telling me how disruptive he is in the classroom. He gets up to sharpen his pencil six or seven times a day. He falls out of his chair and pretends to be a clown when she gives assignments. He trips other students as they walk by his desk. I don't know what I can do about his behavior in class—he's even worse at home."

"Linnea just isn't completing her schoolwork, and even the parts she finishes are done really carelessly. I've been talking with her teacher and we're both pretty puzzled about why she doesn't do better. She invited me to observe her class, and I was so embarrassed. She didn't follow the teacher's instructions, even on simple things I know she can do, like copying her assignment from the board into her notebook. When I asked her later about this, she just gave me a blank stare."

One of the most common reasons children are referred to the school psychologist is that someone—a teacher, a parent, or both—suspect a difficult or inattentive child has ADHD, or Attention Deficit Hyperactivity Disorder.

Psychologists have studied ADHD since the beginning of this century, and the thinking about its cause and its treatment has changed with the times. The most recent developments occurred in the early 1990s, and our recommendations for action stem from these most current views.

While you may be at your wits end with a child you suspect has ADHD, the good news is there are techniques you and your child's teacher can use that will help your child learn appropriate behavior for school and for home.

WHAT WE KNOW NOW

Strictly defined, Attention Deficit Hyperactivity Disorder is exactly what it says: it is a term applied to children who cannot focus their attention or sit still for as long as their age indicates they should be able to.

But in practice, ADHD is not so easy to pin down, and there are always conflicting views about its cause and how to manage it. While no one claims to have uttered the last word about ADHD, most experts agree that it is not strictly a neurological problem treatable primarily with drugs as they thought in the 1980s. Instead, most see it now as a neurodevelopmental disability, a behavioral problem that occurs in some children who have inherited a certain biological makeup. While we can't yet define that biological makeup, and while not everyone who has the biological makeup will develop ADHD behavior, still, the research shows that we cannot rule out that some people are biologically more likely to develop ADHD than others.

That means parents don't cause a child to develop ADHD, but parents and teachers can be instrumental in helping the child who has ADHD change his behavior so that he is much more socially and academically adept.

It's also important to know that not very many children actually have it. Some estimates are that 3 to 5 percent of all children actually have ADHD; other estimates are as high as 8 percent, even though about 25 to 50 percent of all referrals to school psychologists are for suspected ADHD.

Many of those are referred because they are children who are difficult to deal with. But while arriving at an ADHD diagnosis is not an easy, black-and-white matter, children who have it conform to a more specific profile than simply being difficult. Children who have ADHD:

❏ are more often boys than girls.
❏ are usually between ages 6 and 9 when diagnosed, but have definitely shown ADHD behavior before age 7.
❏ behave in a majority of the ways listed below for more than six months.

WHEN SHOULD I BE CONCERNED?

If you think your child may have ADHD, look carefully at his behavior before you jump to conclusions. Notice if your child has shown at least eight of these behaviors for at least six months:

❏ often fidgets with hands or feet, or squirms in his seat at school. (Adolescents report feeling generally restless).
❏ has difficulty remaining seated when required to.
❏ is easily distracted by extraneous events.
❏ has difficulty waiting his turn in games or group situations.
❏ blurts out answers to questions before they have been completed.
❏ has difficulty following through on instructions.
❏ has difficulty sustaining attention when working or playing.
❏ shifts often from one uncompleted activity to another.
❏ has difficulty playing quietly.
❏ often talks excessively.
❏ often interrupts or intrudes on others, in games or conversation.
❏ often does not listen to what is being said to him or her.
❏ often loses things he needs for school, like pens, notebooks, etc.
❏ often engages in physically dangerous activities without considering the consequences, like running into the street without looking.

Many parents could read this list and believe their child must have ADHD because most children behave in some of these ways, some of the time. But children who have ADHD differ in that they aren't responding to their environment the way other children are. In other words, most children will figure out how to stop fidgeting (at least for a little while) when they are told that if they don't, there will be a negative consequence, like time out. A child with ADHD does not stop unless someone helps him to with the kinds of approaches explained in the next section.

WHAT CAN I DO TO HELP?

There are many techniques that help children with ADHD, but it might be useful to know first those that have been used but shown not to help in most cases, so that you can whole-heartedly focus on those that do.

❏ *The Feingold Diet.* Popular in the 1970s and 80s, Dr. Walker Feingold, a California physician, claimed that ADHD behavior was the result of undetected allergies to additives, preservatives, dyes, and salicylates in food. Few studies ever showed a link, and this is no longer routinely recommended.

❏ *Reducing sugar intake.* Studies have not conclusively shown that sugar produces significant effects on children's behavior or learning, although a few children have been shown to become more lethargic after excessive doses of sugar. Sugar has not been shown to have a role in clinically defined ADHD.

❏ *Megavitamin therapy,* also known as *orthomolecular therapy.* Studies have shown massive doses of vitamins have no positive effect on ADHD and may have some long-range negative effect on the child's liver if it has to constantly process more than the normal amount of nutrients.

❏ *Sensory integration training.* It was hoped these physical exercises done with an occupational therapist to develop better visual-motor coordination would help establish normal brain function to correct typical ADHD problems, but research has shown little or no benefit from these exercises.

❏ *Chiropractic treatment.* Manipulation of the bony plates of the skull to release tension or pressure on the brain has not been shown to have an effect on ADHD.

❏ *Ocular-motor training.* Eye-movement exercises (also known as optometrics, visual perspective training, or ocular-motor exercises) used for some children with reading disorders, learning disabilities, and sometimes ADHD. There is no research that supports this type of therapy for ADHD.

❏ *Play therapy.* A technique used by social workers, psychologists, psychiatrists, and other mental health workers with children who have emotional disorders, but which has no effect on ADHD because it is a behavior disorder. (Although emotional problems may develop if ADHD is not properly treated.)

❏ *Biofeedback.* Uses relaxation exercise with electronic monitoring of muscle tension, which is then fed back to the person through displays of light on a panel or TV monitor, or through different pitches of tones. The individual learns to acquire better control of muscle tension and physical reactions to stress. While this is useful for other problems, it has not so far proved useful for children with ADHD.

❏ *Neurofeedback.* Also called EEG biofeedback, this was based on findings that, for some unknown reason, children with ADHD have less electrical activity in the front portion of the brain. This treatment seeks to help children learn to control and increase electrical brain activity associated with attentiveness. Studies are unclear about neurofeedback's effectiveness in all respects except one: it is very expensive.

What *does* work is a day-by-day approach in which you teach your child how to control those parts of his behavior that have been outside his control. Russell A. Barkley, psychologist and author of *ADHD: What We Know* (see Further Reading at the end of this section), has an eight-point plan for parents to use in changing the behavior of their child who has ADHD. His plan can also be helpful for dealing with a difficult child whether or not he has been diagnosed with ADHD. If you are already working with a school psychologist and you know your child has ADHD, you might speak with her about incorporating any of these ideas you are not already using.

Barkley suggests that parents:

1 *Use more immediate feedback and consequences.* Children with ADHD need more praise than most children, more quickly. The type of consequence you use (praise, compliments, physical affection, or rewards like extra privileges or an occasional food treat), is not as important as the timing: it must occur immediately. For example, when your fourth-grader remains focused on his homework for 15 minutes straight without succumbing to distractions, don't wait until dinnertime to praise him.

2 *Use more frequent feedback and consequences.* You'll need to find something to praise your child for every few minutes in order to help him remember to keep working toward his home and school behavior goals. Barkley suggests parents remind themselves to make frequent positive comments by placing smiley-face stickers at their own eye level, setting a kitchen cooking timer for brief, varied intervals, or using a vibrating pager, which Barkley calls a *motivator,* programmed to be a silent reminder to praise your child.

3 *Use more substantial consequences.* Children with ADHD usually need larger, more significant and sometimes more material (like money) consequences for positive behavior, especially at the beginning of your behavior-change efforts.

4 *Remember to use positives before negatives.* Many children with ADHD misbehave so often, you could be punishing them constantly if that's all you pay attention to. Mild punishment (time

out, revoking small privileges) can be useful as a last resort, but Barkley says you should use it infrequently and selectively and always in conjunction with a reward program.

5 *Be consistent.* Unpredictability is one of the main reasons behavior-change programs fail. No one is perfect with how they enforce family rules, but be sure that over time, you are consistent in your expectations of your child and in the consequences you've set up for both good and inappropriate behavior. Even though your child may not respond exactly the way you want him to in the first days of your behavior-change efforts, if you remain consistent, you are likely to see changes begin after a week or two. You are also likely to see the good results reach a plateau after a few more weeks, and weeks later, you may see your child testing the limits and even regressing. The long-term changes in behavior you're aiming for typically happen in fits and starts, and some days it may seem you and your child take one step forward and two steps back. This is where the importance of consistency comes in, and where your behavior shows your child that you won't quit the plan, that you are patient enough to stay with it (and him), and that you have seen too many good changes in him to go back now. You may also consider adjusting rewards and punishments to keep your child motivated. And, don't be afraid to consult the school psychologist again when you hit a low point. Be sure through all this, that you and your spouse are on the same track in how you reward and punish behavior and in how you both react to behavior at home, as well as away from home.

6 *Anticipate problems.* You may be able to head off inappropriate behavior by anticipating times you know will be tough for your child. Not only will you save yourself the frustration and embarrassment of a public confrontation, but you will be able to plan your behavior reinforcement strategy. For example, if you know that in the past, walking into the school with your first-grader has resulted in a confrontation because he runs in the hall and throws his coat on the floor, stop before you enter the building and have him review the specific rules he usually has trouble following. (For example he should say, "I will remember to walk in the hall and hang up my coat.") It's important that your child *say* the rules, because it helps him to make those rules part of him, rather than something you tell him to do.

You can also review the reward to be earned if he behaves well, and the punishment he'll have if he does not behave well. Then be prepared to carry it out. Your quick, predictable response to his inappropriate behavior is the key to change.

7 *Keep your perspective.* As you work with your child to help him change his behavior, try to think of yourself as his teacher and coach. It's hard not to lose your cool when dealing with a child who is as difficult as children with ADHD can be, so you may need this psychological distance.

For his *eighth* step, Barkley suggests that you practice forgiveness when you are dealing with a child who has ADHD. Each evening, review the day's events in your mind, and silently forgive your child for the times his behavior has been less than what you would like. Forgive others who may misunderstand your child's difficulty or your efforts to work with him. And last, forgive yourself for your own mistakes in managing your child that day. After you've forgiven yourself, try to also give yourself credit for the times you did exactly the right thing with your child.

WHAT WILL A PROFESSIONAL DO?

If you or your child's teacher suspect your child has ADHD, you don't have to wait to call the school psychologist. Even if it turns out he does not have ADHD, the psychologist may be able to help you with strategies that will work for you. And if your child does have ADHD, the psychologist can help you and your child get on a path toward better academic and social functioning. In any case, it's good to know whether or not your child has ADHD. Children with ADHD who don't get help learning how to control their behavior only develop more serious social and academic problems as they get older. If there is no psychologist at your school, or if your child is home-schooled or attends a private school, contact the psychologist at a nearby school in your town, even if your child actually attends school in another town. That psychologist will probably help you or at least refer you to someone who can.

There is some difference of opinion about who should provide the ADHD diagnosis, and you'll need to check with your school district to see what their policy is. Some districts require the school psychologist to collect information and make the diagnosis; in others, all possible ADHD cases are referred to physicians even though there are no medical tests that confirm ADHD, and physicians use the same kind of information as psychologists to make a diagnosis. It is, however, a physician or psychiatrist who must prescribe medication if your child needs it, but it is the school psychologist who will coordinate behavior-change efforts between the teacher and the parents. The school psychologist and nurse will also be involved in monitoring the effects of medication.

In making a diagnosis, the school psychologist should be interested in keeping the focus on your child's educational as well as behavioral needs, so that both can be improved. Her focus should not only be to determine if he has ADHD, but also rule out other problems—frustration, lack of motivation, nervousness, or depression. (See also Motivation, Nervous Habits, Depression, and Learning Disabilities.) Your school psychologist should:

❏ observe your child in the classroom and at recess.

❏ have you and your child's teacher complete some behavioral checklists such as the Child Behavior Checklist by Achenbach for parents and teachers, the Revised Behavior Problem Checklist for parents and teachers by Quay and Peterson, the Conners Teacher Rating Scale, or the Conners Parent Rating Scale. She may also use other tests such as the Academic Performance Rating Scale to determine your child's academic level and his level of intellectual functioning and information processing skills. (See Appendix D, Test Samples.)

❏ interview you, your child, and your child's teacher. As the parent, your input will be critical in helping the psychologist understand your child. A complete assessment will probably include interviews with your child, either alone or with you. Because there is no one technique for diagnosing or working with children who have or who are suspected to have ADHD, there are many combinations of interviews and testing a psychologist may use to learn about you and your child. (See Evaluation and Testing in Part 1).

In designing a behavior-change program for your child with the teacher, the school psychologist will most likely recommend that the classroom teacher and the parents adhere to some basic principles, such as providing:

❏ clearly defined rules and expectations
❏ consistent routines for completing work
❏ clearly stated teacher expectations for your child's behavior
❏ an effective seating arrangement in the classroom, placing your child in a seat where the teacher can best implement the plan
❏ frequent praise and immediate consequences from the teacher
❏ responsibilities in the classroom, such as handing out papers

In addition, Barkley recommends that the teacher consider:

❏ decreasing your child's workload to fit his attention span or breaking assignments up into smaller pieces your child will be capable of doing
❏ planning frequent breaks during the day and letting all the children exercise briefly near their desks
❏ rewarding children for how they solve a problem, not for the speed with which they solve it, in order to help children with ADHD control their impulsive behavior
❏ developing self-monitoring strategies for the classroom which can help them learn to control their own behavior. One technique for younger children is an exercise called "Turtle." Whenever the teacher says the word "turtle," the children are to stop, pull their arms and legs in like a turtle, and think for a moment about whether they are following the rules or the task they were assigned before they go back to the activity they'd drifted away from.
❏ controlling frequency of reminders. While immediate and frequent feedback is necessary for children with ADHD, too much reminding about rules is easily tuned out by the child. Clearly stated, or written, rules are enough. It

is the immediate reaction to the child's actions that produce behavioral change, not constant reminding.

Children with ADHD who cannot respond to the kinds of structured, consistent home and school behavioral-change plans described here may need medication to help them control their behavior. This is another area full of controversy. While your physician may recommend medication for your child, the decision about whether to use it or not must rest with you and must fit with your family's values. It may help you to know that the medications most commonly used for ADHD are not addictive, nor do they produce side effects that last significantly beyond the time your child takes the medication. ADHD medications fall into three categories:

1 *Stimulants:* Central nervous system stimulants are the drugs of choice for ADHD symptoms because they do the best job of lessening impulsive and aggressive behavior and increasing a child's ability to concentrate. While behavior, academic accuracy, and productivity clearly improve for children taking these medications, it is not clear that overall academic achievement improves too, without additional academic help.

Stimulants most commonly prescribed for ADHD are methylphenidate (sold as Ritalin), d-amphetamine (sold as Dexedrine), and pemoline (sold as Cylert). Effective dosages vary with the individual, and your child should be carefully monitored when beginning medication to determine what dosage is best for him. Some children take medication only on school days; others find it's best to take it over weekends and school vacations, too.

The most commonly reported side effects are insomnia, appetite reduction (particularly at noon), and temporary growth suppression, which can be handled by increasing your child's calorie intake at other times of the day. Some children have stomachaches or headaches when first taking the medication, which means they need a smaller dose to begin with. About 1 to 2 percent of children will develop motor or vocal tics when they are treated with stimulants. If your child already has a tic, be sure to tell your physician about it before your child takes a stimulant.

2 *Antidepressants:* For children who cannot take stimulants, some physicians prescribe tricyclic antidepressants like imipramine and desipramine. These medications produce increased attention and decreased impulsivity, and may also elevate the mood of children who were depressed. But because the effects of these medications may diminish over time, these cannot be used as long-term therapy for ADHD as can the stimulants.

Side effects for some children may be drowsiness during the first few days, dry mouth, and constipation. For some, these can trigger heart arrhythmias or temporary eye problems mimicking nearsightedness.

3 *Antihypertensives:* One drug usually used to control high blood pressure in adults, Clonidine, has been found to help ADHD symptoms. It decreases aggressive behavior and outbursts in children with ADHD, but not as dramatically as the stimulants.

4 *Combining medications:* One type of drug is usually effective, but some children may be best helped by combining one or more of these drugs. This should only be done by a physician well-trained in treating children with ADHD with these kinds of medication.

See also:

❑ Depression
❑ Learning Disabilities

❑ Motivation
❑ Nervous Habits

Further Reading

Alexander-Roberts, C. *The ADHD Parenting Handbook: Practical Advice for Parents from Parents.* Dallas: Taylor Publishing, 1994.

Barkley, Russell A. *ADHD: What Do We Know?* New York: Guildford Publications, 1992.

Bain, L. *Parent's Guide to Attention Deficit Disorder.* New York: Dell Publishing, 1991.

Hartmann, T. *Attention Deficit Disorder: A Different Perception.* Penn Valley, CA: Underwood-Miller, 1993.

Ingusoll, Barbara. *Your Hyperactive Child: A Parent's Guide to Coping with Attention Deficit Disorder.* New York: Mainstreet Books, 1988.

Kennedy, P., Terdal, L. & Fusetti, L. *The Hyperactive Child Book.* New York: St. Martin's Books, 1993.

Moss, R. & Dunlap, H. *Why Johnny Can't Concentrate: Coping with Attention Deficit Problems.* New York: Bantam Books, 1993.

Moss, D. & Schawarty, C. *Shelley, the Hyperactive Turtle.* Rockville, MD: Woodbine House, 1989.

Quinn, P.O. *ADHD and the College Student.* New York: Magination Press, 1994.

Quinn, P. & Stein, J. *Putting On the Brakes: Young People's Guide to Understanding Attention Deficit Hyperactive Disorder (ADHD).* New York: Magination Press, 1991.

C H A P T E R 5

Anger Control

"Kimberly has been having angry outbursts during class, her teacher tells me. Two or three times a day she shouts at a classmate or gestures as if she'd hit someone. It seemes like she's having the 'Terrible Twos' all over again in fourth grade."

Even though it can be unsettling to watch someone (and sometimes to be the one) getting red in the face and yelling, it's important to remember that anger does have some positive uses in our culture. For example, it can help people define and resolve conflicts, and it can provide a way to get strongly felt differences out on the table.

Being angry and showing it from time to time is not abnormal, but if you have a child you think is angry very frequently, if he is still having what you would describe as tantrums on a regular basis after about age 6, or if his anger seems overwhelmingly intense or aggressive, you may find helpful some ideas on how to help him figure out why he's angry, and then to learn to manage his anger or to express it in acceptable ways.

WHAT WE KNOW NOW

Babies express anger when they cry, flail their arms, and kick their legs. At around 18 months, many children begin having tantrums when they are angry. Tantrums peak around the end of the second year, and thankfully, decline after about the third birthday. That's because by about age 3, most children begin to see that language is a more effective tool for getting what they want.

But as you've no doubt noticed, language doesn't always completely replace outbursts. That may be because children mimic what they see around them, and the attentive child sees plenty of anger in the normal middle-class home, where they are two to three times more likely to see incidents of anger than they are to see incidents of affection.

Perhaps our children see so much anger in adults because anger has so many uses in our culture. We use anger:

❑ as a way to open up communication and define issues,

❑ as a pathway to aggression in sports and in portrayals in movies and television shows,

❑ as a safety valve, providing a healthy way to release built-up frustrations,

❑ as a normal part of the grieving process when a loved one has died, or when a child has lost a parent or a way of life through death, divorce (see Divorce/Single Parents and Appendix C, Helping Children Through Crises) or separation.

At school, anger can be a reaction to academic difficulties (see Learning Disabilities, Giftedness). It can also signal a certain kind of aggression, which is how some groups of schoolchildren define their social roles: angry threats and challenges help determine who's toughest. (See Friends.)

Just like adults, some kids get angry more easily than others. Children who are normally "high strung," like a pressure cooker that's at near-capacity steam all the time, take very little provocation or difficulty to make them explode. Others may have simply not yet learned the skills required to manage their anger. And some childrens' anger may be a reaction to serious situations in their lives, such as abuse or illness.

In any case, it's important to understand why your child is angry at school, as well as how to help him learn to manage his anger in appropriate ways. Children who do not have or learn this ability may develop problems with making or keeping school friends and can become easy targets for teasing and provocation from other children.

WHEN SHOULD I BE CONCERNED?

If your child's anger regularly leads to physical attacks on others, it's cause for concern because that kind of significant physical aggression is rarely displayed in school.

You should also be concerned if either your elementary-aged child or your adolescent is:

❏ angry frequently and gets into arguments with classmates every day, for example. However, if your child gets over his anger quickly, even daily anger is not significant unless your child typically gets angry and stays angry all day.

❏ more intensely angry than other children the same age, and she often cries, hits others, rips up her paper if she gets something wrong or if she's having difficulty with it, tips over her desk or knocks over her paint if she doesn't like the picture she's done.

❏ unresponsive to her teacher's attempts to calm her, and yells at or hits her.

❏ easily angered over things that don't seem that serious to you, like changes in classroom routine.

❏ overwhelmed by angry outbursts that seem to last an especially long time, more than five minutes of tantrum-type behavior. You should also be concerned if he has extreme difficulty regaining control of himself.

❏ feeling angry about something in almost every part of her life, and she often feels generally angry rather than being angry at a specific event or person. (See Depression.)

You might also be concerned if you see a significant change in how your child handles certain situations; for example, if you see him becoming very angry over things that haven't bothered him before.

WHAT CAN I DO TO HELP?

Children are most likely to show inappropriate anger at school when there is something amiss in at least one of four areas: academics, relationships with friends, problems at home, or simply because the temperament they were born with makes it easy to get angry.

Your first task in helping a child who can't manage his or her anger is to understand why they are angry and help them to understand if they don't. That means listening. Angry children need adults who are open and who can respond with empathy, in a calm and understanding manner. Simply criticizing him for becoming angry, or becoming angry yourself, won't show him how to express anger appropriately or how to replace anger with composure.

You can begin to understand why your child is angry by asking him (at a calm time) what made him so angry and having him identify if it was a feeling inside of him, like frustration, or a reaction to what someone said, like teasing (see Bullies and Victims). Some children may not want to talk with you about their anger, particularly adolescents. In that case, you can seek the help of the school psychologist first, instead of trying to figure out what to do yourself.

The goal of working with an angry youngster, from kindergarten age through high school, is to get him to see that he always has a choice about how he will respond to things like his own frustration or teasing from others. He can choose to yell, to hit, to have a tantrum; or he can choose to tell the teacher or the classmate how he feels and why (see Conflict). Encourage him to tell you which action gets the best results.

You can also help your child learn to control his anger by:

❐ praising him when he is not angry or when he has handled a difficult situation with at least a little composure.

❐ making an agreement with your child that for a certain period of time he will not act out his anger, or he will act it out in agreed-upon appropriate ways. Begin with a manageable time-frame for him—say, two hours—and reward him for succeeding. (See Appendix A—Motivators.) Let the teacher know of your plan, so she too can reward your child.

❐ having your fifth grade or younger child keep a diary of feelings, using pictures if written words are too difficult. Encourage children to describe the problem that made them angry, how they reacted, what happened as a result of their reaction, whether their reaction was a good way to handle the situation, and what might have worked better. Help them to find

better reactions if they have trouble with that.

❐ acting in ways you would like to see him act. For example, you can express your own anger in words that will help resolve a conflict, showing your child that the anger itself is not necessarily the problem, but the expression of it is.

You might also consider offering karate lessons to your child. For some children, regardless of age or gender, karate offers a way to learn discipline as well as offering a physical outlet for pent-up anger.

WHAT WILL A PROFESSIONAL DO?

If your child won't talk with you about his anger, or if you don't see an improvement in your child's behavior even though you have worked to understand his anger and modeled appropriate behavior, it's time to contact the school psychologist for help. It's also time if you think your adolescent is turning to drugs or alcohol because of his anger. Some youngsters will ask to see the school psychologist themselves, and others are referred by a teacher or a principal because of disruptive behavior.

If the psychologist is doing a full assessment, usually because your child's anger is affecting her school performance, she will likely have her complete some self-report tests such as the Child Behavior Checklist or the Piers-Harris Children's Self-Concept Scale (see Evaluation and Testing, in Part I, and Appendix D—Samples from Tests and Assessments). She may ask your child's teacher to complete a behavior evaluation form, too, such as the Achenbach Teacher's Report Form. And in trying to determine if your child has learning problems or is bored with her class level, she may also do some academic testing, having your child complete a test such as the Woodcock-Johnson Tests of Achievement, as well as reviewing scores from standardized tests your child may have already taken. The psychologist is also likely to observe your child in order to better define his anger, and perhaps will ask you and the teacher to help by noting:

❏ when and where your child becomes angry. For example, is it only during unstructured times, only on the playground, or is it always associated with certain subjects?
❏ how he acts it out (threats, yelling, tears),
❏ what happens immediately before the outburst, and
❏ what happens immediately after the outburst.

You may also be asked to be on the lookout for evidence of issues that could be provoking your child's anger, such as academic frustration (see Perfectionism, Learning Disabilities, Giftedness, Anxiety, ADHD), grieving, illness, abuse, divorce (see Divorce), or problems with peers (see Friends). Evidence may show up in the words he yells, or in the particular type of situation that almost always trips your child's anger switch.

The psychologist may then work with your child to learn the specific skills he needs to manage his anger in the situations that bother him most. Many psychologists offer groups teaching conflict resolution (see Conflict) or social skills. For middle and high school students, there may be peer mediation programs that cash in on the strength of peer influence at these ages, or special groups for children of alcoholics or of substance abusers. In some cases, the psychologist may also refer to an outside counselor for help.

See also:

❏ ADHD
❏ Anxiety
❏ Appendix A—Motivators
❏ Bullies and Victims
❏ Conflict
❏ Depression
❏ Divorce—Single Parents
❏ Giftedness
❏ Learning Disabilities
❏ Perfectionism

Further Reading

Eastman, M. & Rozer, S. *Taming the Dragon in Your Child: Solutions for Breaking the Cycle of Family Anger.* New York: John Wiley, 1994.

Fein, T. I. *I.A.M.: A Common Sense Guide to Coping With Anger.* Westport, CT: Praeger, 1993.

McKay, M. *When Anger Hurts: How to Change Painful Feelings into Positive Action.* New York: MJF Books, 1989.

Rubin, T. I. *The Angry Book.* New York: Collier, 1987.

Samalin, N. & Whitney, C. *Love and Anger: The Parental Dilemma.* New York: Viking Penguin, 1991.

Tavris, C. *Anger: The Misunderstood Emotion.* New York: Simon and Schuster, 1982.

CHAPTER 6

Anxiety

"Matthew, 9, seems to enjoy school, but he becomes so anxious before and during any kind of test, that he just 'freezes' and can't remember a thing. And his grades are beginning to show it."

"Lately, Sarah, 14, has had trouble getting to sleep, and she's complained of a stomachache at least once a week for the last month or so. She talks about her school work constantly and asks me to check her homework for errors over and over."

Anxiety is a normal, often positive, part of life. It's healthy anxiety that spurs a sixth-grader to complete an extra poster, to illustrate her science project, and it's the good kind of anxiety that pushes the tenth grader to study an extra half-hour for his French exam.

But too much anxiety can be paralyzing. When it is, it can interfere with, or, in some cases, shut down a child's academic progress or social life. Knowing what to do when helpful anxiety turns hurtful can help you and your child keep a healthy outlook on this powerful feeling that can push us to excel, or push us over the edge.

WHAT WE KNOW NOW

Everybody is familiar with the term *anxiety* and with how it can make them feel. For children, it is difficult to distinguish anxiety from fear, but generally anxiety is thought of as apprehension about future events. By contrast, fear is a response to a situation, such as a child being afraid of an animal, afraid of speaking in front of the class, or afraid of the class bully. Anxiety can be a long-term feeling—for example, if your child feels anxious about her school per-formance in general, always uncertain whether she is really a good student and whether she is actually liked by her teachers and peers, no matter what her grades are or how many friends she has. Anxiety can also occur only in a specific setting—for example, when your child has to take her midterm exams.

Anxiety is a normal response to any situation in which we cannot know the outcome ahead of time. It is a message to the brain which says, "Get ready for a challenge!", and different people in the same situation will normally experience different intensities of anxiety. You may know (or perhaps you have) "high strung" youngsters who normally react more dramatically than other kids to the first day of school and midterm exams. Just as infants and preschoolers show different degrees of separation anxiety when mom leaves for a few hours, so do primary-age children, and secondary youngsters show different ways of reacting to anxiety-producing situations, depending on their own personalities. In addition, adolescents often have a more extreme approach to anxiety, either showing a "so-what" attitude (less than usual anxiety), or an "oh, no" attitude (far more anxiety than usual).

So there's a broad range of what's normal when we're talking about anxiety. It depends on that person's personality, where they are in their own development (very young children and adolescents tend to be more anxious), and what's normal in their family (anxious children often have anxious parents).

WHEN SHOULD I BE CONCERNED?

No matter who you are or what your family is like, anxiety has become too much when it keeps your child from being able to do something as basic as fully focusing during the school day. For some children that means anxiety strong enough to keep them from raising their hands to answer a question in class for fear they'll get it wrong and everyone will laugh. (See also Assertiveness and Shyness.) For others, it means anxiety over forgetting something important to them, such as their lunch money, even though they know their school has a voucher system that would allow them to have a lunch anyway. These may sound like small things to an adult, but when a child's anxiety over small things becomes the focus for the entire day, it's time for you to be concerned. If your child's behavior is not that dramatic, but you still wonder if he is overly anxious, you can get a general picture of the appropriateness of his behavior by comparing what he does with what other children his age do.

You can also notice if your child:

❐ has morbid fears of accidents, or that illness will strike his parents or other people who matter to him.

❐ needs lots of reassurance about how he's doing in school, how well he's done his homework, whether his friends really like him.

❐ frequently wants to stay home from school. (See also School Phobia.)

❐ is markedly self-conscious about his hair, his clothes, everything.

❐ has frequent physical complaints like stomachaches, also trembling, motor tics, sweating or clammy hands, excessive talking, pacing, squirming that shows you the child is "wound up."

A primary-age child might also:

❐ have trouble falling asleep and want parents in the room with her.

❐ worry a great deal about future events, like a test or her appearance in a school play.

A secondary-age youngster might also:

❐ show extreme concern over meeting school work deadlines.

❐ worry constantly about the quality of their school work.

❐ be more preoccupied than their friends are with how they are seen by their peers, with grades, or with athletic acceptance.

❐ cling to parents when out in public.

There are a number of reasons a child can become extremely anxious. Some of them are:

❐ parental expectations that set standards the child sees as unattainable.

❐ extremely high personal needs for achievement.

❐ rejection by her peers. (See also Friends.)

❐ acceptance by a new set of peers whom the child believes will hold her to a higher standard.

❐ inconsistency in treatment by parents or teachers, so that life becomes unpredictable.

❐ permissiveness or neglect, so that the child has no clearly defined limits.

❐ constant criticism, so that the feeling of being judged never goes away.

❐ constant frustration, so that the child feels

unable to reach her academic or her social goals.

❏ parents who are anxious themselves and unwittingly teach their children to become anxious.

WHAT CAN I DO TO HELP?

One of the most effective things you can do at home to help an anxious child is to really listen to and understand what she has to say. A technique called Active Listening can be helpful. To use it you:

❏ encourage your child to talk openly about whatever it is that makes her anxious.

❏ never interrupt her or "speak for" her.

❏ never question what she has to say or try to "reason" her out of feeling what she feels.

❏ never "correct" her feelings, as in saying "You shouldn't feel that way. . . "

❏ show that you understand and respect what she's saying by nodding and listening quietly.

Your calm acceptance of what she has to say and your reassurance that many problems in life are to be expected, handled, and forgotten can be a starting place to overcoming anxiety.

You can also talk with your child about things that make you anxious and how you handle them. Helplessness is a key element of anxiety, and letting your child know that there are solutions to even the toughest problems can be a step toward losing that helpless feeling.

Some other activities you can do at home to help both primary and secondary age youngsters manage anxiety:

❏ Help your child learn to relax. Simple slow, deep breathing might be enough for some children. Or, try the techniques in a book called *Beyond the Relaxation Response,* by Dr. Herbert Benson, and guide your child through them. Even though a secondary-age youngster could do the techniques on her own, she might appreciate your help. Part of Benson's technique is to have your child lie down and close her eyes while you instruct her to tense one part of her body at a time—her jaw, for example—and then relax it, moving slowly through her whole body. Without making this a major chore, you could start out doing this twice a day, before school and before bed.

❏ Teach your child to tell positive stories. Have your younger child tell you a scary or strange story. Then tell her a similar story, but have the hero or heroine figure out how to vanquish the monster or win the friends. Without describing what you are teaching her, you can be giving your child valuable lessons in how people work out tough problems and overcome anxiety.

❏ Teach your child to use positive imagery. Many children can quickly learn to relax when they are faced with an anxiety-producing situation by picturing a calm, pleasant memory. You can practice this during the relaxation sessions described above. Calling to mind that day at the beach instead of fretting about how she'll ever remember all her history facts can calm pre-exam jitters.

❏ Teach your child to use positive self-talk. We all silently "talk" to ourselves, and that talk can be very negative. If your child is telling herself things like, "I'll never be able to do math as well as Amy," or "I always get the lowest spelling score," it's not surprising she feels anxious. Help your child figure out good things to say to herself like, "When I start to get upset about giving my report, I remember how to relax and I do fine," or "I know how to do my best, and that's all I need to do."

❏ Encourage your secondary-age youngster to open up to you about things that are most anxiety-producing to him. Then brainstorm with him about ways he might be able to address those anxieties. Sometimes when they are closely examined, some anxieties, such as speaking in front of a group, may really be about feeling unprepared. And sometimes, doing whatever is possible can at least leave your youngster with the satisfaction he's done his best, no matter what the outcome.

Last, don't underestimate the effect of physical contact. For some kids it's powerfully reassuring if you'll go one step farther than talk and show them you'll stand with them through difficult times with hugs and cuddling. That applies to your first grader as well as to your high-schooler, who may be much too big for your lap, but not too big to curl up with on the couch.

You also could talk to your child's teacher about changes that may help him manage test-taking with less anxiety, for example:

❏ eliminating or modifying time constraints on tests if possible.
❏ modifying the amount of material included on a test by breaking it into two smaller tests.
❏ allowing your child to take a test during recess or after school if class time is too stressful for him.
❏ allowing your child a water or bathroom break during a test to catch his breath.
❏ substituting a term paper for an exam, or modifying the exam so it's not always all essay or all multiple choice questions.

You can help your child manage test anxiety by getting an exam schedule from the teacher so that you'll know when one is coming up. Then encourage your child to prepare for the test well in advance, with the reward being that the night before he can study a little, and then you can share a relaxing, fun activity.

Keep in mind that the object of all the these activities is to help your child learn how to manage anxiety, not to eliminate it or to eliminate the cause of anxiety, like tests.

WHAT WILL A PROFESSIONAL DO?

It's time to contact the school psychologist if you feel for any reason that your child's level of anxiety is more than you can successfully deal with at home. In this case, it's better to ask for help sooner rather than later, when your child may have already developed a sense of failure or incompetence because of his anxious feelings.

The psychologist will want to talk with your child, with both parents, and with the teacher about the child's anxieties to try to determine their basis. If she can identify a basis (another child who is threatening to yours, for example), then the psychologist can work with the teacher and parents to head off the cause of the anxiety.

If the basis is not so clear, more evaluation may be warranted, but in most school districts, the psychologist may not have the time or resources to do that unless your child's anxiety is so severe that he may have undiagnosed learning problems, or be in need of special education services. If neither of those are the case with your child, at this point, the school psychologist may suggest private counseling for you and your child.

If the psychologist suspects your child may need special learning services from the school, she will further evaluate your child by having him fill out some self-reporting inventories such as the Children's Manifest Anxiety

Scale or the State-Trait Anxiety Inventory for Children, or by having you and the teacher complete a similar inventory about your child, like the Personality Inventory for Children (see Appendix D for description).

Depending on how the psychologist interprets what the inventories show about your child, and depending on what she has learned about your child from talking with you and your child's teacher, some techniques the school psychologist (or a private psychologist, if that is the route you are taking) might use to help your child become less anxious are:

- *Cognitive behavior modification:* a technique in which your child is taught to recognize how her own thoughts trigger her anxiety, and how to change her thinking process to control this.
- *Desensitization:* a relaxation technique in which your child is encouraged to think of a safe, happy situation; then of an anxiety-producing one. Over time, this pairing of positive and negative feelings can help your child learn to respond positively when confronted with a negative situation, making her less sensitive, or vulnerable, to negative situations.

See also:

❐ Assertiveness
❐ Dependency
❐ Depression
❐ Fears
❐ Friends
❐ School Phobia

Further Reading

Benson, Herbert M. D. & William Proctor. *Beyond the Relaxation Response.* New York: Times Books, 1984.

Feiner, J. *Taming Monsters, Slaying Dragons: The Revolutionary Family Approach to Overcoming Childhood Fears and Anxieties.* New York: Arbor House, 1988.

Greist, J. H. *Anxiety and Its Treatment: Help Is Available: Advice from Three Leading Psychiatrists in the Field of Anxiety Treatment.* Washington, DC: American Psychiatric Press, 1988.

CHAPTER 7

Assertiveness and Shyness

"I know Shakima is a bright student, and she does all her homework. But her teacher tells me Shakima is so shy that she never volunteers to answer in class, and even when the teacher calls on her, Shakima won't always answer. I'm afraid her shyness is going to hurt her academically if she doesn't grow out of it soon."

"Mason told me that a girl who sits next to him copied off his paper during a test today. He knew she was doing it, but he didn't have the nerve to hide his paper or to tell the teacher."

"Paula was kept in at recess again today for pushing another child while they were standing in the lunch line. I say she's just being assertive and letting other kids know she's going to stand up to them if they give her a hard time. But the teacher says Paula's being aggressive, not assertive. What's the difference?"

Children need to know how to stand up for themselves. They also need to know when to back off. And parents become concerned when they see their children using too little assertiveness, too much aggression, or vice versa.

Most children don't learn all these social skills without direction from a parent who understands the fine line between aggression and assertiveness, who can see the difference between shyness that's a result of temperament or cultural training and shyness that grows out of low self esteem.

You can give your child that direction, and it will stand him in good stead in his social life as well as at school, where being either overly assertive or overly shy can have repercussions on your child's academic performance.

WHAT WE KNOW NOW

A key aspect of understanding how to help your child learn the social skills she'll need in school (and in the rest of her life), is first understanding the differences in terms we'll use.

Your child is using assertive behavior when she expresses her thoughts, feelings, and beliefs in direct, honest, and appropriate ways that do not violate the rights of others, and when the message does not humiliate, degrade, or dominate the one she's talking to. An assertive person can express her personal opinions but also respects the opinions of others who differ with her. Assertive people speak in an even tone, look the person they are speaking to in the eye, and speak calmly.

Your child is using nonassertive or passive behavior when she does not honestly and directly express her thoughts and feelings, allowing her own rights to be violated. That's what happens when your child allows another child to copy from her paper at school, or when she is talked in to giving away her favorite pen even though she didn't want to.

Nonassertive behavior is often accompanied by nervous giggling or inappropriate laughter and little eye contact.

Your child is using aggressive behavior when she expresses thoughts, feelings, and beliefs in a way that violates the rights of others, the goal being to win a fight or to dominate the other person, no matter what the cost. Aggressive actions can include finger-pointing, shouting, staring, a sarcastic or a condescending tone of voice, or physical contact like hitting.

Children learn how assertive to be from family and friends, and later from people at school. If your child is having trouble with assertiveness, it could be because she learned a limited repertoire of responses, or she might be "stuck" at a certain behavioral stage and need some help learning how to move on to better ways of handling conflict or social relationships. (See Conflict.) We know that sometimes children are unable to speak up for themselves because of:

❏ a lack of self-esteem (see Self-Esteem)
❏ a fear of not being able to measure up to unrealistic standards they set for themselves (see Perfectionism) or they feel are set for them (see Here's the First Step. . . , in Part I)
❏ an overwhelming need for peer acceptance (see Friends)

No one has figured out how many children have problems with assertiveness, although it's clear by the number of referrals to school psychologists that focus on this issue, that there are quite a few. But researchers have a fairly good idea of how many children would describe themselves as shy. Surveys conducted by the Stanford Shyness Clinic show that 80 percent of school children describe themselves as having been shy at some point in their lives.

Being shy, or avoiding social interaction, can have its positive points: Shyness can be a kind of protective device that allows young children time to adapt to new people or situations. Shy older children or adults are sometimes looked at as people who value privacy, are more introspective, and are good listeners.

But even allowing for the fact that everyone has a different temperament, and some people are comfortable seeking out more social interaction than others, still, children who are very shy can experience some negative academic effects when they are too shy to interact with teachers or classmates.

Research shows that shyness in children can be strongly related to poor self-concept, feelings of failure, and negative self-statements. Whether you see your own child's shyness as a negative or a positive attribute will have a lot to do with what you know about your child's personality, how your child is doing academically and socially, and what is appropriate for your heritage: for example, in Asian American and Latino families a kind of shyness or reticence around people who are authorities is a sign of respect.

As with assertiveness, children learn from the people around them the social skills that allow them to interact with others. Sometimes children are shy because they don't feel they know how to be friends with others their age; other times, they may feel they have the skills, but are afraid or uncertain about using them.

WHEN SHOULD I BE CONCERNED?

You should be concerned about your child's assertiveness when your child:

❏ is always the doormat, or always the one to comply with others' requests, even when she doesn't want to.

❏ feels angry or upset about events that happen in school, but is unwilling to speak up about it, even though, for example, she got in trouble for something she didn't do.

❏ is usually passive, won't make eye contact when she speaks with you or with friends.

❏ is too assertive, never compromises with peers, always has to have things her way, never tries to see anothers' side of the story, is usually a demanding playmate.

❏ has a hard time finding someone to play with him because his classmates say he is too bossy.

You should be concerned about your child's shyness when your child:

❏ won't ask questions in class, won't volunteer answers or help

❏ won't ask the teacher for extra help

❏ develops physical symptoms, like a stomachache, in anticipation of class plays or working on a group project

❏ always prefers to work independently rather than in a group

❏ won't attend social events like after-school activities; for adolescents, won't go to school dances or parties

❏ becomes extremely anxious when the teacher calls on him—for example, getting red in the face

❏ resists taking any kind of leadership role

❏ has been outgoing and suddenly becomes a loner. If your attempts to talk about this change with your child are not successful, contact the school psychologist immediately, because it could be a sign of a more serious problem. (See Depression, Suicide.)

WHAT CAN I DO TO HELP?

If you are concerned about your child's shyness, you may need to be the one to contact the teacher first. Quiet, compliant children don't often stand out in a classroom, and the teacher may not think of your child's shyness as a problem.

To help your child with shyness, you can:

❏ have your child make a list of things she'd like to be able to do, such as have a certain child over or do a class project with another child. Role play with him how he might ask the child to come play, or to work on the project with him. Then go over the possible responses he might get from the other child. Evaluate with him which are realistic and act them out. He'll feel more comfortable acting on his wishes if the results are not so foreign.

❏ help reduce the amount of anxiety she may be feeling in social or academic situations. (See Anxiety.) For example, have her practice her oral report on you until she feels comfortable saying it. Check with the teacher on cutting the length of your child's first presentation and then increasing the length slightly each time in later presentations. In social situations, replay with your child what she would have done at her classmate's birthday party if she hadn't been too shy to join in the games. You can help ease her way the next time by doing things like playing some of those games with her, so that they are not unfamiliar.

❏ arrange with the teacher for your child to work with one other child on a project instead of a larger group. She'll have the plus of social interaction with one person, and if your child is too nervous to make a class presentation, perhaps her partner will. Giving your child an out once in a while as she's learning new social skills may also help reduce her anxiety.

❏ arrange with the teacher to use your child for one-on-one peer tutoring in any skill your child is particularly good at. When your child is in a position to tell someone else something she knows well, it will give her practice at talking with others, and for many children, shyness vanishes the more confident they feel. Don't spring this on your child; always clear plans like this with her first.

There are other things you could suggest to the teacher, such as:

❐ sending your child on school errands with a classmate

❐ giving your child classroom responsibilities like feeding pets, washing the blackboard, turning on the computers.

❐ planning ahead of time with your child to ask her a question in class to which she's already rehearsed the answer. If your child can answer in front of others, the teacher gives her a small reward later.

You can also look at the chapter on Dependency for ideas on how to help your child be more independent, as well as at the chapter on Responsibility. Independence and responsibility give a child confidence, which in many cases can reduce shyness.

If you want to help your child with assertiveness issues, you'll need to first talk with your child about his behavior, and which parts of it you disapprove of. Take one incident at a time and ask him how he could do it if he had it to do over again. (See Conflict for specific techniques.)

Talking to your child in a way that models the behavior you'd like to see from her helps, too. For example, you could say, "Katie, I understand you gave away your favorite pen. How did you feel about this? Were you uncomfortable telling Jeff you didn't want him to have it?" Talking this way gives your child feedback by:

❐ describing rather than labeling behaviors you are concerned about

❐ being objective rather than evaluating her behavior

❐ being specific rather than general about your concerns,

❐ and requesting her reaction to your comments.

If you can talk with your child without accusing and judging, you can then help her to work out some other ways of reacting than the one that concerns you.

For children up to about fifth grade, you can use hand puppets to act out situations, having the puppets respond assertively, passively, and aggressively as described above. This way you can be sure your child understands the differences between these types of behavior.

WHAT WILL A PROFESSIONAL DO?

If your child is too assertive or too passive, the school psychologist may want to observe your child to get a better look at how he communicates to help determine if your child's behavior is the result of low self-esteem or a lack of social skills. Some possibilities are:

❐ If the root of your child's behavior seems to be a lack of social skills, the school psychologist may suggest he join a social skills training group in which students act out or discuss different ways to handle difficult social or academic situations.

❐ If your child's behavior seems to stem from low self-esteem, the school psychologist may suggest some short-term counseling to find out why your child sees himself this way and how to bolster his self confidence.

❐ If your over-assertive child is simply acting out, the school psychologist may suggest a behavior management plan in which your child receives positive consequences for good behavior and negative consequences for over-assertive behavior.

Once you, the school psychologist, and your child's teacher have tried some of the strategies listed here and in the section above, and if you don't see a change in your child's behavior, the school psychologist may want to continue with a more in-depth psychological evaluation. This could offer more information on why your child may be behaving this way, which in turn can suggest some alternative strategies.

For a very shy child, the school psychologist may use a technique such as visual imagery, in which he teaches your child to spend a few minutes each day imagining herself doing things that in real life are very difficult for her, for example:

❏ laughing, talking, and asking questions in a group

❏ standing in front of the class giving a report. Everyone in class is interested, paying attention, asking questions. Your child sees herself effortlessly answering the questions, holding their attention, speaking clearly.

Thinking of oneself as more confident can translate into more confident action.

The school psychologist may also suggest that your shy or passive child join an assertiveness-training group where she can practice speaking her mind directly and without fear.

See also:

❏ Anxiety
❏ Bullies and Victims
❏ Conflict
❏ Depression
❏ Friends
❏ Perfectionism
❏ Self-Esteem
❏ Suicide

Further Reading

Glenn, H. & Nelson, J. *Raising Self-Reliant Children in a Self-Indulgent World*. Rocklin, CA: Prima Publications, 1988.

Silberman, M. & Wheelan, S. *How to Discipline Without Feeling Guilty: Assertive Relationships with Children*. Champaign, IL: Research Press, 1980.

C H A P T E R   8

Bullies and Victims

"Josie was adamant about not going to school again yesterday. When I asked why, he wouldn't answer me. I think he's afraid."

"For the third time this month, Chris' principal has called to tell me he's picking fights with younger kids, or yelling at them, harrassing them after school. His father has spanked him more than once for fighting. I just don't know what else to do with him."

Violence in schools has increased at an alarming rate over the last decade. By 1992, in an average month, about a half million attacks, shakedowns, and robberies occurred in public secondary schools across the country. Nearly 8 percent of urban middle and high school students miss one day of school a month because they are afraid to attend.

Underlying these dismaying statistics is the fact that about one in seven school children behaves like either a bully or a victim. If you suspect that your child acts in either of these ways, you can take some comfort in knowing that both are behaviors your child has learned. And, just as he or she learned how to be a bully or a victim, that behavior can be unlearned, with your help.

WHAT WE KNOW NOW ABOUT BULLIES

A child is bullying when he fairly often oppresses or harrasses someone else, either physically or verbally. Boys are most often the ones who do the bullying, but there are some girls who bully, too.

There is no single reason a child learns to

bully, but we do know that it seems to be caused by a number of factors. Some of them are:

❏ The child's own temperament.

❏ A home environment in which parents consistently act aggressively to get what they want from family members, co-workers, and others.

❏ Too little supervision; no one to show children that there are ways other than aggressive behavior to get what they want.

❏ The message that bullying is worth it. Every time a parent, a teacher, or a peer gives in to bullying behavior, they give the message that it was worth it for the child to be aggressive or just plain obnoxious.

❏ Harsh physical punishment. Punishing a child with harsh, frequent spanking, teaches a child that it is OK for bigger people (parents) to bully smaller people (kids). Not surprisingly, children who bully usually pick on smaller, younger, or weaker children.

❏ Poor self-concept. (See also Self-Esteem.) Children who get more negative comments directed to them than positive ones don't feel good about themselves. Eventually, they expect the world to be negative toward them, so they strike first by bullying. Picking on others also makes them feel superior, and they get plenty of attention for it. For these children, negative attention or a negative reputation is better than no attention at all.

❑ A peer group that supports bullying behavior. (See also Friends.) In some cases, a child will bully others in order to fit in with a peer group or to win friends in a "tougher" group. (See Gang Risk box, below).

WHAT WE KNOW ABOUT VICTIMS

A victim is the child who, for a fairly long time, has been the focus of aggression from others, with someone often picking fights, teasing, or ridiculing him or her. This is not a one-time victim, but someone who has not learned how to be assertive enough to protect himself.

There seem to be two kinds of victims. One is the passive victim, who is anxious and insecure. She appears to do nothing to provoke attacks and never defends herself. The other is the provocative victim, who is considered hot-tempered and who irritates or teases others and tries to fight back when she is attacked.

While there is less research on victims, we do know that most victims:

❑ are anxious, sensitive, and quiet.
❑ tend to have few, if any, good friends at school.
❑ seem to somehow signal to others that they are insecure and that they probably won't fight back if they are attacked or insulted.
❑ are often those who appear emotionally or physically weak, or who complain or seek attention from children and adults.

They may also be those children who are overprotected by parents and school personnel, so they don't develop their own coping skills. (See also Dependency.)

WHEN SHOULD I BE CONCERNED?

Children younger than about 5 are normally more physical in the ways they settle disputes, and they have plenty of disputes over things like who owns which notebook or which box of markers, and who sits next to whom at lunch. But by the time they are between 5 and 7, most children should have verbal skills strong enough to settle most disagreements without physical attacks, without becoming either a bully or a victim. If your child is older than this and still uses physical aggression or harrassment as a first resort in disputes, or easily ends up the on-going object of other children's derision, you should be concerned.

You should also be concerned if:

❑ The teacher or other parents report to you more than once that your child is fighting over possessions (for younger children) or over status or power issues (for older children). Any youngster can lose their temper and strike out occasionally, but if your child is frequently in trouble at school for fighting, or if you see a pattern emerge in which your child is always fighting with—or being picked on by—a particular child or group, you should be concerned.
❑ Your child refuses to talk about large parts of his day at school, or if he becomes anxious or fearful about going to school or getting on the bus.
❑ Your child tells you he feels helpless about life in general, or tells you he thinks he's ugly, a wimp, or stupid. Any marked decline in self-esteem should be a red flag that something is wrong.

Of course you should also be concerned if your child comes home from school with a physical injury or if his school books, reports, papers or other items are mysteriously missing or destroyed.

WHAT CAN I DO TO HELP?

You should address bullying or victimlike behavior immediately, any time it occurs. Don't think your child will grow out of either of these without your help. Once a child is 8 to 10 years old and still behaving like a bully or a victim, it becomes significantly more difficult to change these long-term habits.

You and your partner, along with the teacher and playground monitor, will need to agree on a strong, consistent, positive course of action, like the one outlined below, to help your child learn not to bully or to be a victim. And, you will need to let your child know as clearly as you can that bullying is completely unacceptable and hurtful to others, and that she's strong enough to learn not to be a victim.

There are five key anti-bullying strategies you can use:

❏ *Be positive.* For every negative comment ("You flunked your spelling test again!"), try to make five positive comments to your child ("I saw how hard you tried to resolve that argument peacefully with Jill. Good job."). It will be difficult at first, but try hard to "catch" your child being good.

❏ *Rethink how you discipline your child.* Instead of spanking, substitute removal of privileges, time out, or extra household tasks as consequences of bully behavior. See Appendix A for lists of appropriate privileges to revoke.

❏ *Have your child practice appropriate behavior.* When you see your young child bullying, stop the behavior immediately and have him practice appropriate behavior. For example, if your son hits an after-school playmate to get his toy, have him rehearse (at least three times) the

words to use to ask for (and receive) the toy. For older youngsters, have them verbally replay the situation in which they bullied, and then help them come up with a more appropriate course of action.

❏ *Review your own behavior.* Children imitate behavior they see in their homes. If you and your partner yell at and bully one another, this would be the time for you to begin changing your own behavior to model the way you'd like your children to behave.

❏ *Arrange for supervision.* Either you, your partner, or the teacher or playground monitor should supervise the situations in which your child is most likely to act like a bully.

If your child tends to be a victim, try these kinds of strategies:

❏ *Be positive.* When victims feel better about themselves, they are more able to develop the coping skills they need with other children. Find ways to comment on what your child does well instead of dwelling on what she seems incapable of doing or the reasons she's being picked on.

❏ *Encourage your child to stay with those children or adults she feels comfortable with.* To be alone is to be vulnerable. Suggest she change seats on the school bus, or sit next to the driver.

❏ *Talk to your child about remaining calm.* Have your child practice saying, "Stop bothering me," and standing up straight, speaking calmly, slowly and firmly, and then walking away from someone who is bullying her. Displays of temper, frustration, and anger are all great entertainment for bullies.

❏ *Encourage your child to try shrugging off or laughing at mild taunts.* A sense of humor and the ability to laugh at oneself are helpful lifelong tools.

❏ *Check your own behavior and attitudes.* You may appreciate your child's uniqueness, but are you dressing your child or encouraging traits that may be making them easy targets for bullies? Or are you extremely passive with others, and feel like a victim yourself? You may be unwittingly teaching your child to be a victim.

❏ *Arrange for supervision.* Be sure you or another responsible adult, like a teacher or playground monitor, can be there in situations your child is likely to be victimized, so that you can stop the behavior and have both children rehearse appropriate behavior.

WHAT WILL A PROFESSIONAL DO?

Many school psychologists offer a social skills training group, which can teach both children who act like bullies and those who act like victims more effective, positive ways of dealing with conflict.

You might also ask your school psychologist to work with the teacher to find ways to make a victimized child look more competent in front of the class, or to have the bully model for the class better ways to resolve conflicts. For example, the child who is more aggressive might be asked to role-play something positive to do when someone calls him names. A skit like this can reinforce the bully's getting attention for positive action and the victim's standing up for himself in an appropriate way.

See also:

❏ Dependency
❏ Friends
❏ Self-Esteem

Is Your Child at Risk for Gang Membership?

There are probably as many reasons for why some youngsters become gangmembers as there are youngsters who do not. But studies have shown that certain behaviors and situations do more often lead to gang membership than others. The chart below shows how it can happen.

Low Social and Economic Status, combined with:

❏ Lack of adult bonding, training in antisocial behavior
❏ Poor parental discipline and monitoring
❏ Conduct and aggression problems at home
❏ Conduct and aggression problems at school
❏ Rejection of adult norms
❏ Academic failure
❏ Rejection by low-risk peers
❏ Rejection of low-risk peers—Commitment to high-risk peers

If you think your child may be flirting with gang membership, here are some risk factors to look for:

❏ Your youngster doesn't come home at all some nights, or is gone for several nights in a row.
❏ Evidence that your youngster is abusing alcohol or drugs, or that his abuse of these has increased.

Is Your Child at Risk for Gang Membership? (cont.)

❏ Abrupt changes in your child's behavior and personality.

❏ Newly acquired or unexplained "wealth," often showered on or shared with others. This can be anything from a bag of candy shared with younger children to a gold chain worn by an older youth.

❏ Requests to borrow money, or reliable evidence that your child is borrowing from others.

❏ "Hanging around," but no discussion of problems with others.

❏ A dress style adopted by only a few: specific colors, style, or item of clothing; a particular hairstyle; or other symbols of identification.

❏ Talks about a "new family" (the gang).

Further Reading

Besag, V. E. Bullies and Victims in Schools: A Guide to Understanding and Management. Philadelphia: Open University Press, 1989.

Olweus, D. Bullies at School: What We Know and What We Can Do. Cambridge, MA: Blackwell, 1993.

McLaughlin, M. Urban Sanctuaries: Neighborhood Organizations in the Lives and Futures of Inner-City Youth. San Francisco: Jossey-Bass Publications, 1994.

CHAPTER 9

Cheating

"Elgin's teacher called today to let me know that during a test, he was clearly copying the answers from a classmate's paper. I was so embarrassed. He's in the third grade; I thought we'd taught him right from wrong."

No parent is happy to get a call or a note from school informing her that her child has been caught cheating. Although it may seem like a disaster, it might help to know that infrequent or one-time cheating can be the result of a developmental stage or an academic problem more than of a real character flaw on your child's part.

While cheating is certainly not acceptable behavior, it might also help you to know that at least 40 to 50 percent of students are reported to have cheated at some time during their academic careers. That is, they used crib sheets, copied answers from someone else's paper or allowed theirs to be copied, plagiarized or had someone else do their work under their name. It may not be thrilling to find that your child is part of this group, but you can know that as a parent, you are not alone in trying to understand more about childhood cheating, its contexts, and what you can do about it.

WHAT WE KNOW NOW

Teachers and parents alike often see cheating as a character flaw in the student, and react with anger and disappointment that a child would choose to cheat. In fact, cheating and the reasons a child does it may be more complex than that, and several factors may be behind a child's cheating. For example, children are more likely to cheat when they:

❏ feel alienated from parents or peers,
❏ feel they are incompetent or less competent than their peers,
❏ have an intense fear of failure,
❏ have a very high need for approval,
❏ have a high need for immediate gratification.

Outside factors can also provide a nudge toward cheating, such as extreme parental, academic, or social pressure and school work that is too easy or too difficult.

No matter what the cause, it's important to look at the context in which the cheating occurred in order to figure out what to do about it. Three things to consider are:

❏ *The stage of moral development your child is in.* As with many social skills and concepts, children learn the rules of moral behavior as they are intellectually able to absorb them. Your young child may see no moral implications of cheating simply because she is too young to understand them.
❏ *How your child sees cheating as a behavior.* A child who truly believes there is nothing wrong with cheating is very different—and may have serious problems—from one who knows

cheating is wrong but doesn't resist temptation.

❏ *What's accepted at your school or in your child's classroom.* It could be that your child has cheated because his friends do and because the consequences for getting caught have not been particularly strong. It could also be that the classroom set-up makes it easy or even inviting to look at someone else's paper during a test.

WHEN SHOULD I BE CONCERNED?

It's important to try to keep some perspective about this issue, and avoid overreacting. Of course, you should be concerned any time your child, or your child's teacher, tells you he has cheated. But if it is a one-time occurrence, address it as such, use some of the techniques in the following section to help your child learn not to cheat, and move on. It won't help to remind your child over and over of his transgression. A one-time mistake is worth addressing, but is best left behind once addressed.

You should be concerned, though, if your child:

❏ says she depends on cheating to pass tests and feels it is her only choice,
❏ develops a consistent pattern of cheating,
❏ does not feel remorseful when she is caught, or
❏ if she tells you others copy her work and she can't stop them.

WHAT CAN I DO TO HELP?

Any time you are dealing with an undesirable behavior from your child, be sure you let her know that you still love and respect her, even though her behavior has not been what you would want. You will always get better results with your child if you start from the basis of a warm, positive relationship.

Keep in mind too, that punishment alone does not give your child the opportunity to learn. Try to fit any punishment you do give to the crime, and have it come as soon as possible after the incident. For example, you could assign your child to write a short paper for you on why she cheated, why in that particular subject, and why she shouldn't cheat in the future.

Talk with your child about why she cheated. Discuss your expectations for her, her expectations for herself, and the teacher's expectations. Try to get a sense from this conversation if your child feels there is too much competition in the classroom, or if she's feeling too much pressure to succeed. (See Competition and Cooperation, Perfectionism.) Review your child's schedule: Does she have time to study, or is her schedule crammed with too many extracurricular activities? Ask her about how she goes about studying. Perhaps she doesn't have the skills or habits to study effectively. (See Study Habits.)

Be sure your child knows the consequences of cheating:

❏ she won't know the material,
❏ she won't develop a good concept of herself as a learner,
❏ she is likely get a low grade or a zero—and/or incur disciplinary actions at school ranging from a stern lecture in elementary school to suspension in some high schools.

If your child tells you she has cheated, encourage her to tell the teacher. Often first-time offenders have the option of redoing the paper or test on which they cheated.

If others are copying from your child's paper, talk with your child about how to say no (see Assertiveness and Shyness). You might also speak with the teacher who might then address the class about copying from others. But be discreet so that your child doesn't become known as a tattler.

WHAT WILL A PROFESSIONAL DO?

The primary issue for a child who has developed a pattern of cheating is to figure out why she is cheating, and to make sure the classroom environment is not conducive to cheating. The school psychologist may first want to talk with your child to find out if she knows why she cheats and if she understands that what she is doing is wrong. The psychologist may also talk with your child to get a clearer picture of why she has cheated and if her cheating is simply to do better in school or if it is part of a larger problem that may exist for her outside of school. (See Lying.)

In working with the classroom teacher, the psychologist may suggest that she:

❏ set up clear consequences for cheating, such as loss of classroom privileges or loss of recess, library, or computer time.

❏ encourage children to ask questions, if they tend to cheat because they don't understand assignments or test questions.

❏ talk about test anxiety to defuse some of the tension about tests. (See Stress, Competition and Cooperation, Lying, Perfectionism.)

❏ consider making changes in her classroom so that cheating is less possible. She could use physical barriers to cheating, such as closer monitoring during tests or making more space between desks. And she can develop emotional barriers by leading group discussions and activities concerning cheating and its ramifications. The more everyone in the class sees cheating as a negative act, the less likely they are to do it.

See also:

❏ Anxiety
❏ Assertiveness and Shyness
❏ Competition and Cooperation
❏ Lying
❏ Perfectionism
❏ Stress
❏ Study Habits

Further Reading

Ekman, P. *Why Kids Lie: How Parents Can Encourage Truthfulness.* New York: Scribner, 1989.

CHAPTER 10

Competition and Cooperation

"Even though she's been singled out as Student of the Week more than once for her good grades, Tracy won't really try when she's faced with a difficult assignment. Just the other night, she told me she didn't need to do some extra studying for her social studies test because she's smart."

"We know Jared is a talented athlete, but now, at 13, we're wondering if he should continue on his soccer team, where he's been high-scorer for three years running. Before games he complains of headaches, he's nauseated, and most of the time we have to fight to get him to go to practice."

Competition and cooperation often share an uneasy alliance in our society, especially where children are concerned. On one hand, there are those who believe all forms of academic and athletic competition are harmful to children, and they would like to see it consistently avoided in favor of cooperative play and ungraded work. And at the other extreme are those who see the emphasis on cooperation as unrealistic, and favor competition in all arenas as the necessary, and sometimes painful, crucible in which childrens' characters are forged.

In truth, both competition and cooperation play key roles in our society and in the lives of our children, and neither is, of itself, bad or good for all children. It may even be that neither is really the issue; that the true issue is our reaction to winning or losing.

No matter how we feel personally about cooperation and competition, our children run into these issues every day in the classroom and on the playing field. The challenge to parents is to understand these issues and their own reactions to winning and losing well enough to guide their children toward healthy attitudes about competition, and pass on the ability to work and play cooperatively.

WHAT WE KNOW NOW

Competition is a strong characteristic of American culture. Left to their own devices, children in primary and early secondary grades often dream up competitive games with rules, structure, winners, and losers. While it's a natural urge at this age for children to work hard to show they are better than their peers, losing at one of these made-up games doesn't seem to have a negative effect on their self-esteem. That's partly because decision making about the game is shared, everyone participates more or less equally, and winning seems to be slightly less important than belonging. It also seems that when it occurs naturally and kids have some control over it, competition can be a powerful teacher about self-discipline and social relationships, as well as the skills necessary to the game.

In the classroom, too, there is individual competition, and rewards for competing well can be strong motivators propelling students to greater academic performance and achievement, promoting higher standards, and making everyday activities more interesting.

But when competition is misused or overused, it can result in stressed-out, burned-out kids with low self-esteem. For example, when adults become involved in childrens' activities, as they do in many sports, the emphasis can easily switch from the belonging, participation, and fun of spontaneous competitive play, to the importance of ability, skill, and winning of organized sports. When a teacher overuses competition in the classroom, it's easy for some children to stop trying, because in a simple competition for grades, the smartest children are most likely to come out on top, no matter how hard children with lesser abilities try. And when a parent sends subtle (or not-so-subtle) messages to a child about how vitally important it is to get the best grades and be on the best team, a child who wants to please pushes herself fiercely, competing with herself to do better and better.

The bottom line for most children in the classroom or on the playing field is that they'd rather play than win. One survey done by J. R. Thomas reported in *Education Digest* showed that 72 percent of children in youth football said they'd rather play on a losing team than sit on the bench on a winning team. Keep this in mind as you decide how to handle competition issues with your child.

WHEN SHOULD I BE CONCERNED?

Your family's values should be the first criteria you use in deciding if competition is a problem for your child. Some parents revel in competitiveness, and others find problematic even relatively small amounts of competition in sports or in academics. Your job will be to find a balance between your beliefs and the fact that our society, inside and outside of school, is based more on competitiveness than on cooperative efforts.

Behaviors that can signal to a parent that a child is having trouble with competition look the same for primary and secondary children. Any one of these behaviors is cause for concern. Notice if your child:

❏ becomes extremely upset at herself or others for losing a game or not achieving an academic goal, so that she is feeling down for days afterward.

❏ does a lot of blaming others for a loss—for example, claiming that the other students cheated to do better or that the referee made unfair calls.

❏ is so preoccupied with the competitive activity that other activities are neglected.

❏ thinks of himself as truly superior to others because of his athletic ability or better grades.

❏ links her sense of self-worth to the number of contests she has won or people she has "defeated."

❏ believes that winning is more important than fair, skillful work or play.

❏ no longer finds the competitive activity fun, and his enthusiasm has waned along with his ability to concentrate.

❏ reports she has emotional or physical complaints associated with competitive activities: an upset stomach before the game, sleeplessness, nightmares.

Any competitive situation can be particularly difficult for children who generally tend to be anxious (see Anxiety) or dependent (see Dependency). Some children who are burned-out on competitiveness become under-competitive and won't try at all, which may indicate another problem.

Competition: How Your Child Rates

SITUATION

1	2	3	4	5
not competitive at all				extremely competitive

❏ *Academics:* (for example, how competitive is your child when working on a term paper project with others or aiming for a midterm grade in French.)

❏ *Sports:* (for example, how does she handle competition in an individual-oriented sport like gymnastics, a team sport like soccer, or her individual exercise habits).

❏ *Friends:* (for example, does she see winning friends primarily as a competition for popularity?)

❏ *Other skills or activities:*

Current total rating (the average of all four areas) =_____

Ideal rating =_____

WHAT CAN I DO TO HELP?

Before focusing on how your child deals with competition, take a look at how you handle winning and losing. What do you do when it's your child who shanks a serve in a volleyball game to give the opposing team the winning point? Or when, in the second-grade spelling bee, it's your child who places next to last? How much emphasis do you place on your child's success when he scores the winning run at Little League, or places highest in her class on the math test? If you feel you attach blame to your child for losing, or that her worth to you is closely knit with how she does in sports or in academics, you might consider talking out your feelings with a caring spouse or a counselor. Certainly, it is valuable to encourage your child to always do her best, but beyond that, the ideal is to feel you have

the same emotional connection to and the same esteem and love for your child, win or lose, pass or fail.

Before you can help your child with competition issues, you and your partner will need to clearly understand and agree upon your approach to competition. Individually, write down what you think are the pros and cons of competition for your children. Then spend some time together, without children, and share your lists, talking out your differences until you have a single list or description of how you both would like to see your child engage in competition.

Then take a look with your partner at how you see your child behaving in a variety of competitive or potentially competitive situations. Use the chart above to help clarify your thinking. Personalize it by writing in specific situations you may be concerned about. Once you have rated your child's competitiveness on the scale of 1–5, average the numbers to arrive at a total competitiveness rating and compare this to what you think would be ideal. Or, you can look at the individual situations and think about whether a highly competitive attitude is appropriate in some situations and not in others.

You can do the same kind of chart for cooperativeness in your child. Of course, being cooperative and being competitive sometimes overlap, as when your child plays a team sport. But it might give you a better overall picture of your child if you complete both charts.

When you are ready to talk with your child about competition, you might invite her to go through the same process, rating herself in different activities on both competitiveness and cooperativeness. Then talk with her about where she feels comfortable on those scales or where she'd like to be.

When you talk further with her about competition, be sure she:

■ understands there are appropriate and inappropriate areas for competition. It's acceptable to compete in sports and, at times, for school grades; it's not acceptable to be competitive about friendships or social activities, or to be obviously competitive about material things like clothes. (See Friends.)

■ understands you love her no matter what the outcome of her competition.

Then, if you see consistent signs—like those listed above—that competition is a problem for your child at school or in sports, check in with her teacher. If she agrees your child is having difficulty with being either over- or under-competitive, you can:

■ ask if she would be willing to organize her class so that students work in teams some-times, as well as individually. Group work can take some of the pressure off both individuals who are too competitive and those who shy away from competition.

If your child has a problem with internal competition, competing intensely with herself, pushing herself severely to get top grades, and making negative comments about herself when she doesn't measure up to her own standards, you can work with her to develop a more reasonable attitude by helping her change how she talks to herself. Begin by going over your ideas and her view of competition, as described above. Then, before a big exam, for example, make a small chart for tallying positive comments ("I'll try my best." "It won't be the end of the world if I don't get an A+." "I'll ask for help if I need it."), and negative comments ("I'll die if I don't get every single spelling word right." "I'll never get into college if I don't ace every math exam."), and set up a reward system (See Appendix A, Motivators) for positive comments.

You can also arrange to reward self-supportive comments after the exam, like, "I know I did my best, no matter what my grade is." Review the chart with your child a few days after the exam, and talk about what the chart tells you about how she talks to herself, and how she can continue to focus on making that talk more positive.

Contact the teacher if you are working at home on your child's internal competition. Ask the teacher for ideas on how to help your child achieve some balance in her self-competitiveness in the classroom, and let her know what you are doing at home. Be clear with the teacher about the difference between your appreciation for her ability to motivate and inspire your child, and your concern over the potentially self-destructive lengths to which your child may be going to excel.

For sports activities, you can also:

❏ Point out and talk about the supporting players when you're watching sports on television. Not everyone is Michael Jordan, but they are still valuable to the team.

❏ Change the way you reward your child so that you also reward the effort, not always the end result. For example, you can say, "I'm proud of the courage you showed in trying out for the team, even though you didn't make it. You were brave to take such a risk without knowing the outcome."

❏ Point out the less obvious values associated with being on a winning team. You can say, "I'm glad your team is winning, but I'm especially pleased you're getting a chance to learn about cooperation, team effort, and keeping your cool under pressure."

❏ Literally cheer the effort rather than the outcome. Shout things like, "Good try," and "Good hustle," from the sidelines, and congratulate your child for hard, honest play whether her team won or lost.

❏ Remind your child that people are competitors not because they win, but because they keep on competing.

❏ Remind yourself that a certain amount of your child's fretting about a loss is normal and healthy. You can talk about losing as an inevitable part of life, and help her see what can be learned from loss.

It might help you in guiding your child toward healthy attitudes about competition to know that ages 6 to 12 are the most critical for a child in developing her sense of self and confidence. During this time, it's especially easy for a child to dramatically take to heart the results of any kind of competition. Consequently, it may be best during this time for you to avoid reinforcing the extremes you see in competition—the very competitive players or the children who won't compete at all—in order to help your child find a healthy balance between competition and cooperation.

WHAT WILL A PROFESSIONAL DO?

Call the school psychologist if you find your home remedies like those listed above aren't working, or if you are uncomfortable with any aspect of your child's reaction to competition, even if it's only occurred for a short time. For example, there's no sense in waiting to ask for help if your child has complained of an upset stomach nearly every day before school for a couple of weeks, or if she has been depressed for days after each of four or five Saturday soccer game losses. In some cases, just having a conversation yourself with the school psychologist may give you enough understanding and direction to know whether you need to pursue more specific help.

If you decide you do need more help, the school psychologist will want to talk with both parents in greater detail about your views on competition and cooperation, and to see what your expectations are of your child. She'll then want to observe your child in a variety of settings: in the classroom and at recess, for example, and then talk with your child about competition issues. In addition, the psychologist may ask that she complete some personality inventories (see Evaluation and Testing, in Part I), to help her better understand your child's level of self-confidence and self-esteem, and in order to rule out other problems like depression or anger. (See Self-Esteem, Anger.)

Once she has a clear picture of how your child feels about competition, the psychologist can then work with the classroom teacher to increase or decrease the amount of competition for your child. In some cases, the psychologist may recommend short-term counseling to help your child understand and deal with issues surrounding competition.

See also:

❐ Anxiety
❐ Dependency
❐ Evaluation and Testing, in Part I
❐ Friends
❐ Self-Esteem

Further Reading

Gordon, T. *Parent Effectiveness Training*. New York: Plume Books, 1975.

Johnson, D. W. *Reaching Out: Inter-Personal Effectiveness and Self-Actualization*. Englewood Cliffs, NJ: Prentice-Hall, 1990.

CHAPTER 11

Conflict

"Estelle just falls apart if anyone raises their voice to her. It seems that if there's a conflict about anything at school, I hear from her teacher that Estelle just runs away or leaves the room in tears. I'd like to see her learn how to deal with conflict in a positive way."

"I've really had it with Jonah. He's been in three fights at recess this week alone. He's got a different excuse each time; I don't know what to do any more."

For most of us, children and adults alike, conflict of one sort or another is an everyday part of our lives. By adulthood, most people have learned to handle conflict at least somewhat comfortably. But some adults, like some children, have not, and for them it may seem there are no other choices than fighting or walking away.

No matter how you rate the way you deal with conflict, it's important your child learns good conflict resolution skills, not just to make life run more smoothly, but because those skills contribute to healthy overall social and emotional development. Without these skills, children are likely to not only have poor relationships with others their age, but it may also reflect problems with self-esteem.

The good news is there are plenty of creative, constructive ways of dealing with conflict, and just like other skills, you and your child can learn them.

WHAT WE KNOW NOW

Conflict is a normal part of life. It arises from all kinds of things, from simple misunderstandings and frustrations to expecting too much or too little of oneself or of others. By definition, conflict is any kind of disagreement. It can be fighting over which television channel to watch, fighting over pencils at school, or arguing over a seat on the bus. And conflicts can range from mild disagreements to serious acts of violence, such as teenage shooting and gang warfare.

Two typical ways many people see as the only options for dealing with conflict are:

■ *to withdraw* from it, which certainly defuses the conflict but is likely to leave the withdrawing child with more feelings of frustration, decreased self-esteem and insecurity, and may ultimately lead to the child taking on the victim's role. (See Bullies and Victims.)
■ or to *respond aggressively*. There's a lot of media support for taking this role; verbal or physical violence is often shown as an acceptable way to settle conflict. But in fact, children who use aggression or violence regularly are not learning the kinds of social skills that will help them make their way in the world as adults.

In real life—both in school and out—there are many other ways to deal with conflict. They include negotiating, compromising, and sharing. Most children learn at least some of these skills naturally by playing games in which they must take turns, by flipping a coin to see who goes first, and in the classroom by negotiating with other children—for example, to determine who will be the teacher's helper on different days.

By school age, most children have enough language and problem-solving abilities to work out conflicts without verbal or physical aggression. There are five basic skills a child must have to do this:

1 *Feeling-detection Skills,* which means being able to identify your own feelings as well as those of others. Naming feelings is the first step toward controlling them.

2 *Communication Skills,* which include the ability to tell others of one's needs and feelings.

3 *Problem-solving Skills,* which include the ability to see both sides of a problem in order to reach a middle ground.

4 *Anger Control,* which includes the ability to respond nonaggressively to a difficult situation.

5 *Appropriate Use of Assertiveness,* which means a child can stand up for herself without becoming violent or overly aggressive.

Given good role models and encouragement to settle conflicts in positive ways, many children will simply acquire these skills over the course of their preschool years. Children who do not usually fall into one of four groups:

❏ They really don't have the skills to resolve conflict, or they don't generally know how to act in a conflict situation, so they do whatever occurs to them at the moment,

❏ They actually have the skills to deal with conflict in constructive ways, but they don't know how to use them appropriately,

❏ They cannot control their anger or their frustration enough to use other social skills they may have, or

❏ They cannot control their feelings, and they don't have the skills to use, anyway.

WHEN SHOULD I BE CONCERNED?

You should be concerned when you see your child developing patterns of withdrawal from conflict or aggression in the face of conflict. Both of these are behavior habits that are difficult to break and that can have long-term effects on the way your child relates to others.

You should also be concerned if you see that your child just can't seem to solve any of his problems on his own (see Dependency) or without resorting to aggression (see Bullies and Victims).

You should also be concerned if:

❏ your child becomes extrememly anxious when confronted with a conflict (see Anxiety), breaking into a sweat, crying, becoming immobilized with fear (see Fears).

❏ simple issues become big issues on a daily basis.

❏ your child's teacher tells you that your child constantly fights on the playground, or disrupts class with fighting.

❏ your child says his classmates make fun of him in school and he doesn't know what to say to them.

❏ other kids take your child's belongings (lunch, pencils, pens) and he doesn't do anything about it.

❏ your child or the teacher tells you he couldn't pay attention in class or do assignments because he was so upset about a conflict he had that day.

❏ your child tells you he doesn't want to go to school (see School Phobia).

❏ your child typically ends up doing all the work on a group project, but doesn't complain to other kids or to the teacher. (See Assertiveness and Shyness.)

❏ your child complains of being talked into doing things at school he doesn't want to do or that he regrets, like letting a classmate copy his paper.

❏ your child constantly makes fun of class-mates.

Many of these problems are common-place, one-time events, and you can help your child learn how to deal with them better by using the conflict resolution techniques in the following section. Since constructive conflict resolution is a learned behavior, as is being a bully or being the victim, it is best if you can work with your child on acquiring positive skills earlier in his school career rather than later, when it is harder to break long-standing habits.

WHAT CAN I DO TO HELP?

One of the first things you can do is to think about how your family handles conflict in your home. Children model, or copy, what they see. Take, for example, what may happen when your child has related the details of a disagreement between him and a classmate at school. Do you find it difficult to see the other child's point of view, and do you find yourself becoming just as defensive and angry at him as your child was? If you see yourself in that example, keep in mind that your child is prob-ably learning by example not to see both sides of an issue and to blame someone else for the conflict. You may have an opportunity here to learn more about your own style, talk about it with your child, and then work with him toward better methods of conflict resolution.

That will entail talking through some basic steps with your child:

1 Tell your child he has choices in how he responds to conflict.
2 Encourage him to talk openly about conflict situations after they happen and express his feelings about the situation.
3 Ask him if he can see the other side in the situation. If he can't, describe the other side for him.
4 Talk about what the other person was prob-ably feeling during the conflict.
5 Your child must be willing to solve the problem, and perhaps the best way to ensure he is would be to remind him of consequences of his behavior. Aggressive or passive behavior each has its own uncomfortable consequences.
6 Reminding your child that he can change the outcome by changing the way he responds to conflict may be a helpful motivator.

Next, have your child think of ways in which the problem you've been talking about could have been solved, and figure out what would be the outcome if he had acted that way.

You might also use family time to talk about how fighting helps or does not help to solve a problem. As a family, talk about how your child feels about fighting and its conse-quences, and ask him for ideas on how a con-flict could have been solved without fighting or without giving in to doing something he didn't want to do. Some guidelines to this kind of discussion, which helps build conflict-reso-lution skills, are:

❏ each person gets a turn to speak
❏ no one can interrupt another person
❏ each person has to listen to the one speaking

You can also write out the steps for solv-ing conflicts, and post the steps in a prominent place, such as on the refrigerator, so that your child can refer to it. Make a chart like the one shown in the box below, leaving space for comments. Another way to use the list of steps is to write it on a chalkboard or have your child start a notebook so that he can use the list to help him work out or review different disagreements.

Your child is likely to need clear guidelines and support from adults to keep situations from getting out of hand while she is learning how to resolve conflicts. Some guidelines for how to act during a disagreement might be that your child can:

❏ talk but not yell
❏ talk but not hit
❏ walk away if he needs time to calm down and think of ways to resolve the conflict
❏ ask an adult for help in solving a problem (This is for a young child.)

WHAT WILL A PROFESSIONAL DO?

If you are concerned that the way your child handles conflict is affecting his classroom behavior and thereby his school work, talk first with the teacher to see if her perception of your child matches yours. If it does, the two of you should meet with the school psychologist. She will want to observe your child in both structured settings like the classroom and unstructured settings like recess or lunch, and she will want to talk with your child about how she feels when she is in conflict situations.

Many schools offer social skills training programs they can purchase as a package from a publisher, which include some work on conflict resolution skills, or they may offer classes specifically for conflict resolution, usually meeting weekly in small groups.

Steps for Resolving Conflicts

······································

❏ *Identify the problem*
❏ *Identify how the other person sees the problem*
❏ *Name your feelings*
❏ *Name the other person's feelings*
❏ *Agree* to solve the problem
❏ *Think* of ways to do it
❏ *Name the consequences of each way*
❏ *Pick the best ideas and do it/them*

DID IT WORK?

In these groups students act out problems and how they could solve them, younger students perhaps using puppets or drawings, older students role-playing or discussing. No matter what the specific plan of activities for these groups is, they should all address the five basic skills for conflict resolution listed above under What We Know Now. The goal of groups like this is to teach these five skills, and to give children enough practice in using them so it translates to real life. It usually takes a couple of months before you'll notice a change in your child's behavior. You might hear your child using different language, like "We have a problem here," or "How do you see it?" And your child may try to guide you through the problem-solving steps. These are great times to reward your child with praise as she practices her new skills.

It may be useful for your child to join a group like this, but be sure you know and support what they are teaching, and that this is consistent with what you teach at home. Plenty of practice at home and at school is key to learning conflict resolution.

If your school does not have a group like one of these, or if it is not appropriate for your child, the school psychologist will work out techniques that are appropriate. For example, if your child tends to withdraw from conflict, the psychologist may work with the teacher to be sure that the teacher can step in when this happens so as to help your child and the one she's having a disagreement with practice the steps to conflict resolution listed above. Or if your child seems to be angry a lot of the time, the school psychologist may want to meet with her to try to get to the root of the problem. Sometimes constant anger reflects deeper issues, like depression or a reaction to the death of a loved one.

The school psychologist may also suggest that the teacher use cooperative learning techniques in the classroom to foster conflict reso-lution skills. For example, she would assign projects to children in groups or couples instead of individually, giving them guidelines as to how to work cooperatively toward a goal.

Younger children need clear guidelines for learning how to resolve conflicts. But once your child learns the basic steps, she may be ready to work in peer mediation—usually by about fifth grade—in which students help other students resolve conflicts. Many middle and high schools now have peer mediation groups where students can learn conflict reso-lution skills to help their peers resolve con-flicts.

See also:

❑ Anger Control
❑ Anxiety
❑ Bullies and Victims

Further Reading

Gordon, T. *Parent Effectiveness Training*. New York: Plume Books, 1975.

Johnson, D. W. *Reaching Out: Inter-Personal Effectiveness and Self-Actualization*. Englewood Cliffs, NJ: Prentice-Hall, 1990.

C H A P T E R 1 2

Creativity

"I've always thought of Iris as a very creative child. Now that she's in the fourth grade though, she doesn't seem to take the time away from friends to draw or daydream the way she used to. Can a child just lose their creativity?"

Everybody is creative. Putting old ideas together in a new way is the essence of creativity, and everyone does that every day in the process of adapting to changing situations.

But the definitions we tend to pin on people we think of as especially creative are not nearly so simple. If you're interested in helping your child sustain her creativity, or if you'd like to encourage a little more creativity in your child, it will help if you understand how creativity develops in children and how you can support it.

WHAT WE KNOW NOW

When people identify a child as creative, they are usually talking about that child's degree of creativity. That means the degree to which the child comes up with unusual or unconventional ideas which others would call novel, valuable, different from previous ideas or approaches, or beyond the commonplace. In some school districts, children who have a high degree of creativity may be identified during elementary school and included in a Talented and Gifted program. In others, you may find that creativity is not so highly valued or easily recognized.

Not everyone at school (and sometimes at home) is thrilled when a child shows these kinds of abilities. Children, those called creative as well as those who are not, get a lot of pressure from the adult world to conform, to do what is expected of them—in short, to be ordinary. A child with an especially creative way of doing things or looking at the world can rock the boat, uncomfortably at times, for adults trying to see that the child somehow "fits in." As a child grows, there is usually less and less support for creative approaches. For example, a small child who uses mom's saucepan as a car or a doll bed is likely to get plenty of encouragement for her creative play. But within a few years, that same child is likely to get far more praise if she uses the saucepan for cooking than if she uses it as a hat.

Your child's thinking patterns go through several stages as she matures. In the earliest, before she is able to frame her experiences in cause-and-effect thinking, she has no trouble accepting fantastic and fictional ideas, and the line between fact and fantasy or a wish and reality is easily blurred. That's why at this young age, a saucepan makes perfect sense as a doll bed, if that's what her play calls for at that moment.

At this preschool age, your child may also create charming and startling metaphors, like "barefoot head" for a person who isn't wearing a hat. While it's wonderful to hear these unique ways of seeing things, they are typical of the way many young children speak, and they don't indicate an exceptional degree of creativity. Most children this age don't understand the concept of metaphors, and their creation is quite unconscious. The same child who points out someone's "barefoot head" will think it's silly if you say a person is "full of himself."

As your child grows, she begins to value other forms of thinking and knowing besides the overlapping fantasy/reality she started with. Some of the impetus to do this comes from her own curiosity about other ways of seeing things, and some comes from outside encouragement to figure things out on her own. The free-form associations she may have made as a preschooler begin to settle into more set ideas about what things are and how they are to be used. Children at this age begin to lose the metaphorical associations that can create new relationships—the unconscious ability to see the "barefoot head."

In fact, by the time many children reach the age of 9 or 10, they may find themselves in what some people call the "fourth-grade slump." It's clear to children by this age that adults far prefer conforming behavior over their nonconforming ideas. Some children never pull out of this slump to become creative once again; others simply see a dip in their production of ideas or objects, and eventually work their way back to their creative ways.

Those who do end up being identified as creative people often share certain personality traits that some people may see as a plus and others see as a minus. Some of those traits are:

❏ *Free Thinking.* Toying with ideas may look creative to some people and undisciplined or lacking in goal orientation to others.

❏ *Gullibility.* Creative children may easily get excited about "half-baked" ideas and not see drawbacks or flaws adults see.

❏ *Humor.* While seeing humor in ideas most adults take seriously shows an ability to question and to see other perspectives, it can also be interpreted as mocking and obnoxious.

❏ *Daydreaming.* Fantasy can be helpful to some children in learning and in solving problems. Others can see this as inattentive or spacey behavior.

❏ *Aloneness.* Sometimes the most creative thinking emerges out of solitude, not something many children are encouraged to cultivate.

❏ *Activity.* Ideas often come at times of "doing nothing." But once the idea comes, the creative child can become completely absorbed in the activity. This swing from what looks like laziness to overcommitment can be confusing and hard for others to handle.

Researchers have also identified three types of thinking that help explain the thought processes everyone has and that can also throw light on how especially creative people think. According to this theory, there are three types of thinkers:

- *Convergers,* who use deliberate, explicit and critical thinking. Convergent thinking is necessary in the end phase of creativity, which brings an idea to fruition or makes it into some kind of communicable product.
- *Divergers,* who produce many ideas and varied solutions to a problem.
- *All-Arounders,* who bring both kinds of thinking together. Creative people who are prolific writers, painters, or designers, for example, are probably All-Arounders who can move

back and forth between divergent and convergent thinking.

While the mission of society and schools is primarily to produce adults with basic thinking skills and basic knowledge, it's good for parents and school administrators to keep in mind that this doesn't have to be an either/or situation. Rather, the combination of the basics and the creative aspects of a child's thinking can be a more balanced goal.

WHEN SHOULD I BE CONCERNED?

You should be concerned if you see your creative child become persistently restless, appear or talk about being bored a good part of the time with school, or consistently using his creativity to nonconstructive or socially unacceptable ends. Any of the following examples can indicate that your child has a great deal of creativity and no constructive outlet for it. You might be concerned if your child does such things as:

❏ writing a report for her fifth-grade class, but purposely misinterpreting the assignment by adding her own illustrations in the borders of all the pages, when the report was supposed to be typed manuscript-style.

❏ disrupting the class frequently in clever ways. They may be funny at first, but ultimately, disruption is not a constructive use of creativity.

❏ using his ability with computers to break into the school's record system, or his knowledge of electronics to disable the school's bell system.

On the other hand, you may have a child whom you know is quite creative, but who either stops producing, or who has somehow changed her view of creativity so she hides or masks her abilities. This should also concern you, because it's an indication your child may lack the self-esteem to do things that may set her apart, even in a good way, from her friends, or that would call attention to herself.

WHAT CAN I DO TO HELP?

If your child is quite creative but not getting the opportunity at school to develop it or to have a constructive outlet for it, you can first talk with the teacher to see how much leeway she has in the classroom. Some schools have a very tightly prescribed curriculum that does not allow the teacher to make day-to-day changes to allow for individual differences in children's needs. But most teachers welcome reports or projects on topics within the curriculum. Check with your child's teacher about this.

Some districts have programs for creative children or special clubs or activities that focus on their abilities. If your district or school does not, you can pressure them to meet the needs of creative children, too. It may mean tying in (individually or as a school) with local or regional arts organizations, sports clubs (for gifted athletes), computer stores, or theater groups and finding community volunteers to help develop creative outlets for youngsters. Another possibility is the Odyssey of the Mind program, which teaches children to invent creative solutions to problems. (See Appendix B, Parent Resources)

At home, you can try some of the following activities with younger children to exercise their creative minds, whether you think your child is particularly creative or not:

❏ When you're in the car, or perhaps when you're busy in the kitchen and your child is hanging out with you, play a game called

"What if. . . ?" You can start; eventually, your child will want to start. Ask a question like, "What if no one invented the car? How would we do these errands?" Or "What if it started to pour rain and we were in a covered wagon? What would we do next?"

❑ Have a costume box. Up to about age 8 or 9, and sometimes past that age, youngsters love to dress up and pretend they are someone else. Even an older child might find that a pirate hat or a frontier bonnet sparks creative pretend play.

❑ Provide unstructured play materials. A box with old magazines, art supplies, and some discarded jewelry can be a treasure trove of ideas. Keep in mind that many toys and games available now allow little creativity on the part of the child—they are set up so that the child only has to respond somewhat passively to the action of the toy.

While unstructured play is fertile ground for creativity, a somewhat structured environment is also necessary. Creative children, like all children, need a reasonably predictable household and clear boundaries on their behavior. They also could use a place where they can be quiet and just think, a place to work on projects, and some control over their time and how they use it.

For older children and teenagers, these same rules apply too. You might also be aware of:

❑ Encouraging your youngster to experiment and explore in constructive ways. Practice listening and observing what your child does without being judgmental. Praise is always wonderful—unless it is "empty" praise—but be careful to support your child in failed efforts as well as in dazzling successes. Sometimes efforts that don't produce expected

Whose Creativity?

Computer games and video games continue to be the top toy of the moment. They certainly supply your child with lots of visual stimulation, plenty of practice at the rapid processing of information, and work on hand-eye coordination. But if you're looking to foster creativity in your child, think twice before assuming that computer games are where it's at.

There's no question the games themselves are creative. Most people would agree that extremely creative people dreamed up the games and brought their ideas to fruition. But unless your child is designing a new computer game, that's where the creativity ends. In fact, too many hours spent playing computer and/or video games, where the only thing required of your child is steady vision and fast fingers, is more likely to put a damper on your child's creativity than it is to foster it.

results are stepping stones toward more exciting creations.

❑ How you and your family use television. Visual images can be stimulating, but television has enormous potential for passive distraction, both for you and for your children. It can be a major block for creative energy.

❑ Setting an example both with your attitudes and your deeds. When you honor and act on your own curiosity, enthusiasm, and "crazy" ideas, you model for your youngster not only how to do it, but that you find it acceptable to step out of the ordinary at times. Your acceptance of her need to step out, too, can help her build the confidence to use her creativity well.

It's also helpful to your child if you give some thought to what kind of thinker your child is: Converger, Diverger or All-Arounder. You probably can't—and shouldn't try to—make a Converger into a Diverger. Some children will grow up to be scientists or mathematicians; others will write or dance. Very few will be strong in both areas. While there is nothing wrong with encouraging a child to see other ways of thinking, overall, it will help your child enormously if you can put the emphasis on where her strengths lie, rather than trying to change those strengths.

WHAT THE PROFESSIONAL WILL DO

Your school psychologist can offer a wealth of knowledge about creativity. She should be able to:

❏ answer your questions about creativity and its relationship to intelligence and learning,

❏ advise you on its relative importance in your child's classroom or school life,

❏ help you to discuss with the teacher the nature of the curriculum, the opportunities it presents for creativity, and how to enhance those for children for whom this is important, and

❏ help you also discuss with the teacher whether it would be better for your child to have a more flexible set-up at school, as in an open classroom.

The school psychologist can also assess your child to measure her ability levels, but the assessment of creativity usually comes from a consensus of those who know the student and who have seen her work.

See also:

❏ Friends
❏ Motivation
❏ Self-Esteem

Further Reading

Day, J. *Creative Visualization with Children.* Shaftsbury, England: Element Books Ltd, 1994.

Johnson, M. *Understanding and Encouraging Your Child's Art: How to Enhance Confidence in Drawing, Ages, 2–12.* Los Angeles: Lowell House, 1993.

Johnson, M. *Teach Your Child to Draw: Bringing Out Your Child's Talents and Appreciation for Art.* Los Angeles: Lowell House, 1990.

C H A P T E R 13

Dependency

"Josh is 10, but he can't seem to get his schoolwork started on his own. He wants the teacher to sit with him and describe, step by step, what he should do."

"We know Marty, who is only in second grade, has a hard time with reading, so her brother and sister and I read assignments to her she says are too hard, which is almost all of them. Are we doing the right thing?"

It's normal, and even healthy, for children to be dependent on others, particularly when they are very young. Your daughter needs to know you will fuss over her when she's ill; your son needs to know you will be waiting to take him home when he's finished with baseball practice.

But dependency that keeps your child from trusting himself to check and correct his homework, from thinking independently in class, or from making friends at the beginning of a new school year, eventually robs him of self-confidence.

WHAT WE KNOW NOW

Dependency becomes a problem when a child consistently relies on others to make decisions for her, or depends on classmates or parents to do things that she really is capable of doing herself. Some dependent children behave that way only when they are around certain people, like the kindergartner who never remembers how to tie his shoelaces when Mom's around, but who has no problem doing it when his teacher expects him to. Others are dependent in certain settings, like the fourth-grader who seems to understand her math homework when she's at home, but can't work a problem at school without help.

Some children become so dependent they go one step farther, to learned helplessness. These children appear uninterested in trying to do anything, certain that they'll fail anyway. The helpless child "knows" she'll fail her history test no matter how hard she studies. And failure represents defeat, not motivation to plan how to do better next time.

Dependency and learned helplessness can show up in children of any age. But it's important to try to recognize dependency as early as possible so that you can work with your child to help her become more self-reliant before she reaches adolescence, when the normal emotional turmoil of puberty can make learning more difficult.

There is almost never a single event that triggers dependency; it's a pattern of behavior that has gone on for years, and it can have many kinds of roots:

❑ It can grow out of relationships that teach your child that the way someone else behaves or approaches a problem is almost always better than the way she does. These can be relationships with overprotective parents, with brothers and sisters, with friends, or with adults.

❑ It can be a method some children use to feel powerful or to gain attention. Even though the dependent child's words may sound powerless, ("Help me, take care of me. I can't read this book by myself.") their pleas for far more help than they need do indeed attract far more adult attention and protection than they would get if they were self-reliant.

❑ It can be a result of guilt, as when a parent gives in to a whining fifth-grader's demands that the parent sit with her while she does her homework, because the parent is afraid she's away at work too much anyway, or because the parent feels sorry for a child with a disability or a health problem.

❑ It can be the result of permissiveness when parents have trouble setting limits for their children. Parents are easily manipulated when they are uncertain of their "right" to enforce rules such as homework completed before television time, or because they are afraid their children won't like them if they are "tough" and insist their child learn to do homework independently.

WHEN SHOULD I BE CONCERNED

Behaviors that can be red flags to parents who wonder if their child is overly dependent are not the one-time occurrences. They are consistent, ongoing patterns you see repeated over months or even years. But keep in mind that there is no objective scale for judging if dependency is a problem; in fact what may seem like problem behavior to one parent or to a teacher, may be perfectly appropriate in another family. Generally, you should be concerned when you are not comfortable with the degree of depen-

dency you see in your child. One way to measure that is to look at the following list. Your child may have a problem if you and your child's teacher have seen a majority of these behaviors (say, three out of five) in your child for more than six months.

For children in primary grades, notice if your child:

❑ Prefers to stay with teacher or monitor at recess rather than joining other children.

❑ Constantly checks in with teacher for more directions, approval, reassurance, and advice.

❑ Doesn't want to participate in new activities in class unless the teacher sits with the child and helps every step of the way.

❑ Consistently saves class work or homework to do when a parent is available to help.

❑ Doesn't want to go to school. This can also be an indication of other problems (see School Phobia).

For children in middle and high school also notice if your child:

❑ Avoids pairing up in class to work on projects, preferring to appeal directly to the teacher.

❑ Doesn't have fairly equal, give-and-take friendships with children of the same age.

❑ Clings to or relies heavily on one or two other students, beyond what you would call a normal best-friend relationship.

❑ Consistently prefers to remain at home rather than join in after-school activities or clubs.

❑ Clings to adults in public.

❑ Consistently accepts what others tell her rather than expressing her own opinions.

WHAT CAN I DO TO HELP?

At home, you can begin working one small step at a time to change the behavior pattern you and your child are used to. Once again, these are patterns that have been established over long periods of time, and you will need patience in changing them slowly over the next months.

You can start by examining your own behavior and noticing where you take on your child's concerns as your own. For example, some parents use the first person plural in talking about their child's school work, as in, "How hard are our spelling words this week?" If this is something you do, catching yourself and changing your language will help both you and and your child begin to see as separate entities his job as student and your job as parent.

The next step is to begin encouraging your child to be independent enough to make mistakes, which can be difficult for a parent who has overprotected that child. You can start by telling your child how much you care for her, and how much you believe in her ability to think for herself. Then be prepared to praise and encourage every effort she makes to do something her own, whether the end result is successful or not. Praise the process, not the product. Let her know how proud you are of her for taking a chance or becoming involved.

Have a talk too, with brothers and sisters who read for, or talk for, your dependent child. Helping a child become more self-reliant takes a consistent approach on the part of each person who deals with her. It also takes follow-through, so be prepared to make good on your plan of action: creating opportunities for and expecting more self-reliance, and praising the effort every time.

At school, contact your child's teacher and let her know of your concerns. If she sees similar behaviors in class, then it is most effective if the two of you work together to target the behaviors that most concern you both, and then develop strategies to deal with them, using the activities below as guidelines. You'll need to check in with the teacher about every two weeks so that you can discuss your child's progress towards self-reliance, and adjust your approach if need be. The key is for you and your child's teacher to work together so that your strategies and rewards are consistent.

If your teacher does not see a problem in class, she may refer you to the school counselor, school psychologist, or social worker, or you may feel comfortable trying some of the activities listed below.

To teach self-reliance both at home and at school, you will need to be prepared with:

❏ *Clear explanations of behavior you expect.* Tell your child what you want him to learn from these activities (how to take care of himself in school and at home, for example), and what the consequences will be if he does not. For example, before a primary-age child can wake himself up for school, he needs to know how to set an alarm clock and what time to set it for in order to be ready for school on time. He'll also need to know that if he isn't ready on time, his ride (or the bus) will leave without him.

❏ *Firm resolve.* Everyone stumbles as they learn a new skill, and so will your child. You must be prepared to let him bear the brunt of the consequences for his own actions, rather than bailing him out to save him from failure. At the same time, you must be ready with praise for his efforts and encouragement to keep trying if he doesn't succeed immediately. Be sure the praise and attention you give your child are for efforts toward self-reliance more often than for her old "helpless" ways.

❏ *Rewards for effort* more often than for success.

❏ *A little creative thinking* in tailoring the self-reliance activities listed below to fit your family and your child. While several are things you can do at home, stay in touch with your child's teacher to be sure home self-reliance carries through to school.

For Primary Students

❏ *Wake up/Wake me up.* Be sure she knows how to use an alarm clock, then take turns being the one who wakes the other on school mornings. Your allowing her to be responsible for waking you on some mornings shows you have confidence in her ability to do the job.

❏ *Home/School Box.* Expect her to keep track of her school things that come home by providing a special place to put them. It's not the parents' job to find last night's homework or that missing spelling book.

❏ *Timed Homework.* For the child who has trouble working independently, go over his homework assignment once with him to be sure he understands it, then set a timer for five minutes. He is to work independently for that time. After the first week, set the timer for ten minutes. Continue increasing the independent work time, rewarding your child for working independently.

❏ *Assignments.* Work with your child to break homework assignments into smaller portions. Independent work—and success—are more likely if the amount of work required is presented in smaller chunks.

❏ *Self-Reliance Chart.* Make a weekly chart on paper or on an erasable marker board. List the specific behaviors you'd like to see your child achieve, for example:

- doing homework independently
- studying spelling words without reminding
- telephoning one new friend in class

- waking self in time for school

Have your child check off which she did each day, then offer rewards based on how many times she behaved in a self-reliant way. If it's not possible for her to do some of the things on the list yet, revise the list so that the behaviors are within her reach, then change the list as the behaviors become easier for her.

For Secondary Students

❏ Talk with your child about your own middle school and high school years when being self-reliant may have been difficult for you. Share the ways in which you became more confident and independent.

❏ Make it a habit of yours that you tell your youngster at least once a week what he does right in school, to begin building a foundation for self-confidence.

❏ Encourage your middle- and high-schoolers to use a journal to track self-reliant behavior. Suggest they target behaviors such as those in the list for primary-age children, then track with them how often they achieve, or come close to achieving, those behaviors. Have age-appropriate rewards as payoff for their efforts.

WHAT WILL A PROFESSIONAL DO?

It's time to call the school psychologist any time you feel uncomfortable with your child's level of dependency at school, and equally uncomfortable with working for change on your own. It's also time to call if you have worked on your own and tried some of the activities listed above and, in spite of about a semester's worth of effort, your child still behaves in dependent ways you and your child's teacher find unacceptable. For example, your primary-age child still cannot complete assignments without assistance.

If, after talking, you and the school psychologist agree there has been no change in your child's school behavior during the previous semester to about six months, the psychologist should suggest that she conduct a more thorough psychological evaluation to rule out other problems, such as certain kinds of learning disabilities (see Learning Disabilities) or social skills problems. This kind of evaluation should include:

❐ observations in school in both a structured setting, like a classroom, and in an unstructured setting, like during recess.

❐ talking with both parents about the child's behavior outside of school. While a school psychologist only addresses school-related behavior issues, it's important for her to have a complete picture of a child's life in order to effectively address the school issues.

❐ talking with the teacher about specific school behaviors that concern her.

❐ a written behavior rating scale, such as the Child Behavior Checklist, to be completed by you and your child's teacher evaluating how often the behaviors that concern you occur.

❐ having your child complete a self-reporting inventory, such as the Piers Harris Children's Self-Concept Scale or the Achenbach Youth Self-Report, on which your child evaluates his own behavior.

The results of these tests may show that your child would benefit from individual or group counseling. (See Evaluation and Testing, in Part I.)

All of this should result in a specific plan that targets changing specific behaviors in positive ways. The psychologist's plan may look a lot like some of the activities you have tried, such as the self-reliance chart, but the difference will be that the psychologist will be able to more closely coordinate home and school efforts, adjusting the strategy to fit your child.

The key to effective treatment by your school psychologist in this case is that she evaluate your child's behavior in more than one setting to get a clear picture of which situations trigger the child's dependency and which situations reinforce it.

See also:

❐ School Phobia
❐ Evaluation and Testing, in Part I
❐ Learning Disabilities

Further Reading

Blechman, E. A. *Solving Child Behavior Problems At Home and At School.* Champaign, IL: Research Press, 1985.

Dinkmeyer, D. & McKaye, G. D. *The Next Step:* *Effective Parenting Through Problem Solving.* American Guidance Services, Inc. 1987.

Rich, Dorothy. *Megaskills.* New York: Houghton Mifflin, 1992.

C H A P T E R   1 4

Depression

"Lisa, my sixth grader, is the star of her softball team, on the honor roll, and a cheerleader. But when I found her crying in her room for the umpteenth time this month, she told me she felt awful because she is too fat, too ugly, and doesn't deserve to have friends. I don't understand how she could feel so bad when everything in her life seems so good."

"Sam can't seem to stay awake in class, he complains constantly of mysterious aches and pains we can't find any basis for, and he seems like he doesn't care about anything. He's only in the fourth grade, but he acts like a burned-out old man. What can we do for him?"

Until recently, many professionals in the mental health field did not recognize childhood depression as a psychological problem. The assumption was that although pre-adolescent children could feel sad, it was not significant enough to be addressed seriously. The same was true for child suicide, which, until recent years, was often viewed as accidental death because many people didn't believe children could feel deeply depressed enough to act on those feelings.

Perhaps childhood depression has also been underestimated because in our culture, we typically see youth as a carefree, happy time, and many adults cannot imagine how a child could have anything to feel depressed about. It's easy to think a child is just "going through a phase" if they are sad or uncooperative, when in fact, they may be suffering from depression, which can interfere with learning.

But current research shows that many children do take their school work and personal lives seriously enough to become depressed at times. Those most easily affected are children characterized as well-behaved,

sensitive, and interested in pleasing adults. In addition, many experts agree that today youngsters can face increased pressure and demands at home and at school, which may come from more disrupted families, frequent moves by parents, and higher expectations for academic performance—all of which can contribute to childhood depression. Experts still disagree on the nature, extent, and the symptoms of childhood depression, but, as parents, you can be aware of behaviors that may signal problems and you can relate to your children in positive ways that, in some cases, may help ward off depression.

WHAT WE KNOW NOW

Everyone feels sad sometimes. Most often though, time and a little extra attention will help a youngster bounce back from the disappointing loss of a basketball game, a poor grade on a test they thought they'd aced, or the shifting loyalties of school friends.

Less than 10 percent of children ever become severely depressed, and girls seem more likely to become depressed than boys.

But no matter what a child's gender or age, short-term sadness that turns to longer-term depression can throw a monkey wrench into home life and school life alike, making it difficult for your child to learn.

If your child is acting sad and is not performing well at school, it may seem simple to arrive at the conclusion he's depressed. But because depression is a complex combination of symptoms, it's actually not at all easy to diagnose or to separate the cause of the depression from the effect of the depression. For example, your child's depressed behavior may be the result of low self-esteem, not the cause, and simply addressing the depression won't do anything for his self-esteem problem. (See Self-Esteem.)

Another difficulty in diagnosing depression is that in some cases, depressed children don't act the way you might think they would; they may seem more angry or irritable than sad, or just more forgetful or "spacey" than usual, so that it can be difficult to pinpoint depression rather than another behavior issue or learning problem as the cause. And, sometimes, depression turns up as an important side issue after another problem is addressed, as it does for many children who are acting out then found to be at least somewhat depressed too.

There are lots of reasons why some children become depressed, and experts now recognize that for any one child, several factors at a time are usually contributing to how they feel. Most psychologists agree there are two main factors that may play a part in most depression:

- *Biological*: including a genetically inherited tendency to become depressed, and imbalances in the brain chemicals that affect moods.

- *Psychological*: including disturbances in parent-child relationships, threats to self-esteem that may come from school activities or difficulties with academics, and the loss of loved ones through death, divorce, moving, or rejection. (See Divorce/Single Parents, Moving, or Friends.) Some children may also simply have a way of looking at the world or interpreting actions and everyday experiences that, for them leads to depression.

WHEN SHOULD I BE CONCERNED?

Any time you see a change in your child's behavior that worries you, you can consider it a signal from your child that something is wrong. You may want to check with the school psychologist when you see such signs of depression as those listed below. You should get help immediately if your child seems preoccupied with death or thoughts of suicide, especially if she is in adolescence, when the likelihood of her suffering a serious depression is somewhat greater than when she was younger.

Another reason to check with a school psychologist sooner rather than later in this case, is that for many children by the time their school work is affected, they may have already been depressed for a long time. It can take weeks or months of depression before a child loses motivation, becomes slower at accomplishing even basic academic tasks or problem solving, or is unable to remember facts and assignments.

As you will see by the extensive list of symptoms below, there are lots of feelings and behaviors that can be part of depression. You should be concerned if your child shows several of the symptoms described below for a month. Another way to know when to be concerned is to keep in mind this rule of thumb: If your child feels sad enough to be unable to focus on school work or to see friends most days of the week for a month, and if you are not able to lift him out of the sad mood with treats or attention, then it is time to be concerned.

In young children who are depressed, you might see an increase in physical complaints such as stomachaches and headaches, or agitation, anxiety, and fears related to school. (See Anxiety, School Phobia.) For older children and adolescents, you might see more antisocial or sulky behavior, and they may become withdrawn and detached from school work or extracurricular activities they used to like, or they may become more emotional than usual. Physical symptoms for an adolescent may also include dramatic weight loss or gain, a significant change in sleeping habits (sleeping a great deal more, or being unable to sleep), or an increase in fatigue.

For children who may not act sad, but who may still be depressed, you could use these guidelines—adapted from *Childhood Depression: School-Based Intervention*, by psychologist Kevin Stark—to determine when you should be concerned:

❏ *Decreased academic performance:* Children who are depressed may become unmotivated (see Motivation) or apathetic. They often have difficulty concentrating, are more easily frustrated by school work, and may be more irritable than usual and lash out at people trying to help them. In addition, there may be an unexplained decline in grades; an increase in missed assignments or messy, careless work; or complaints from your child that he is too tired to complete assignments. He may also give up easily or say he's not interested in subjects he used to love.

❏ *Anger:* You should be concerned if your child seems angry the majority of the time for about a month. The less his anger is attached to events around him—for example, he just feels angry, not angry at the teacher or a classmate—the more likely he is to be depressed. (See Anger.)

❏ *Boredom or loss of pleasure:* You should be concerned if your child feels bored more than half of her waking hours for about a month or has lost interest or pleasure in at least half of activities she used to love. For example, a depressed 14-year-old girl voted by her classmates to be one of the school cheerleaders, said it meant nothing to her and that she felt nothing when her name was announced, even though cheerleading had previously meant the world to her.

❏ *Crying:* Depressed children often cry more than usual, and more easily, although some who are seriously depressed say that even though they feel like crying, they cannot. If your child is crying more than usual and more easily than he usually would, for about a month, you should be concerned. You should also be concerned if your child tells you he has felt like crying almost every day for quite a while but cannot.

❏ *Feeling unloved:* It's normal for a child to accuse you of not loving her when you have disciplined or punished her, but a depressed child feels this way at other times as well. You should be concerned if your child tells you this—even once—in a heartfelt manner, when you are sure she is not reacting to discipline or trying to manipulate you.

❏ *Negative self-evaluation:* You should be concerned if your child perceives herself as inadequate or unacceptable in at least three of these major areas: scholastic achievement, athletic ability, intelligence, physical appearance, personality, and personal possessions. Negative self-evaluation is closely associated with suicidal behavior.

❏ *Hopelessness:* Children who do not see any possibility for a solution to their problems, and who express hopelessness along with other symptoms of depression are at higher risk for suicide.

Children who are depressed may also show:

❏ consistent, pervasive guilty feelings over things they really could not have controlled

❏ indecisiveness that keeps them from making and sticking to decisions (see Dependency).

❏ a persistent pattern of poor peer relationships

❏ social withdrawal or an unwillingness or inability to become involved with friends or family

❏ a lot of interest in death or suicide, or in ways in which people could, or do, kill themselves.

WHAT CAN I DO TO HELP?

If you think your child is depressed, it's best to consult the school psychologist and work with her as described below in What Will A Professional Do? She can then act as a liason between your efforts and the teacher. Your child's teacher will most likely not be asked to intervene in a therapeutic way in the classroom, primarily because it takes someone with specific training in psychology to be effective, but it will be helpful for her to know what your child may be struggling with. The school psychologist may also ask the teacher to provide more positive feedback to your child, as well as ask for her observations of your child's progress.

In addition to informing the teacher and

working with the school psychologist, you can be helping your depressed child cope with school and home issues by:

❏ giving frequent, genuine praise. Accentuate what your child can do well in school.

❏ planning for special, enjoyable events, and talking about them ahead of time to help your child keep at least a partially positive focus.

❏ maintaining a predictable school and family routine as much as possible to minimize changes and the anxiety they may cause.

❏ encouraging your child's participation in games, activities, and discussions that will help her practice concentrating or thinking through problems, which is very difficult for most depressed children.

WHAT WILL A PROFESSIONAL DO?

If you are nonetheless concerned that your child is depressed, the school psychologist can be available for you to talk with. She can also provide you with a referral to an outside psychologist and then act as a liason between you and the teacher.

If the school psychologist agrees that it is likely your child is depressed and that her academic performance is being affected, she will want to assemble a multidisciplinary team (see Evaluations and Testing, in Part I) to look more closely at your child's behavior, possibly through a full evaluation, which will rely heavily on clear and accurate reports from you and the teacher about your child's behavior in the classroom and at home. You and the teacher might also be asked to complete a behavior rating form (see Psychological Evaluations, in Part I, for a description of the process) such as the Child Behavior Checklist (see Appendix D for examples of tests mentioned in this section). In talking with you and evaluating the data, the psychologist will be looking both for symptoms of depression like those listed above (see When Should I Be Concerned), and for changes in your child's behavior, such as becoming noticeably less social than usual, or showing decreased school performance.

Of course, the school psychologist will also talk extensively with your child and observe her in the classroom. During interviews with your child, the psychologist will be assessing her mood and the degree to which she shows the symptoms listed above. She may ask your child specifically about depression and suicide, if it seems warranted. And she will most likely have your child complete some self-report inventories to understand her view of herself and how she feels. Tests the psychologist might use are the Children's Depression Inventory, the Junior-Senior High School Personality Inventory, or the Piers-Harris Children's Self-Concept Scale.

Some psychologists may also use a less structured approach with a method called *projective techniques*, which involve such activities as having your child complete drawings, supply words to complete sentences that describe her feelings or beliefs about herself, make up stories to go with pictures, or interpret inkblots. (See Evaluation and Testing, in Part I.)

All of these techniques are aimed at finding in your child's behavior recurring themes—where they exist—of sadness, depression, anger, or an inability to cope successfully. You will be informed in detail of the psychologist's findings, so that you can work with her on deciding the next step for your child, which could be:

❐ following the initial evaluation with more testing to get a clearer idea of what is bothering your child,

❐ developing an in-school plan for action with the school psychologist, or

❐ immediately seeking outside psychological help for your child which may include the use of medications to alleviate depression.

An in-school intervention may be recommended by the multidisciplinary team. (See Special Education, in Part I.) That could include special education help for your child if members agree that her academic progress is being affected by her depression to such a degree that she cannot produce work, or that she is falling significantly behind her class level, and that the problem has existed for a significant amount of time, about six months.

In special education, your child can get academic help so that she can at least keep up academically until the depression can be addressed, or she can receive in-school counseling from the school psychologist or a social worker, or she'll receive both forms of aid. Keep in mind that no matter what the multidisciplinary team recommends, you have the final say about what is best for your child.

See also:

❐ Anger
❐ Anxiety
❐ Dependency
❐ Divorce/Single Parents
❐ Evaluation and Testing, in Part I
❐ Friends
❐ Self-Esteem
❐ Suicide

Further Reading

Greist, J. H. & Jefferson, J. *Depression and Its Treatment.* New York: Warner Books, 1994.

McCoy, S. "Danny's Descent Into Hell." *Reader's Digest,* (January 1988).

Divorce/Single Parents

"Doug has been so quiet since his father and I separated. It seems he's adjusting to the changes because he does what I tell him and doesn't seem upset. But his grades have been falling, and it's beginning to worry me."

For many children, life in a single-parent family can be challenging, whether it is caused by divorce, by death, or even if that's the way it always was because the mom chose to be single. In the United States today, it's estimated that a majority of children will live in a single-parent family at some point in their lives. Although in many communities, life without father (which is by far most often the case, a fact that's underscored by the complete lack of studies on school behavior in mother-less children) is no longer an oddity, it can still carry some unique challenges for children and mom alike. For the most part, these are parenting issues, and you can find sources for more information on single parenting under Further Reading at the end of this section. In addition, single parenting may affect your child's academic life in specific ways, and it will be helpful to see how you can help your child meet that challenge.

WHAT WE KNOW NOW

There is no one way that children in single-parent families behave in school. Some children do have significant problems, but keep in mind, especially if you are newly divorced or widowed, that others weather this drastic change without collecting harmful emotional scars or seeing their school experience seriously damaged. The best predictor of how your child will handle this change is to look carefully at how he has always handled change. Children who already have academic or social problems in school and who tend to be thrown off track by most changes, are likely to continue to have the same difficulties, or have somewhat more of them, during and after a divorce. And children who are flexible, adaptable, and who do well in school continue to do well, responding to this challenge for the most part in the same positive ways they respond to other challenges.

For children who do have difficulty adjusting to a single-parent family, it's important to know that adjustment can be a fairly long, uneven road. A child may seem fine at first, then hit a low spot months, or even years, later. Some children may not feel the full emotional effect until they become adolescents and begin developing their own relationships.

How divorce will affect your child depends on several factors:

1 Her age at the time of the divorce. School-age children are at greater social and academic risk. They commonly react with depression, withdrawal, grieving, fear, fantasies of responsibility for the break-up and of possible reconciliation, anger, shame, decreased school performance, a sense of loss or rejection, and conflicts over which parent to express loyalty to.

The reaction of adolescents can be similar to those of younger children. In addition, they may feel anxious about the future and their own potential marriages. In some cases, however, adolescents may more easily adjust to their parents' divorce because their relative maturity helps them understand the circumstances surrounding the divorce.

2 *Your child's gender.* Divorce more seriously affects boys initially and in the long term than girls, and older boys show more significant emotional and academic problems than younger boys.

3 *Length of time since the divorce.* Most children seem to adjust to divorce over a period of years.

4 *Parents' own emotional stability.* Although during the first years after the divorce, parents may not be at the peak of their parenting prowess, the more emotional stability they can show their children, the better. Most parents begin to stabilize emotionally the second year after a divorce; parenting difficulties begin to subside then, too.

WHEN SHOULD I BE CONCERNED?

It's normal for many children, whether they are in first grade or seniors in high school, to be angry during or after a divorce. You should be concerned if your child's anger seems excessive compared to how he would have acted before the divorce. You should also be concerned if he seems to be angry almost every day, if he is more intensely angry than you've previously seen him, or if his anger is interfering with his school work or relationships with friends. (See also Anger Control.) While nightmares are common and normal among younger children, you should be concerned if the nightmares are making your child afraid to go to sleep, or if he is losing enough sleep that he is consistently tired at school. And, of course, adolescents who act out their anger by abusing drugs or becoming blatantly sexual are cause for concern.

It's also cause for concern if your child of any age won't talk to you about the divorce or her reaction to it, or if her anger is unduly centered on one parent or the other.

At school, you should be concerned if you see your child losing interest in academics or in her friends. Other causes for concern at school are:

□ not finishing homework when she never used to miss an assignment (see Perfectionism), or becoming a perfectionist when she was never that careful.

□ a sudden drop in grades

□ difficulty concentrating

□ younger children who suddenly don't want to go to school (see School Phobia), or who develop unexplained stomachaches or headaches regularly (see Depression)

□ adolescents who seem uncharacteristically insecure or who jump into more adultlike relationships than is appropriate for their age.

WHAT CAN I DO TO HELP?

Some experts recommend you let the teacher know as soon as you tell your child that you are getting a divorce. Others caution that, being human, some teachers will look for problems where none exist if they know you are divorcing. Keep in mind that your child will probably tell everyone anyway. And you may want to think about how much detail will be helpful to tell the teacher about your divorce.

During and after a divorce or a death in your family, it's important for you to offer your child the most supportive, stable environment you can, to balance the huge changes your family will be going through. Do not move to a different town or even a new house unless it is absolutely necessary. Most children of any age do better when their support systems (familiar teachers, school, friends, and relatives) remain intact.

You can also:

❏ have the other parent continue involvement in your child's school as much as possible,

❏ ask extended family or friends for additional help or emotional support. If there is no male (or female) in your child's life, consider enlisting a willing friend or relative to spend time helping your child with homework, taking him to the library, or helping him learn how to work with new computer software.

WHAT WILL A PROFESSIONAL DO?

Your child's teacher should be able to tell you what kinds of support services the school psychologist at your school offers, or you can contact the school psychologist directly. In many districts, school psychologists offer individual counseling for children who have lost a parent through death or divorce. Others offer a variety of counseling groups for children of divorce, tailoring them to focus on common issues, like learning to live in two households at once. These kinds of groups typically use techniques such as role-playing, discussion, and drawing pictures (for younger children) or (for older children and adolescents) producing more sophisticated artwork or videos to help them adjust to their single-parent family.

See also:

❏ Anger Control
❏ Anxiety
❏ Depression
❏ School Phobia
❏ Self-Esteem

Further Reading

Alexander, S. In Praise of Single Parents. Boston: Houghton Mifflin, 1994.

Anderson, J. The Single Mother's Book. Atlanta: Peachtree Publication, 1993.

Bustanoby, A. Being A Single Parent. New York: Ballantine Books, 1985.

Christopher, G. Anchors for the Innocent: Inner Power for Today's Single Mothers and Fathers. Chicago: Human Capacity Press, 1993.

Francke, L. Growing Up Divorced. New York: Fawcett Crest, 1983.

Kennedy, M. & King, J. The Single Parent Family: Living Happily in a Changing World. New York: Crown Trade Paperbacks, 1994.

Goldstein, S. & Solnit, A. J. *Divorce and Your Child*. New Haven: Yale University Press, 1984.

Krementz, J. *How It Feels When Parents Divorce*. New York: Alfred A. Knopf, 1993.

Leman, K. *Living In a Step Family Without Getting Stepped On*. Nashville: Thomas Nelson Publication, 1994.

Mattes, J. *Single Mothers By Choice*. New York: Times Books, 1994.

Reed, B. *Single Mothers Raising Sons*. Nashville: Thomas Nelson Publication, 1988.

Wassil-Grilmm, L. *Where's Daddy: How Divorced, Single and Widowed Mothers Can Provide What's Missing When Dad's Missing*. Woodstock, NY: The Overlook Press, 1994.

C H A P T E R 1 6

Drug Abuse

"Terrill told me lots of her friends had smoked pot by the time they were in middle school. She swears she hasn't tried it, but I'm worried she won't be able to resist if everyone else is doing it."

Drugs and alcohol may not be a regular part of your child's life now. But you can bet that at some time before she is out of high school, your child will likely be faced with the temptation from her peers to try something you would probably prefer she not use: a beer at a party, or a joint, or a line of cocaine. Studies show that all of these and more are available to most youngsters, beginning now as young as age 9 or 10 in some areas.

It's good to talk with your child long before the temptation arises about your house rules on drugs and alcohol. You can begin by clarifying for yourself your own attitudes about these substances, which will in turn help you to formulate a useful response if you find your child has experimented with them. If you suspect your child has already crossed the line from experimentation to abuse, more knowledge about the issues involved in substance abuse can help you know where to get help and how to develop effective ways of handling the problem.

WHAT WE KNOW NOW

Some people who deal with drug and alcohol issues believe that any use of these by adolescents or younger children is abuse. Others believe that responsible use is permissible, although their definition of responsible use includes delaying the first use of drugs or alcohol and then not using much of either drugs or alcohol very often or in risky circumstances, as in driving a car. What you consider permissible will have a lot to do with your own values, as well as what the law allows.

In any case, the sad news is that each year a large number of teens begin using drugs and/or alcohol. One national survey showed that 93 percent of high school seniors had tried alcohol and 61 percent had tried marijuana. While the average grade for first use of alcohol is ninth grade, about half of high school seniors report using alcohol before high school, and some surveys show that elementary-age children are drinking, too. Inhalants, such as fumes from certain kinds of glue or paint thinners and aerosol cans, are the drug of choice for some younger adolescents, while alcohol and marijuana are more likely to be chosen by some older adolescents.

There is no doubt among educators and psychologists that drug and alcohol use among children and adolescents is a major social problem. The continuum they see of how youngsters move from one substance to another begins with experimentation with tobacco, beer, wine, and hard liquor. Marijuana use usually starts after youngsters have tried alcohol. Some adolescents go on to experiment with such depressants as Valium or Quaaludes, stimulants such as amphetamines or cocaine, and psychedelics such as LSD. Opiates, such as heroin, are most often the last substance tried. Not surprisingly, most initial use takes place in a social situation. The good news in all of this is that a large number of adolescents experiment with drugs or alcohol and do not repeat the experience. Some use drugs occasionally without suffering any negative consequences. And most make a conscious decision at some point to go no further with drugs or alcohol.

Of course, this doesn't mean you should wink at your child's experimentation. But it might help give you a little perspective to govern how you react if you find out your child has had a drink with her friends or smoked a joint. If you can manage not to overreact, you can use the incident as an opportunity to open lines of communication about drugs and alcohol with your child, and to be honest with her about your concerns and about what is and is not permissible in your household and under the law.

For some youngsters, drug and alcohol use is not a one-time thing, but rather a constant, compulsive act eventually resulting in physical, emotional, and social deterioration. There are lots of reasons why some adolescents fall into this destructive pattern. Some of the prominent ones are:

❐ Social factors including the influence of parents, siblings, and friends who use drugs and alcohol, and unstable family situations.
❐ Psychological factors like lower self-esteem, confidence, and assertiveness (see Self-Esteem, Assertiveness and Shyness), high need for social approval from peers (see Friends), high

levels of anxiety (see Anxiety), and a tendency to be impulsive and rebellious.
❐ Behavioral factors, such as acting out in school, getting lower grades, and having no interest in extracurricular activities.

Psychologists have identified five stages of adolescent drug use:

1 Initial exposure to drugs through peers, media, and family influences.
2 Learning the mood swing, when a youngster finds that using the drug makes her feel good. This usually happens in a social setting with peers.
3 Seeking the mood swing, when usage progresses from occasional to regular weekend use, to occasional weekday use, and finally in some cases, to regular weekday use.
4 Preoccupation with the mood swing, when most of the adolescent's time is devoted to obtaining drugs and getting high. Solitary use, as opposed to social use, is typical of this stage, along with dealing drugs in many cases.
5 Using drugs to feel normal, or to get through the day.

Needless to say, adolescents who progress through all five stages have a serious substance abuse problem. Even those who stop at one of the early stages may be setting up a lifelong pattern of mild abuse, which also has its consequences on your child's health and emotional welfare.

WHEN SHOULD I BE CONCERNED?

There are many signs your child could be experimenting with or regularly using drugs or alcohol. You should be concerned if you note:

❐ a decrease in school attendance
❐ a decrease in academic performance

- displays of unusual degrees of activity or inactivity
- deterioration of your child's personal appearance
- changes in appetite or sleeping habits (increase or decrease)
- slurred or incoherent speech
- lack of motor coordination
- unpredictable displays of temper
- your child is wearing sunglasses at inappropriate times
- your child develops a new pattern of spending most of the time at home alone in her room
- borrowing or stealing money
- wearing long-sleeved shirts at inappropriate times (to hide needle marks)
- getting into trouble with legal authorities
- a radical change in your child's peer group
- withdrawing from church, school, or community activities
- association with known substance users
- appearance of intoxication with or without the smell of alcohol
- red, watery eyes, runny nose, shortness of breath
- possession of unexplained expensive articles or large sums of money
- possession of drug paraphernalia, such as incense, pipes, eye droppers

WHAT CAN I DO TO HELP?

Try not to overreact the first time you find your child has experimented with drugs or alcohol. This is an opportunity to open up communication with her about these issues. Remember that many youngsters experiment once and never use these substances again.

You can also:

- *Be a good role model.* Parents' habits and attitudes about alcohol and drug use influence their children's behavior. Drinking in front of your child is not necessarily harmful, but drinking too much and in risk situations (like while driving) can be, because children will do what you show them—not necessarily what you tell them. Far more than many adults realize, children notice why their parents drink, when they drink, how much they drink and what they do while they're drinking.
- *Help your children have a positive self-image.* Children and youngsters who feel good about themselves are less likely to use alcohol and/or drugs to help them feel good. (See Self-Esteem.)
- *Learn to listen to your child.* Real listening is more than not talking. Try:

  - Watching your child's facial expressions and body language to uncover how she really feels.
  - Rephrasing your child's comments to show you understand what she said.
  - Using your own body language (make eye contact, nod your head, smile when appropriate) and tone of voice to give support and encouragement.
  - Using encouraging phrases to keep the conversation going, such as "Tell me more about it."

- *Talk with your child about substance use.* Choose an appropriate time, for example, when a television news program deals with the issue. Find out how your child feels about the issue and clearly explain why she should not drink or use drugs.
- *Encourage healthy activities.* When a child has positive interests, she may be less likely to experiment with drugs or alcohol out of boredom. Family activities as well as such things as school clubs, scouts, music, sports, or other hobbies are all good choices.

❏ *Set family rules regarding substance use.* Children should know clearly what your views are on substance use and what the consequences will be for going against those. You can also tell your child clearly what you expect them to do in situations where they may be pressured to use alcohol or drugs.

❏ *Teach your child to deal with peer pressure.* Role-play with her situations where peer pressure may come into play, and show her how to say no. See the Saying No box below for details.

❏ *Know the early warning signs* of drug and alcohol use listed under When Should I Be Concerned? If you suspect your child is smoking pot, for example, you have even more reason to talk with her about drugs. If you ignore it, her drug use will not go away. In fact, youngsters often assume their parents know about their use or their experimentation, so if you say nothing, your youngster may think you are silently condoning her actions.

❏ *When you talk about drug use, try hard to stay calm.* Your youngster is likely to be extremely defensive the first time you bring up her use of drugs or alcohol. Your job will be to remain calmly focused on the drug issue, ignoring all the side issues she's likely to bring up. Remember to reassure your youngster that you love her, but not her actions. If you feel you need help with these discussions or in deciding what to do after your child tells you of her drug use, call the school psychologist and read the What Will A Professional Do? section, below.

Find out from the principal if your school has a substance abuse prevention program. Your support will help your child, and can help the program continue. If they don't have one, volunteer to get information from your local police department. Most departments now either teach the drug prevention program called D.A.R.E., or at least offer information on it.

Other places to find substance abuse edu-

Saying No

Most people make better decisions in difficult situations if they are prepared for those situations. You can help your child prepare for peer pressure to use drugs or alcohol by practicing what to say or do instead of giving in.

Try Role-Playing. Pretend your child is at a party and some kids walk in with drugs. What do you say?

"I don't want to."
"It's not good for you."
"I don't need drugs to have a good time."
"I want my brain to stay the way it is."
"Drugs make you stupid."
"I don't do drugs, they're bad for my health."
"I need to be in shape to play soccer."

Make a Contract. Encourage your child to make a pact with a friend or group of friends not to do drugs or use alcohol.

Make a Deal. Tell your child that sometimes talk doesn't work and the only way to avoid drugs is to walk away, to leave a party, or to leave friends who have been drinking rather than ride home in a car with them. Make a deal with your child that you will pick him up any time, any place, no questions asked. Or offer to pay his cab fare home.

cation programs outside of school are your local hospital, Alcoholics Anonymous, Narcotics Anonymous, a local mental health center, the National Institute of Drug Abuse, or the National Clearing House for Alcohol and

Drug Information (call 1-800-662-HELP). You can also speak with your pediatrician or someone from your church or synagogue.

WHAT WILL A PROFESSIONAL DO?

If your son or daughter is already involved with drugs, not just in a first-time experimentation, talk to your school psychologist to find out about a drug rehabilitation center for your child. Remember, school personnel cannot get your child involved in outside counseling of any kind without your approval. Some school psychologists also run a counseling group for substance abusers. Usually, these will be small groups of youngsters led by the psychologist to focus on why they are using drugs, on education about drugs, and on how to deal with peer pressure to use drugs or with difficult family situations.

If you feel you need help talking with your youngster about drug use, or you just suspect she may be involved in substance abuse, you can also call the school psychologist. He will be able to help you keep the lines of communication open between you and your child, or to reopen them, and to help you keep track of whether your child's use of drugs or alcohol is affecting her school performance.

If your child confesses drug use to the school psychologist, he will not automatically turn your child over to the police, but will focus first on helping your child and you. However, if your child discusses serious drug use with the psychologist that she has not told you about, because drug use is so hurtful to her, the psychologist will let your child know when he begins talking with her that he must involve you, too.

Schools have very strict policies regarding drugs on school grounds. If your child is found with drugs in school, the police will probably be called. They will most likely also be called if your child is suspected to be under the influence of drugs or alcohol, which could result in a suspension for your child.

Whether your child confesses serious substance abuse to the school psychologist, is found with drugs at school, or is under the influence at school, you will be called by the psychologist or the principal. That's not the kind of phone call any parent relishes, but if it happens to you, try to keep in mind that the school psychologist is a source for help for both you and your child.

See also:

❐ Anxiety
❐ Assertiveness and Shyness
❐ Friends
❐ Self-Esteem

Further Reading

Baron, J. *The Parent Handbook of Drug Abuse.* Drug Abuse Program of America. 1981.

Dupont, R. L. *Getting Tough On Getaway Drugs.* American Psychiatric Press, 1985.

Meyer, R. *The Parent Connection: How to Communicate with Your Children About Alcohol and Other Drugs.* New York: Franklin Watts, 1984.

Milgram, G. G. *What, When and How to Talk to Children About Alcohol and Other Drugs: A Guide for Parents.* Center City, MN: Hazelden, 1983.

Polson, B. & Newton, M. *Not My Kid: A Parent's Guide to Kids and Drugs.* New York: Avon Books, 1984.

Fears

"Ellie hasn't wanted to go to school three days this week because the weather has been cloudy. She's so afraid of thunder and lightning, on even partly cloudy days we really have to do some heavy convincing to get her to go to school. She says she's so scared it might thunder that it's impossible for her to concentrate."

Fear plays a part in just about everyone's life at one time or another. For children, fear is a normal part of their development, and the expression of fear is a positive, healthy aspect of growing up. Normal fears are one way in which children learn to adapt to their environment and deal with things they find stressful. In fact, it's fear that plays a role in keeping children safe; without some degree of fear, playing in traffic would be just the same for them as playing on the playground at school. And it is parents who intentionally or unintentionally instill some fears in children, warning them not to run into the street, touch a hot stove, poke a screwdriver into an electrical outlet, or perhaps not to go outside during thunderstorms. Instilling certain fears serves an important purpose both for your child (protection), and for you (peace of mind).

But while having some fear is generally healthy, for some children it can be intense enough to be socially or academically paralyzing. Understanding which fears are normal and when they have become something more serious will help you to help your child.

WHAT WE KNOW NOW

Fear is usually described as a person's reaction to a threatening situation. For example, a child would be afraid if she was being chased by a growling dog, or if he saw the class bully approaching him on the playground with clenched fists.

Phobias, on the other hand, are a special form of fear which has some additional qualities. A phobia:

❏ is a fear of the consequences of an object or situation, more than of the object itself. For example, a person could have a phobia about being bitten by the dog, not about the dog itself

❏ is out of proportion to the situation,

❏ cannot be explained or reasoned away

❏ is beyond your child's voluntary control

❏ leads your child to avoid any situation in which he might encounter the thing he's afraid of

In addition, phobias tend to go on for a long time, say for a year, and to not change with your child's age or continued development. And they are so intense that your child becomes, in some sense, incapacitated when faced with the thing that scares him.

Both fears and phobias have their basis in anxiety. (See Anxiety.) A child feels anxious about an event, a situation, or even the possibility of a bad experience, and then learns to

Is Your Child Afraid? Or Is She Anxious?

FEAR	ANXIETY
A thinking (cognitive) process	An emotional response
An intellectual appraisal of a threatening situation	An emotional response to that appraisal
Used in reference to something likely to happen in the future	Occurs when the person either is exposed to the situation or just thinks about it
Is activated when the person is physically or psychologically exposed to the situation	Same as above
Can be separated into "realistic" (based on a sensible assumption) vs. "unrealistic."	Cannot be evaluated on this criterion; is an affective response, not an intellectual one.

be afraid of it, sometimes to the point of phobia. It's important to note the word *learns*. Most fears and phobias are ways of thinking your child has somehow learned, even in children younger than school age, when fears tend to be less reality-based. The good news is that with the right techniques, these learned behaviors can be unlearned. The table above comparing characteristics of fear with those of anxiety might be helpful in further showing the difference between the two.

Children from infancy to young adulthood have fears and phobias in a fairly predictable pattern. Studies have shown that younger children, from ages 2 to 6 typically have four or five things they're really afraid of. By the time they are between the ages of 6 and 12, they ordinarily have as many as seven things that scare them, with adolescents reporting about the same number. The table below shows the kinds of things children of

different ages normally fear.

WHEN SHOULD I BE CONCERNED?

You should be concerned if your child has far more than the average number of fears for children, between about four and seven things that make him really afraid. It's also a concern if the intensity of his fears is so great they become incapacitating to him, preventing him from participating in school. You should be concerned, for example, if your child is so afraid of a bee sting she can't walk to school with the other kids, wait for the bus, or even go to physical education class after a bee was spotted in the gym. The same is true if your child's fears are so great they interfere with learning, for example, if she is so afraid no one will remember to call her for a special reading group that she can't concentrate on her lessons in class. You should also be concerned if, after reviewing the chart below, you can see that

What's Scary

Ages 2–6	Fears largely not based on reality. Tend to be global, irrational. Scared of monsters, ghosts. Also animals (like dogs and bugs) and the dark.
Ages 7–12	Afraid of bodily injury, physical damage, and natural events such as avalanches or tornadoes. School-related fears emerge, such as fear of failing a test or getting bad grades.
Ages 13–18	Fears about political situations emerge. Also fears concerning personal social situations and bodily injury.

your child's fears are not age-appropriate.

But be sure you also examine your own fears and your attitude about your child's fears before you take any action. First, remember that if you have a strong fear of some kind yourself, it wouldn't be surprising to see that fear duplicated in your child, even if you've never spoken directly of that fear to him. Some children learn more from what we don't say to them than from what we do say.

Also, think about who is bothered by your child's fear. If the fear is not incapacitating to him, and if he's not complaining about it, it could be that your child's fear bothers the adults around him more than it bothers him. Sometimes the only problem with a child's fear is that it doesn't fit with adult demands and expectations for fearlessness.

If your child's fear does not restrict or alter his behavior or his ability to carry out the academic, social, and behavioral expectations you or the school have for him, then it really can't be defined by the school as a problem. For example, your young child's fear of snakes is not a problem, so long as he can still go to school and read about them, learn, concen-

trate, and participate in class. On the other hand, if his fear is of being incorrect, or of being chastised by the teacher, and it is so strong that he never volunteers to answer in class and strongly resists doing homework, then the school will most likely want to address the problem. (See Perfectionism, Assertiveness and Shyness.)

Last, while you should always act on your concerns for your child's behavior, it doesn't hurt to think first about what difference it would make for your child if your action leads to some kind of therapy for him. What do you expect would be different about his life if this one piece was changed? If you can't see that it would make much difference for your child, then perhaps his fear isn't really a problem he needs to address now.

WHAT CAN I DO TO HELP?

It may help to understand that there isn't much you can do to keep a child from having fears. But you can work to minimize their impact by following the suggestions in this section. Keep in mind that if your efforts don't seem to help your child, or if his fears are overwhelming or incapacitating to him, you will need to get professional help for him.

First, you can carefully and honestly review your own fears and your reasons for being concerned about your child, and you can establish a supportive climate at home for your child as he learns what to do about his fears. Then, some of the things you can do are the following:

❏ *Do not discount the emotional response of your child.* His feelings are very real to him.

❏ *Listen to your child.* Sometimes a child's fear is lessened simply by having someone listen and provide correct or specific information about the situation he fears.

❏ *Let your child talk to you about his fear.* He needs to know he has your understanding and support.

At school, check with the teacher to see if she notes your child's fears, and find out if and how they impact his learning, his concentration, or his peer relationships.

If your child has specific fears, such as a strong fear of attending school, look at the chapter on School Phobia. For other things your child might be really afraid of, keep in mind that fear is a cognitive—thinking—process. The more you can do to give your child reasonable, logical approaches to the thing he is afraid of, the better he'll be at overcoming those fears. For example, if your young child is afraid of getting on that big, noisy school bus, you should of course talk to him about what it is specifically that scares him (to be sure there's nothing besides the noise and the size that's upsetting), and then try to address those particular concerns. People who teach classes for adults who are afraid of flying in airplanes do the same thing: they sit the person in a seat on a plane, buckle them in, then have the pilot start the engines. For some peo-ple it's the sound of the engines revving before take-off that scares them; so the instructor explains why the engines need to be revved. For others, the scariest part is the bump they feel underneath the plane after take-off, so the instructor explains that bump is the sound of the landing gear lifting into place, and that later, the dips and shivers travelers might feel in the plane itself are normal air currents, and he might describe how they move over the plane, and so on.

You can do the same thing with the school bus. Plan a public bus ride with your kinder-gartner or first grader, and talk as you ride about how you chose the seat the two of you are sitting in, and tell her that the school-bus driver might help her find a seat if she's wor-ried about that. Talk about the sounds the bus makes, about how different it feels going around corners than a car does, and about how you can hear six different conversations at once from people sitting around you. Once your child knows what to expect from bus rid-ing, getting on that school bus will be less frightening.

WHAT WILL THE PROFESSIONAL DO?

The school psychologist will not become fully involved unless your child's academics are being significantly affected. If they are not, the psychologist can act in an advisory role to steer you to other sources of help that would be appropriate in your situation.

If the school psychologist does become involved, she will want to do a functional analysis of your child's fear, focusing not on whether your child is fearful, but on the nature of your child's fear, how it developed, and why it persists.

An assessment of this kind would consist of:

❏ Interviews with parents about how and when your child's fear developed, with lots of detail so the psychologist can understand what is causing or perpetuating the fear. You may also be asked to fill out a Child Behavior Checklist or the Personality Inventory for Children (see Evaluation and Testing, in Part I; also Appendix D, Samples from Tests).

❏ Interviews with your child—once again, to get specific ideas about the causes of his fear and why it persists.

❏ Tests for your child to complete, such as the Fear Survey Schedule for Children and the Children's Manifest Anxiety Scale, which ask children to rate the amount of fear they feel in different situations.

❏ Observations of your child in the classroom.

Exactly what the school psychologist does for your child once the assessment is complete will be tailored to your child's needs—once again, only if the fear or phobia affects your child's academics. Because these fears are usu-ally learned responses, the psychologist will focus on techniques that help your child unlearn the fear. One of those commonly used is called *modeling* in which your child sees how other children, or you, face the specific thing he's afraid of with no ill effects. Another is called *successive approximation*, in which your child is exposed to very small doses at a time of that which frightens him until he can handle larger doses. For example, a child who is afraid of loud noises and large crowds is terrified of going into the auditorium for assemblies. The school psychologist would stand with the child outside the auditorium door, where he could see the crowd and hear some of the noise, but not be engulfed by it. On subse-quent occasions, the child would be invited to stand closer, or perhaps just inside the door, until he was finally comfortable staying inside the room for the entire event.

See also:

❏ Anxiety
❏ School Phobia
❏ Evaluation and Testing, in Part I

For Further Reading

Serafino, E. P. *The Fears of Childhood: A Guide to Recognizing and Reducing Fearful States in Children.* New York: Human Sciences Press, 1986.

For specific academic phobias, see the entry under School Phobia.

CHAPTER 18

Friends

"It happened again this week. Zara came home from school telling me she gave away her favorite picture book, the one she brought to show and tell, to a classmate she hardly knows. My husband says it's a sign of generosity. But I'm not so sure."

Making friends at school isn't just a luxury or an inconsequential bonus your child gets for being there. The skills she learns now in making and keeping friends are necessary building blocks for forming and maintaining relationships throughout her life, in academic as well as business and social situations.

While it may be tempting to treat lightly the friend issues your child may have from time to time, keep in mind that through her friendships and her more casual relationships with others her age, your child is also refining what she knows about herself, about her niche in society, and her view of the world compared to that of those around her. Your understanding of the social skills your child needs in order to make friends and be socially as well as academically successful will allow you to help her along the way.

WHAT WE KNOW NOW

The definition and expectations of friendships change with your child's age and with the environment. For example, the interaction between your preschooler and his little friend is far different from what goes on between your fifth-grader and his best friend. And, school-based friendships may play out differ-

ently than the siblinglike friendship between your son and the neighbor boy with whom he's played since they were both six months old. To get an idea of how friendships change with your child's developmental level, see the table below, compiled by Kathryn C. Gerken of the University of Iowa.

However you define friendship, there is a key task your child must accomplish in order to make friends: to learn to relate to others in a way that is acceptable to her friends and to their peers. There are two theories on how your child does that. One holds that she learns through her own experiences with children her age, using trial and error to figure out what works best in attracting and keeping friends. The other holds that your child learns about friendship primarily by watching the adults that matter in her life, such as parents and teachers, and seeing how they go about making new friends and dealing with current friends. The reality for your child probably lies somewhere between the two, with her picking up many unspoken, as well as spoken, cues from you and observing the pleasant results when she comes to appreciate the capabilities, desires, and values of another—and makes a friend.

Some of the skills your child needs in

Making Friends

Preschool years (3–5 years)	Both positive and negative interactions. Likely to spend much time playing alone or next to, rather than with, friends.
5-year-olds	Likely to work with another child. Some children will work in groups. Overall increase in contact with peers.
Middle Childhood (6–12 years)	Recognition of differences in peers. Increase in effectiveness of communication skills. Increase in cooperative work and play. Decrease in overall aggression.
Early Adolescence	Highest level of conformity in the 11–13 year age range. After 13, gradual decrease in vulnerability to group pressure. Same-sex social groups.
Adolescence	Conformity affected by status in peer group and by self-concept. Seek friends who share their values and who understand their life questions.

order to make friends may seem obvious, such as smiling and knowing how to greet others and behave in a welcoming manner to them. But she also needs to know how to:

❑ Be reasonably assertive in a group by being able to invite others to play, initiate conversations with peers, join an ongoing activity or group, and being able to introduce herself to new people.

❑ Identify the feelings of others. She needs to be able to feel sorry for others when bad things happen to them, to let friends know she likes them by telling or showing them, to listen to friends when they talk about problems they may be having, and to say nice things to others when they have done something well.

❑ Have a sense of responsibility about her friendships, responding appropriately to friendly overtures from others, and interpreting their responses correctly. She needs to know how to appropriately question rules that may be unfair, ask permission before using

another person's property, and request permission to leave the house or classroom.

❑ Cooperate and share as she plays. She needs to be able to comply with directions, attend to instructions, cooperate with friends, and request help appropriately.

❑ Exercise some degree of self-control, responding without violence to physical aggression, receiving criticism well, controlling her temper in conflicts, and responding constructively to teasing.

In addition, be sure your child has appropriate clothes and hair styling for her age and in comparison to her classmates. This doesn't mean you should plan on refinancing the house every school year to be sure your child has jeans with the right label. It simply means that your child's style of dressing should generally fit in with that of her classmates. For example, she most likely shouldn't wear sashed dresses and patent leather shoes to school when everyone else is wearing tie-dyed

T-shirts. And while it may be a touchy subject for you, if your child needs to shower more frequently, or needs to use deodorant (many children need to by about fifth grade), be sure you talk with her about it. The same is true for weight issues. If your child is overweight, talk with him about it and then consult either the school nurse or your family physician about how to help your child move toward a healthier lifestyle. While you may be uncomfortable bringing up some of these issues, it will be better for your child if these are resolved at home than if he is confronted on the playground about them.

WHEN SHOULD I BE CONCERNED?

You should be concerned when it seems your child is always, or almost always, alone or if your perception is that your child has no friends or doesn't really know how to make friends.

You should also be concerned if your child consistently:

❐ Doesn't want to go to school (see School Phobia).
❐ Says everybody makes fun of him.
❐ Gives away toys, books, clothing, or treasured possessions to get friends.
❐ Gets along well with adults but not with peers.
❐ Is the victim of jokes and ridicule (see Bullies and Victims).
❐ Is a loner.
❐ Hangs around exclusively with either younger or older kids.

If you have an elementary-age school child, you should be concerned if your child thinks of reasons to avoid field trips or class outings, if she never gets invited over to classmates' homes, complains that other children won't play with her, or avoids playing with others because she doesn't want to share toys and seems to value the toys more than the friends (which is not appropriate past preschool age), and makes excuses for not playing, saying other children are too bossy.

While it's normal for children in kindergarten through about third grade to enjoy acting out a nurturing role, you should be concerned if the teacher tells you that your child always takes the role of the baby. Children who are unwilling to occasionally take the nurturer role can develop problems with being overdependent. (See Dependency.)

If you have an adolescent, you should be concerned if your youngster often claims to be ill on the day of some social activity or event, if she rarely receives or makes phone calls involving her peers, or if she doesn't want to do things with youngsters her own age, preferring to be with her family almost exclusively.

It's also cause for concern if the teacher tells you your youngster is hanging around with friends who are involved in delinquent behavior. (See Bullies and Victims, sidebar on gang risk.)

You should also be concerned if your child has had normal friendships and suddenly drops them. Talk first with your child, then with your child's teacher to get a clear picture of what might have happened. It could be as simple as an embarrassing incident that your child can reconcile with some adult guidance. Or it could mean a more serious problem, such as depression. (See Depression, Suicide.)

WHAT CAN I DO TO HELP?

Parents unwittingly do quite a bit to influence how their children make friends. This is a good time to take a look at your own values as they relate to friends, because children so readily pick up the approaches of adults around them. You might ask yourself these questions:

- Do I foster developing relationships outside the family, for myself and for my children?
- Am I so concerned about my child's social development or so overprotective of my child that I'm actually sending him the message that he can't have friends?
- Am I, indirectly or directly, giving my child the message that I don't approve of his choices of friends, making it easier for him to simply stay home or be alone?

In addition, think about where you live. It's parents who choose a neighborhood, a school for their child, and their own adult friends, setting the scene to some degree for the kinds of friends your child will have. What kind of scene have you set up for your child? Are there children in your neighborhood? Do you live close to or far from the children she knows at school? Have you made it possible for her to have friends over?

Once you've thought about your own point of view concerning your child and his friends—or lack thereof—here are some things you can try that can be of help to him, without making choices for your child or steering him toward specific friends:

❐ First, observe your child with his friends and see if there's something you can tell he's doing that may be a turn-off to others. When you speak with him about this, don't forget to point out some positives along with the negatives you may need to tell him.
❐ Encourage your child to participate in school-related activities such as sports, drama, scouting.
❐ If your child's teacher assigns a group project, encourage your child to invite the group over to work on it at your house.

❐ If your child really has no friends at all, work with him on developing one friend. Inviting one person over to watch a video can be a good start. Sometimes an activity that doesn't require a lot of interacting is a more comfortable way for children to start a relationship.

Overall, encourage your child to talk with you about how he feels about not having friends or why he's hanging around with friends that are undesirable or having problems themselves. Share with him how you deal with friendships and what kinds of things work for you or make you uncomfortable in relationships.

If your adolescent is hanging around with friends you consider to be undesirable, you can:

❐ Tell him of your disapproval of these friends and why you disapprove of them.
❐ Set clear limitations and expectations for your youngster about his behavior.
❐ Check with the school to see where your child has most contact with this social group. For younger children, changing a seating arrangement may help. For teens, switching some classes may make it less likely your child spends the whole day with the group.
❐ Get involved as a family with activities your adolescent might like: skiing, canoeing, mountain biking.
❐ Decide how much effort you as a family and as parents are willing to put into keeping your child away from influences you feel are destructive. You can also seek outside counseling for the family to deal with deeper parenting or family issues that may be involved.

WHAT WILL A PROFESSIONAL DO?

If you are concerned about your child's ability to make friends, first talk with the teacher to be sure the situation is played out in school too, and to see if it is affecting your child's adjustment and/or school work.

If she, too, is concerned, the school psychologist may be called in to observe your child to see what may be hindering him in developing friendships. The psychologist might suggest at this point that the teacher try some classroom techniques that foster group or cooperative learning, in which students must work together to reach a goal. (See Competition and Cooperation.) In addition, she might suggest that the teacher:

❏ Pair your child with another student in class in a buddy system, so they help each other.
❏ Set up a situation where your child can lead a group, such as making him director of a play or skit.

If none of these techniques seem to work after a few months, the psychologist may conduct an evaluation of your child's social skills. In doing that she would ask you, your child, and your child's teacher to complete some behavioral rating scales such as the Piers-Harris Children's Self-Concept Scale, the Child Behavior Checklist, the Teacher Report Form, and the Social Skills Rating System. (See Evaluations and Testing, in Part 1.) These will help her to document social problems, deter-mine where the gaps in your child's social skills are, and then begin to build a personally tailored approach to helping your child learn the skills she needs. Some of the techniques the psychologist might use are role-playing, in which children act out various ways to be with or to make friends; modeling, in which children see others behave in the ways that are expected of them; and, in a small group of students, talking about and practicing the kinds of friend-relationship skills your child needs.

Some of the ways the psychologist can do that are through social-skills training programs that some schools have either as part of the classroom or as a separate activity, or through peer tutoring or mediation in which children of the same age are trained in helping their peers.

See also:

❏ Anger Control
❏ Anxiety
❏ Assertiveness and Shyness
❏ Bullies and Victims
❏ Conflict
❏ Competition and Cooperation
❏ Evaluation and Testing, in Part 1
❏ Motivation
❏ School Phobia
❏ Self-Esteem

Further Reading

Beck, T. *Building Healthy Friendships: Teaching Friendship Skills to Young People.* Saratoga, CA: R & E Publishers, 1994.

Domash, L. & Sachs, J. *"Wanna Be My Friend?" How to Strengthen Your Child's Social Skills.* New York: Hearst Books, 1994.

Dryer, S. S. *The Book Finder.* Volume 3. American Guidance Services. 1985.

Eisenberg, N. *The Caring Child.* Cambridge, MA: Harvard University Press, 1992.

Gurian, A. & Formanek, R. *The Socially Competent Child.* Boston: Houghton Mifflin, 1983.

CHAPTER 19

Giftedness

"He's only in first grade, but Rasheem wants a chemistry set for Christmas, and when we go to the library, he heads straight for the science books. Lately he's complaining that school is boring. My friends say if he's so smart and loves science so much, he doesn't need anything extra at school, he'll figure out what to do. But I'm afraid he'll get so bored he won't do his regular school work."

It's hard for you to put a finger on it, but you've known it for a long time. Your child has always been different from others his age. He began talking much earlier than your friends' children, and when he was just a toddler, he could remember details of stories and repeat them in the right order, no less. His unbounded curiosity, keen sense of humor, ability to focus on a problem forever until he solves it—all of these traits have let you know your child is very bright.

By the time he enters first grade, you're wondering if he fits that school label: gifted. And if he does, what does that mean to him and to you? With some guidelines, you can begin to understand whether or not your child is in fact gifted as schools define the term, and how you can best help your child fulfill his potential.

WHAT WE KNOW NOW

Definitions of the term *gifted* range from what some think is a limited notion of anyone who scores above a particular point on an IQ test, to broader definitions such as the one the federal government came up with in its 1978 Gifted and Talented Children's Act, which also states that special school programming is needed for children who are gifted. The Act defines gifted children as those capable of "high performance" including those who have demonstrated achievement and/or potential ability in any or all of these areas:

- general intellectual ability
- specific academic aptitude
- creative thinking
- leadership ability
- visual and performing arts
- psychomotor ability

Using this definition as a guide, about 3 to 5 percent of school children would qualify as gifted. Other definitions predict anywhere from 2 to 20 percent of the school population as gifted.

Clearly, there is no universal agreement on what "gifted" means, but there is a sense among many educators that children who are gifted need something different from standard school offerings. But whether or not they get something different isn't a given. Even though Gifted and Talented is one of the categories of exceptional children recognized by both federal and state statutes, the school's responsibilty under those laws is only to help discover which children qualify for this category. The laws stop short of requiring a school to provide a special program for them.

If you have a child who has been identified as gifted, you may know that nothing makes you see red quicker than the attitude that since your child is smart, she doesn't need extra programs at school anyway. But, in fact, one of the things we know about giftedness is that it's not just high IQ that means a child will reach his or her potential, it's a combination of IQ and a stimulating environment. If your school does not provide a gifted program for your child, that means you may have to enrich your child's learning experiences yourself. (See What Can I Do To Help?)

If you are still trying to figure out if your child meets the criteria for gifted programs, it will be useful for you to know that identifying children who are gifted is now done using more than just standardized test scores or group evaluations. At least some of the following information should be used by school personnel to reach a reasonable conclusion about whether your child is gifted:

❐ Examination of test scores (see Evaluation and Testing, and Standardized Group Tests, in Part I)
❐ Nomination by teacher, parents, and/or peers
❐ Evaluations of accomplishments such as poems, paintings, or test performances
❐ Creativity and special ability tests (see Standardized Testing, in Part I)
❐ Outstanding ratings by current or past teachers of your child's potential to advance more rapidly (for younger children) or handle more concentrated study (more typical for middle or high school students)

Sometimes a child's abilities are overshadowed by physical or social disabilities, or by not fitting someone else's idea of what a child who is gifted should be like. Children who fall into one or more of the following categories may never be evaluated for this reason, or may be evaluated and not be identified as gifted even though they are. You may need to be more insistent to the school administration about having your child evaluated (or re-evaluated) if she:

❐ Didn't do particularly well on a standardized IQ test. When these tests are too heavily relied upon to identify children who are gifted, it's possible that only high achievers and good test takers are actually identified.
❐ Has a learning disability. Some students with learning disabilities, despite problems with perception, poor motor skills, and poor memory, are highly talented in other areas. Sometimes, once the learning disability is dealt with, the child's other abilities can be more easily recognized.
❐ Has physical, neurological, or communication problems. These children are more likely to have their disabilities assessed than their abilities.
❐ Is a member of a minority group. As a female or a nonwhite child, mixed messages and misunderstandings of cultural and gender differences can make these children less likely to be identified as gifted.
❐ Is young. Very early measures of intelligence, below age 5, are not good predictors of whether your child will do well or poorly in school. You may get a better idea of your child's potential by gathering other kinds of evidence and having your child reassessed as she gets older. (See How Can I Tell If My Child is Gifted?)
❐ Has a behavior problem. Boredom, frustration, daydreaming, lack of motivation (see

Motivation, Depression, Self-Esteem), are all considered signs of a "difficult" child. In fact, they may be signs that a child needs specialized instruction.

It's also important to understand that children who are gifted do not necessarily have evenly developed skills or abilities in all areas. For example, a child who is a gifted writer may not be great at math, but she could still benefit from a gifted program in her best areas.

HOW CAN I TELL IF MY CHILD IS GIFTED?

Given the current trend toward a broader view of giftedness that includes an appreciation of creativity and special talents, you can look at the following factors in your child, no matter what your child's age, to begin to get an idea of whether she is gifted. Keep in mind that not all children who are gifted will have all of these characteristics, especially if the child has a learning disability or one of the other factors described in the section above.

- Curiosity: Look for persistence, lots of questions, more logical and searching questions, keen observational skills, and a desire to learn rapidly.
- Memory: Look for good memory, retention of an extraordinary quantity and variety of information, and a broad, changing spectrum of interests.
- Higher-Order Thinking Skills: Look for an ability to find and solve problems, an understanding of complex concepts, the ability to perceive relationships, to work with abstractions and to generalize, to generate original ideas and solutions, as well as strong critical thinking skills and self-criticism.
- Language: Look for high level of language development, early and accurate use of

advanced vocabulary, the ability to reproduce stories and events with great detail at an early age.
- Precociousness: Look for precocity in physical and intellectual development such as early walking, talking, or reading, and advanced expression of interest or talent in a specific area such as music.
- Attention and Concentration: Look for a longer attention span and an ability to concentrate for longer periods than normal for your child's age, for persistent goal-directed behavior, and for regular periods of intense concentration.
- Social Maturity: Look for a tendency to prefer the companionship of older children and adults and the ability to converse intelligently with them, along with general social maturity above that expected for your child's age.
- Sense Of Humor: Look for a keen sense of humor, often more insightful than that of her peers, and an ability to see subtle humor in a situation.

While it may feel exciting to think your child may be gifted, keep in mind that children who are gifted may have their own set of problems. For example, they may:

❏ Feel different from their peers, which can lead to feelings of isolation, loneliness, and inadequate social lives.
❏ Place unrealistic pressures on themselves to perform. They may develop problems in accepting their own shortcomings, as well as having unrealistic expectations for success or extremely strong reactions to failure. (See Depression, Stress, Perfectionism.)
❏ Have difficult relationships with their brothers and sisters or with their friends because of being singled out for attention. (See Friends, Self-Esteem).

In addition, parents sometimes find it all too easy to put subtle pressure on their children to achieve or succeed, and place so much emphasis on academics that everything else in their child's life (such as playing) pales in importance. And sometimes it's hard for parents to remember there is an important difference between emotional development and intellectual development, and that a gifted nine-year-old child may perform well in an algebra class, but will still be a nine-year-old on the playground.

WHAT CAN I DO TO HELP?

Understanding what traits constitute giftedness will help you in understanding your child. You can also:

❏ Try not to become envious of your child's abilities.

❏ Keep your expectations for your child at a reasonable level. While her intellectual development may be racing ahead, her motor skills for example, will be appropriate for her age. Guard against the feeling that these skills are lagging just because they are developing at a normal rate.

❏ Be supportive when your child feels different because of her intellectual abilities, especially around puberty when conformity and group membership are important. You can point out that everyone is unique in some way; being gifted is simply your child's way of being unique.

❏ Understand that children who are gifted are more likely to have difficulty understanding some of society's double standards. Their moral sense is often well-developed and may conflict with hypocrisy and other social contradictions. You can try to explain why there are homeless people, for example, but a child who is gifted is not likely to be completely satisfied with your explanation. Although that may be frustrating for you, two good things can come out of what may seem like endless explanations about phenomena you can't justify:

■ The fact that your child is unsatisfied with stock or simple answers can contribute to your understanding of her as gifted, and

■ Your frankness in explaining that human limitations keep society from solving every problem can create a context for your child about her own limitations, even though she is gifted.

Many educators agree that gifted youngsters don't simply need more after-school classes or lessons in Japanese in order to fulfill their potential. Some believe that the three most important things you can do for your child are:

■ Encourage him to pursue his own passionate interests,

■ Give him the time to do that, and

■ Give him time off to play, daydream, ride his bike.

You can talk with your child about choosing a passionate personal interest. It can be anything from civil rights to butterflies, robots, ice cream, computer games, or space travel. If it's ice cream, for example, you can guide your child toward a variety of projects in nutrition, physics, chemistry, or history. If it's computer games, encourage her to master the more intricate games, then challenge her to design one of her own or to figure out why and how her favorite game works. For your child who is gifted in art, music, writing, or dance, try encouraging them to make videos or recordings of performances, or in-depth study of notable individuals in those areas.

Find an adult mentor to pick up where your own knowledge leaves off. Ask a chemistry professor at a nearby university, or an expert from a local special-interest club (a model railroaders' club or equestrians' club, for example) to meet with your child periodically, or to help devise and supervise your child's projects.

Another vital resource for your child is a peer group. She might find friends in a special-interest club, or in special classes at school. You could also contact one of the support groups for parents of gifted students which exist in many communities.

WHAT WILL A PROFESSIONAL DO?

Because the trend in identifying a child who is gifted is to involve much more than an IQ test, the school psychologist is not likely to be the only professional to participate in evaluating your child for giftedness. The process is more likely to involve agreement between your child's teacher, a special teacher of the gifted, yourself, and some kind of data like homework and test scores. It's a good idea for you to approach the teacher early in your child's school career to talk about what you are observing in your child to compare with what she sees. Your input can help the teacher begin to see characteristics in your child that might not have been apparent to her before. And, you can share with the teacher ideas or special projects your child has done outside of school to add to information helpful in identifying your child as gifted.

If your school has a program for gifted students, most likely it will be one of two kinds that most schools use separately or in combination:

- a pullout program, in which children who are gifted are removed from regular classrooms for special instruction, or
- an accelerated program, in which children are advanced a grade or placed in a curriculum that covers material more quickly or with more depth than normal classes.

If your child is identified as gifted, you can talk with the gifted and talented teacher and the school psychologist about which would be best for your child and her learning style.

See also:

❏ Creativity
❏ Learning Disabilities
❏ Motivation
❏ Perfectionism
❏ Self Esteem

Further Reading

Alvino, J. Parent's Guide to Raising a Gifted Child. New York: Ballantine Books, 1985.

Enrich, V. E. Gifted Children. Englewood Cliffs, NJ: Prentice-Hall, 1982.

Freeman, J. The Psychology of Gifted Children. New York: Wiley, 1985.

Rimm, S. Keys to Parenting the Gifted Child. Hauppauge, NY: Barron's Educational Series, 1994.

Smutry, J., Veenker, K., & Veenker, S. Your Gifted Child: How to Recognize and Develop the Special Talents in Your Child from Birth to Age Seven. New York: Ballantine Books, 1989.

Webb, J. T., Meckstroth, E. A., & Tolan, S. Guiding the Gifted Child. Columbus, OH: Ohio Publishing, 1982.

CHAPTER 20

Grade Retention

"Laura's first-grade teacher said she thinks Laura should repeat the grade because she was slow in picking up reading, and she seems younger than her classmates. Her birthday is close to the cut-off date; maybe she does need another year to mature. I don't know what to do."

"I was afraid it would come to this. Aaron's teacher wants him to stay back in fifth grade because he hasn't handed in most of his assignments. She says if he hasn't done fifth grade work, he won't be able to handle sixth grade. Maybe staying back will teach him a lesson."

The merits of grade retention have been hotly discussed ever since graded classes were first used in the nineteenth century. But since the 1930s, educators have been questioning whether the stigma of retention outweighs any good it might do.

Today, many professionals in education oppose retention except under extremely limited circumstances. Nevertheless, every year, just over 2 million school children are held back. If your child has already been held back a grade, you might be relieved to know you can work with the school psychologist to help him feel better about himself and start to catch up to other kids his age. And if a teacher has told you she thinks your child should be retained, you'll need to know the pros and cons of retention and some alternatives in order to reach the decision that best suits your child.

WHAT WE KNOW NOW

Retention is requiring a child to repeat a grade, or requiring a child of appropriate age to delay entry into kindergarten (see also School Entry Decisions, in Part I) or first grade.

Before talking about the pros and cons of retention, it's important to remember the big picture: that we send our children to school to learn, and neither retention nor promotion guarantees that. For some children it is difficult, and for a few it's impossible, to fit into the neat chronological age slots by which most schools are defined. Those are the children for whom progressing through school may not take a straightforward, grade-to-grade path. If this sounds like your child, it may be up to you to work with teachers, principals, and school psychologists to find the path that best fits her.

With the exceptions of birth date, maturity, and physical size, the possibility of retention comes up most frequently when the teacher believes a child has not mastered enough skills in one grade to be able to handle that of the next grade. Her concerns are often that:

❏ The child's self-esteem will be damaged by not succeeding in the following grade, and,
❏ If the child does not succeed in the following grade, she will be at risk for eventually dropping out of school.

The research we have shows the opposite is true. Studies of school children's attitudes toward retention show that they see only two things worse than being retained: themselves going blind, and their parents being killed. Research also shows that being held back one time increases a student's likelihood of dropping out of school by 30 percent, not because she is unable to do the work, but because her attitude toward school is so negative once she has been retained.

Studies of children who have been retained also show:

❏ Most do not catch up simply by being held back. Having your child exposed to the same curriculum two years in a row isn't, by itself, likely to correct her academic problems.

❏ Some retained children do better at first, but unless specific problems that caused them to be retained in the first place are corrected, they fall behind again. In a similar way, children who add a transitional year between kindergarten and first grade or who repeat first grade, may do better than their peers for a few months, but any gains they make even out by fourth grade.

❏ Generally, children who are held back get into trouble, dislike school, and feel bad about themselves more often than do children who are promoted. But that is not to say that promotion in itself guarantees that similar problems won't develop. If a child is not doing well, whether she was promoted or retained, the same problems can still come up.

Even though the retention picture sounds pretty bleak, some children can benefit from it. Students who have missed a lot of school because of frequent illness or family moves, and some of those who need extra time to learn English may be helped by being retained, especially if they have a strong self-concept and they don't have significant behavior or academic problems. (See also Moving.) The difficulty is that no one has figured out a reliable way to predict who will be helped and who will be hurt by retention. What you know about your child's strengths and weaknesses, and close monitoring of how she's doing with or without retention will be your best guide.

WHEN SHOULD I BE CONCERNED?

Of course, the best time to be concerned about grade retention is long before anyone suggests it. In most cases, if you are consistently aware of how your child is doing in school and checking in with your child's teacher at least once each marking period, you should be able to see problems on the horizon soon enough to do something about it.

If you are at that point now, you can ask yourself these questions before you become seriously concerned:

❏ Is it later than midyear in the school calendar?
❏ Has your child's work been consistently and significantly below grade level until now?
❏ Does your child's teacher share your view of your child's work?

If you can answer yes to these questions, it's time to be concerned.

There are also times when even the most vigilant parent doesn't pick up the cues or loses touch with the teacher, and the news that she wants to retain your child comes as a shock. No one has to tell you then to be concerned.

Once the idea of retention has been broached, you should be concerned if:

❏ The teacher cannot tell you what she has already done to address your child's academic problems. Have a long talk with her to deter-

Things to Ask the Teacher

- What, specifically, do you expect from my child in each subject area?
- In which areas does my child have difficulty?
- What kinds of difficulties does my child have? For example, can she read aloud smoothly, but has trouble getting the meaning of the story? Or, does he know his math facts but have trouble with word problems?
- Are there other ways to teach the same material? Are there other books or materials that would be more effective in helping my child learn?
- What are some of my child's strengths?
- What are some of the teaching strategies that seem to be working well for my child?
- Does my child have the necessary skills but can't seem to finish work in the same amount of time as other children?

mine specifically why she's recommending retention. See What Can I Do To Help for questions to ask.

❒ The decision to retain your child rests with just one person, the teacher or the principal. Ask that there be someone in addition who reviews your child's work and the decision. This is like getting a second medical opinion. In many districts, it's policy that a team (consisting of the teacher, school psychologist, and principal) reviews all possible retentions.

❒ The recommendation, or talk of a recommendation for retention comes before midyear. In most cases, this is too early to make such a far-reaching decision. Ask that the retention option be set aside for a time in favor of some positive goal-setting and extra help for your child. Rates of development, especially among young children, vary greatly and can change quickly. Your first-grader may still reach an appropriate skill level by May even though she's lagging behind in November.

If your child has already been retained, you should be concerned if you don't see sig-

nificant progress by the end of the first marking period of the new school year. In this case, either your child still has academic problems that are not being addressed, or the fact that he has been retained is having such a negative effect on him socially, that he's not making academic progress.

WHAT CAN I DO TO HELP?

You'll need a clear picture of how your child is doing in school in order to work with the teacher to help effectively. Use the checklist below to help you prepare for a meeting with your child's teacher.

Once you and the teacher have used these kinds of questions to clearly define the problems your child is having, let the teacher know that you understand the goal is long-term improvement instead of a quick fix. Then, ask her to set some goals with you for your child's improvement. For example:

❒ Ask her what would represent reasonable growth in a certain area over the next month, then what you can do at home to help your child meet that goal. For younger children, remember how important it is to read to them each night to bolster reading skills. For secondary youngsters, you might help them set up a more efficient system for keeping track of assignments.

❏ Ask that she send home daily or weekly progress notes to help you both keep track of your child's progress. Arrange to sign the notes and return them to school so she can be certain you received them.

Also explore other options with the teacher, such as:

❏ Whether an open, nongraded classroom would be a useful option for your child. If it is available at your school, it might be worthwhile to discuss moving your child to one of these rooms, either for the current or following year, where she could work at her own pace without the stigma of retention.

❏ Whether tutoring during the school year would help your secondary youngster, or whether he could complete unfinished work during summer school. (See also Motivation.)

If you have tried some of these techniques to no avail, consider having your child referred to the multidisciplinary team for full evaluation for learning disabilities or to rule out emotional problems. (See Learning Disabilities.)

WHAT WILL A PROFESSIONAL DO?

The right time to consult with your school psychologist is the moment grade retention is mentioned by anyone as a possibility for your child. It's never too early to talk with her about your concerns.

One of the best tools a professional—and a parent—can use is constant vigilance to help pinpoint why your child is not learning. If observation and discussion between you, the teacher, and the school psychologist do not provide some answers and a course of action, the psychologist may suggest that a multidisciplinary team meet to further discuss your child's needs. (See also Special Education, in Part I, for a description of this process.)

Finally, if you and the team of educators at your child's school agree, after all, that retention would be the best thing for your child, be sure to set up with them written goals he is to accomplish during the retention year. Consider carefully whether your child should be with the same teacher again. If he and the teacher get along well, and the teacher is willing to individualize instruction for him, it may work fine for him to have her again. But if your child's experience with that teacher has not been a positive one, it's time for a change.

During the retention year, meet regularly with the educational team to monitor your child's progress, and be sure he has special help in the areas he finds difficult.

See also:

❏ Learning Disabilities
❏ Motivation
❏ Moving
❏ School Entry Decisions, in Part I

Further Reading

Note: The editors were unable to find a recent book on this topic written for parents; parents may want to consult the following books, which were written for educators and other professionals:

Shepard, L., and Smith, M. *Flunking Grades: Research and Policies on Retention*. New York: Falmer Press, 1989.

Retention in Grade: Looking for Alternatives. Bloomington, IN: Phi Delta Kappa, 1992.

C H A P T E R   2 1

Grading

"We've just moved to town, and Erin's grades have jumped a whole letter grade or more in each class. I thought her grades might suffer with the move, so I was really happy when I saw her report card . . . I feel like some of the pressure of helping her adjust to a new school is off."

"Our school principal has been talking about going to a different grading system where the traditional letters, A-B-C, aren't used. I hit the roof when I heard that. How are we supposed to tell how our kids are doing if we don't have letter grades?"

If there's one issue that reliably sparks strong feelings in any school, in almost any family, it's the subject of grades. In fact, there is plenty of evidence that grading practices have a significant effect on children and their work habits, attitudes, and self esteem.

While A-B-C-or-D grades may seem like eternal, universal markers of educational success or failure, it's interesting to note that the practice of assigning a "mark" to a student's work is less than 100 years old. It began at about the turn of the century, probably growing out of that day's belief that everything can be measured. What educators, parents, and students have found since then is that while letter grades do serve a purpose, it's not so easy to accurately measure what a student has learned—or has failed to learn.

But understanding what goes into the grading system at your school can help you use that system as a reliable gauge of your child's progress. If you're interested more in ideas for how to improve your child's grades, see Homework, Motivation, and Study Skills.

WHAT WE KNOW NOW

Traditional grades use a symbol—a letter, number, or word—to represent a value judgment concerning the quality of a student's achievement or performance. And while that symbol does convey an idea of how well your child is doing in school, grading is always a trade-off: between efficiency and succinctness versus completeness and detail about a student's progress.

For example, IQ test scores can be expressed as one number, which does tell you something about the student, but that isolated number loses the richness of detail about the strengths and weakness making up that child's score. So it is with grades: all the effort, each individual paper, the quizzes and projects are lost to one letter or number.

But that letter or number is not without meaning. It will help you interpret your child's grades if you understand the philosophy behind the teachers's grades. Typically, teachers expect grades to have one or more of four basic meanings. The grade may reflect how well your child:

❏ has mastered a specific set of skills or body of knowledge

❏ has improved during a specific period of time

❏ has put forth effort in a subject

❏ stacks up against others in her class.

Teachers and students may also look to grades to provide other functions, such as:

❏ feedback to the student which can act as a motivator,

❏ information for parents about their child's progress in general, or

❏ information for employers or postsecondary schools and training centers about a student's mastery of skills, or their mastery compared to other students.

You can only know where your child's teacher places the greatest emphasis in grading by talking with her. When you meet with the teacher at the beginning of the year or at report-card time, have with you the following list and other information from this chapter you find particularly relevant so you can discuss thoroughly with her which of these she emphasizes.

In addition to these areas of emphasis in grading, it will help you to know the four types of grading most often used. They are:

❏ *Grading on the Curve:* Also called norm-referenced grading, in which students are graded relative to each other, so that only a few students score extremely well or extremely poorly, with the rest distributed through the midrange of grades.

❏ *Fixed-Standard Grading:* Also called criterion-referenced grading, in which students are assigned grades based on reaching a preset goal. Theoretically, everyone could get an A if everyone reaches the goal.

❏ *Contract Grading:* Similar to fixed-standard grading, but in this case, the preset goal is different for each individual, and agreed upon in advance by the teacher, the student, and sometimes the student's parents.

❏ *Pass/Fail Grading:* Similar to fixed-standard grading, but the student receives only one of two possible grades, pass or fail, to indicate he did or did not meet the criteria for the class.

In practice, most teachers use some combination of all of the grading methods and areas of emphasis described above, even if they think they are using one. Understanding all of these, and talking with your child's teacher about which she thinks is most important will also help you accurately interpret your child's grades.

Controversy about grading usually centers on the effects of grades on a student's performance. Detractors of traditional letter-grading say that grades:

❏ breed competition among the students, creating educational "winners" and "losers,"

❏ direct students' attention away from learning toward competition, thereby reducing motivation to learn,

❏ lead some teachers to think they're "soft" or ineffective if a lot of their students get good grades,

❏ make students overly dependent on teachers to whom they look for approval, stifling creativity and initiative.

Proponents of traditional letter-grading say that grades:

❏ motivate students to do better,

❏ provide a succinct evaluation of a student's progress,

❏ help students pinpoint areas of relative

weakness for them to work on, and to help them make realistic career or other choices.

Proponents also point out that most alternatives to traditional letter-grading involve words that convey value judgments anyway, making them not substantially different from letter grades.

Although there is only a small amount of research on traditional grading, we do know that once children are in the upper elementary grades, it acts as a motivator for students who are bright, academically engaged, and already interested in getting good grades. Moderate anxiety about grades tends to improve their academic performance. But for low-achieving students of any age, the opposite is true: grade anxiety may lower the grades of those of average or less ability. (See Motivation, Anxiety.) Perhaps even more significant, these students may also become grade-insensitive because they eventually learn that whether or not they try hard in school, they still get poor grades. The end result for them may be that they have little or no motivation to try hard, and they pay equally little or no attention to the outcome because they have learned it will always be poor.

The other clear piece of information to emerge from research is that, as many would suspect, grades are inexorably subjective. While that may seem almost too obvious to mention, whether you're evaluating your child's grades or talking with the teacher about grading practices, it's important to remember so that you can get the question right: it's not whether grades are subjective, but whether the teacher is being subjective about the right things. For example, is she looking at and grading your child's classroom performance— whether he behaves in class and raises his hand

frequently—more than your child's mastery of a subject?

In an effort to make grading express more closely all the things teachers and parents want them to express about the child's academic progress, most educators agree that the best approach seems to be supplementing, whenever possible, traditional letter-grades with comments about skill mastery or effort involved.

But given all the subjectivity involved in grading, the controversy, and the different types and emphases possible in grading, it might be tempting to simply ignore them. But research has also shown that the grades your child receives in elementary school are reasonably good predictors of what she'll get in high school, and her high school grades are the best single predictor of how she'll do in college. Whether all these grades translate to "real-life" accomplishment once your child leaves school is still anybody's guess, although first-time employers may use transcripts to get a clearer picture of the person they may hire, and colleges certainly depend on grades and class ranking for admissions.

While the grades your child earns should be relatively stable over time, there are some fairly predictable points when curriculum changes can produce a change in your child's grades as she adjusts to new expectations. The starred items in the table below show when those changes occur.

WHEN SHOULD I BE CONCERNED?

Since the grades most children earn are relatively stable throughout their school years, you should be concerned if you see a sudden change in your child's grades. If you do, your first step toward finding out the reason is, of course, to talk calmly with your child about

Changes in Curriculum
That May Mean Changes in Grades

YEAR IN SCHOOL	EMPHASIS IN CURRICULUM
First and Second Grade	Rote memory—learning phonics sounds, math facts
Third and Fourth Grade	Rote memory with new emphasis on conceptual skills such as reading comprehension and application of math facts to solve problems.
Fifth and Sixth Grade	Continued emphasis on conceptual understanding and application.
Seventh Grade	More emphasis on independent writing, concept analysis, and application of problem solving skills.

what happened. But also talk with the teacher and find out what may have changed in the classroom. For example, you can ask:

❑ Is the curriculum new?
❑ Have the teacher's expectations for your child changed?
❑ Is there a new teacher with a different style?
❑ Is your child being evaluated differently than before because you have moved recently? (See Moving.)

You should also be concerned if your child seems overly discouraged by grades. Talk with the teacher about the grading system she uses, and look for clues that she is giving your child enough feedback along the way about her performance. If not, work with her on increasing feedback for you and for your child, with home notes to you, notes written on your child's work, and perhaps a weekly telephone conversation with you about how your child is progressing.

Finally, you should also be concerned if you are overly invested in your child's grades. Remember that while a letter or number grade is an indication of your child's progress, it is

never the whole story. And, an A in one subject is not directly comparable to to an A in another subject because of differences in the types of skills required from subject to subject. Nor is an A at one school directly comparable to an A at another school because of differences in philosophy and teaching or grading styles. Ideally, your concern should be more with what your child is learning than with the letter grade, particularly if your child is having difficulty in a subject.

WHAT CAN I DO TO HELP?

Being aware of the day-to-day work your child is doing in school should stave off any unpleasant surprises on report-card day for either of you. That way, when you see problems cropping up, you can address them with your child and your child's teacher before they become great.

To more accurately interpret your child's grades:

❑ Ask to see work samples if your child doesn't bring them home on a regular basis.
❑ If your child does bring school work home, save papers or tests with the teacher's com-

ments so that you can discuss specifics with the teacher.

❑ Save very good papers—as well as very poor papers—your child brings home. This can help in interpreting grades at the end of the marking period.

❑ Talk with the teacher about her grading philosophies, preferably long before the end of the grading period.

❑ Review with the teacher and/or the school psychologist how your child has done on achievement tests or other similar evaluations so that you can begin to get a clear picture of your child's abilities and areas of weakness.

❑ Review with the teacher ways in which your child could improve grades, then make a plan with your child. (See Study Skills, Homework.)

If your child consistently receives below average grades, it could be an indication that she is lacking in the basic skills required to progress. Knowing how subjective grades are, it may be tempting to move her to a school with a reputation for being less competitive or less stringent about academics, but that won't address a lack of basic skills. You need to work closely with the teacher to determine the source of your child's low grades, and then, with the teacher, address your child's needs.

WHAT WILL A PROFESSIONAL DO?

School psychologists aren't usually directly involved in grading issues, but yours can be a valuable resource in talking further about types of grading systems and how they may affect your child. Your school psychologist can also be a helpful resource for you during meetings with your child's teacher in which you discuss grading systems and brainstorm ideas that may be helpful for your child. And last, if you suspect that your child has a learning disability or a personal problem that is causing consistently low grades, the school psychologist can help with testing and evaluating your child to pinpoint the problem. (See Learning Disabilities, Depression, Anxiety, Perfectionism.)

See also:

❑ Depression
❑ Homework
❑ Learning Disabilities
❑ Motivation
❑ Moving
❑ Study Skills

CHAPTER 22

Hearing Problems

"James, 13, has always gotten good grades. We can only think he must be fooling around in class now that he's in middle school, for his grades to drop this way."

"Sara did well academically in first grade, but now, in second grade, she's really struggling, and we haven't been able to figure out what's wrong."

When children like Sara and James don't have a show-stopping problem, but you know something has changed for them to be having the difficulties they are, figuring out how to help can be an exercise in detective work of the subtlest kind. Clues may be hard to recognize, especially when they point in unexpected directions. One direction you may not have considered at all is hearing loss. Studies show that even hearing loss so mild you might not know your child has it, can make it difficult for children to learn to read, or to understand or finish their school work, which can eventually affect how they feel about themselves. And some children who have been tagged as having behavioral problems are simply frustrated or angry because they cannot hear well and may not realize themselves how poorly they hear.

Routine school hearing tests showed that Sara and James both had mild hearing loss, most likely because of previous ear infections. In Sara's case, her seat near the glare of the classroom windows made it hard for her to see the teacher's face for the visual cues she depended on to fill in for what she couldn't hear. And James' grades had suffered because in middle school he was expected to take notes

during class lectures, a nearly impossible task for a youngster who had to concentrate just to hear the teacher.

WHAT WE KNOW NOW

The tests of hearing specialists classify a child as having mild hearing loss if she has lost 40 decibels of hearing, which means that she cannot hear softer sounds such as ticking clocks and ocean waves, or the sounds made by the letters f, g, h, p, k, or s, or the ch, sh, and th sounds. It's not suprising, then, that a mild hearing loss can have an enormous impact on children in first and second grade when they are learning to read.

Ear infections, called *otitis media* by your doctor, are the primary cause of mild hearing loss or conductive loss, as fluid in the middle ear keeps sound waves from being conducted, or passed through the eardrum to the inner ear. A young child can also cause conductive hearing loss herself by putting something in her ear, such as a bean or a bead, that would block sounds from coming in. In any case, conductive loss is almost always temporary as long as it is treated.

An ear infection can turn up after a cold, or it can be caused by allergies, sinus infections, or by measles or mumps in those children who have not been immunized or have not had a second immunization at age 10–12. Hearing loss can occur during an ear infection, or go on for weeks or even months after the infection has cleared up. That's why it's so important to check your child's hearing if you think he is not progressing as you had expected in areas like reading—he may simply be unable to hear the teacher well.

Mild hearing loss can also occur if the prescribed medication dosage for an ear infection was too low to eliminate the infection, or if medication was discontinued too soon because the child no longer had obvious symptoms. In these cases, the child's ability to hear fluctuates as the fluid in the middle ear increases or thickens in response to on-again, off-again medication.

About 60 percent of children have at least one ear infection before the age of 5, and about 20 percent of children have chronically recurring ear infections. Another 20 percent have a fluctuating hearing loss at some time during their school years. Children who already have a hearing impairment, who have Down's syndrome, and who have cleft palates are especially vulnerable to ear infections and the hearing loss they can cause.

Another kind of hearing loss is called *sensorineural*, which is caused by nerve damage deep in the inner ear and is usually permanent. Some children are born with it because their mothers had a genetic condition or certain bacterial or viral infections while they were pregnant. Other children might have permanently lost some hearing as a result of chicken pox or flu, or an ear infection that spread to the inner ear.

No matter what causes it, studies show that even children who have mild hearing loss,

or mild fluctuating hearing loss from ear infections, perform below their grademates in some academic areas, and about half fail a grade or need special help. While it may be easy, as an adult, to discount the effects of a little hearing loss from time to time, it is clear that for children, it can have long-term repercussions on academic success. In short, no hearing loss, no matter how small or how infrequent, should be taken lightly.

WHEN SHOULD I BE CONCERNED?

It's important for you to know that children of any age whose hearing loss is mild, and young children up to about third grade, may not realize themselves that they aren't hearing well, or that their ability to hear well changes, as it does with fluctuating hearing loss. You may need to watch for some of the signals listed below, then have your child tested by an audiologist (see below, What Will A Professional Do?). Once you and your child establish what it is like for her when she can't hear well, she may be able to tell you when it happens, but it's a good idea to keep your child's particular symptoms of hearing loss in mind.

It's also a good idea to remember that mild hearing loss may be more noticeable at times when your child is undergoing a difficult academic transition—for example, in first grade when language arts and reading skills are introduced, in fourth grade when there is increased emphasis on textbooks and class content, and middle school when your child has to adapt to more than one teacher and take notes in class.

You might consider that your primary age child has mild hearing loss if she:

❐ has a history of ear infections, allergies, or upper respiratory infections

❏ has difficulty learning letter sounds, particularly vowels, or if she has trouble discriminating sounds, confusing the short vowel sound of u with the short o, for example

❏ mispronounces words or letter sounds, uses words inappropriately, or confuses words that sound similar, such as on/in, to/through, fat/sat. (But mispronunciations of letters such as r, l, and w before age 7 are usually normal.)

❏ seems to have a smaller or less mature vocabulary (in written work, too) compared to classmates.

❏ has difficulty following directions, or confuses directions and asks that they be repeated over and over.

❏ has trouble following group discussions and is reluctant to participate.

❏ seems inattentive or preoccupied; fails to respond or is reluctant to respond when called upon.

❏ doesn't want to participate in classroom discussions, and when she does, her answers don't seem to address the question.

❏ uses more than the normal amount of gestures or facial expressions to support what she says.

❏ has school behavior problems such as daydreaming; turning to a different activity when the teacher is more than a couple of feet away from him; talking to a neighbor when the teacher is talking; showing a lot of frustration when he doesn't understand the teacher, sometimes leading to outbursts and disruptive behavior.

In addition, your child may rub her ear, speak softly or often say "Huh?" or "I don't know."

Your secondary-age child who has a mild hearing loss may have some of these behaviors, but may also simply not pay attention in class and may frequently ask questions that have already been answered. Children of any age with a more serious hearing loss (such as the undiagnosed sensorineural loss described above) may also appear stubborn and be disruptive in class. Some children with this kind of hearing loss will look up when someone is speaking, then look around before they can tell where the sound is coming from.

WHAT CAN I DO TO HELP?

If you already know your child has mild hearing loss, or if your physician can confirm that the fluid in your child's ears during or after an ear infection may interfere with her hearing, you can schedule an appointment with her teacher to discuss what can be done. Of course, you'll want to arrange with the teacher to be sure your child is sitting in the place that will make it easiest for her to hear well. But you can also arrange with the teacher to:

❏ double-check with your child to be sure she understands assignments without calling attention to her. It's easy for children with mild hearing loss to feel embarrassed about their inability to hear well, so some sensitivity on the teacher's part would be helpful.

❏ repeat answers from children in the back of the class.

❏ clue your child to activities in other parts of the classroom by making eye contact with her, or with a light tap on the shoulder.

If your child has significant hearing loss, you can also ask the teacher to:

❏ provide written instructions for classroom activities and homework in addition to spoken instructions.

❏ either provide class notes or allow someone to be a notetaker for your middle or high school youngster who is not hearing well.

❏ simplify or reword instructions rather than repeating the same thing over and over

❏ wear an amplification device prescribed by your child's audiologist

WHAT WILL A PROFESSIONAL DO?

Any time you are uncomfortable with your child's progress, or in this case, if you see your child's behavior in the lists above, it's a good idea to check with the school nurse or speech-language pathologist. They will review with you the behaviors that concern you and then test your child's hearing if necessary. They can also act as coordinators between you and other professionals if they are needed to further assess or monitor your child.

Those professionals should be:

❏ *Your child's physician,* who will monitor her health and the status of lingering fluid in her ears as a guide to how well she may be hearing.

❏ *An audiologist,* who can test your child's hearing so that you can know if she does have hearing loss, as well as the degree of the loss. If your child has a lot of ear infections, it's a good idea to have her hearing tested more than once a year. And if your child has been diagnosed as having mild or fluctuating hearing loss, you can have the school nurse, or a speech and language pathologist do follow-up testing every month.

❏ *A speech-language pathologist,* who may work with children who have had mild or mild fluctuating hearing loss over a long period of time. She can teach your child to use visual cues to aid understanding, work on vocabulary development and correcting mispronunciations, and act as a liason between you and the teacher to come up with ways to increase language development. She may also be on the lookout for further language concerns and suggest an assessment if she sees other signs of language problems with your child.

See also:

❏ Language Development
❏ Learning Disabilities

Further Reading

Adams, J. *You and Your Hearing Impaired Child.* Washington, DC: Clerc Books, 1988.

Freeman, R., Carbin C., and Boese, R. *Can't Your Child Hear?* Washington DC: Gallaudet University, Washington D.C.

Luterman, D. *When Your Child Is Deaf: A Guide for Parents.* Parkton, MD: York Press, 1991.

CHAPTER 23

Homework

"I know it's good for Jason to do homework. He knows he's supposed to do it. But still, it doesn't always get done, and we fight about it all the time. I'm at my wit's end."

Homework, like green vegetables, is one of those things that most parents realize their kids should have because it's good for them. But in reality, both are pretty hard to swallow. If you're a parent who's weathered one too many homework wars, you'll know that sometimes, it's tempting to turn your head rather than go another round.

But it doesn't have to be that way. Understanding why homework is assigned, when you should and shouldn't help your child, and how to do that can make a big difference in your child's—and your—after-school hours.

WHAT WE KNOW NOW

The function of homework is one point many educators agree upon: well-designed assignments boost achievement levels among all abilities of students because they not only augment classroom activity, but they teach responsibility and self-discipline, too.

Educators, and parents, also agree that homework works best when everyone knows exactly what they are supposed to do.

Teachers should give homework that: parallels classroom instruction and curriculum, and comes with clear and complete explanations. For maximum learning, they should also provide immediate feedback. In other words, they need to grade, check, or comment on the work

and return it as soon as possible, preferably within a day or two of receiving the assignment.

Parents should supervise. That's all. Even if you think homework is a waste of time, or that a particular assignment is useless, it's important to remember that one of homework's primary functions is to teach responsibility. Your child will be missing a valuable lesson in responsibility if you don't require that he complete his assignments, nor will he learn responsibility if you do the homework for him as a result of heavyhanded helping. Homework is not a responsibility you share with your child; it's your child's responsibility. Your job is to provide structure, encouragement, and an occasional clarification or review.

Students should complete the homework and check it to be sure it is correct. Keep in mind that each child's capacity to be thorough with homework changes with her age, grade, and other circumstances such as health, family situations, peer groups, and how the child gets along with that year's teacher. There's nothing wrong with cutting your child some slack under certain conditions. But as a rule, being consistent about insisting that homework be complete and correct will work best for you and your student.

Understanding the four types of homework that teachers most often give can help

GRADE	TIME PER NIGHT	ASSIGNMENTS PER WEEK
1–3	10–45 min.	1–3
4–6	45–90 min.	2–4
7–9	1–2 hrs.	3–5
10–12	1.5–2.5 hrs.	4–5

clarify the reason behind the assignment, or provide a guideline if you review completed work. Those four types are:

❐ *Practice homework.* This is how children learn such basic skills as spelling, math facts, and science terms. There's no way around a certain amount of memorization and drill to help kids remember, for instance, how to spell *receive*, what 3 × 12 equals, or what the word *photosynthesis* means.

❐ *Preparation homework.* A teacher may prepare his third-grade class for an upcoming unit on animals and the environment by assigning library reports on animal families and what adult animals need in order to take care of their young. In preparation for a similar unit, a middle school or high school teacher may assign background reading, such as Rachel Carson's *Silent Spring.*

❐ *Extension homework.* Your child can broaden her understanding by comparing and contrasting what she's learned in the classroom about the women's suffrage movement, for example, to another situation, such as the Civil Rights movement of the 1960s.

❐ *Creative homework.* These are challenging assignments that ask kids to use a variety of skills to integrate, extend, and apply what they've learned. For example, a creative assignment to profile leading figures of the European Renaissance could result in a videotaped talk show featuring "guest stars" from that historical period.

The last two types are most often given to children in late elementary, middle, or high school, but some teachers find ways to incorporate facets of each type for even the youngest students.

How much homework should you expect for your first grader, compared to what your middle schooler gets? NASP suggestions appear in the above table.

WHEN SHOULD I BE CONCERNED?

If homework is always an issue at your house and you are simply tired of fighting with your child about it, then you should be concerned and look for a different course of action.

Or, if notes from the teacher or a report card shows your child is consistently missing assignments, handing in incomplete work, or shows declining academic performance, it's time to look for a new approach.

On the other hand, you may be concerned that your child is not getting enough homework, or that the homework is too easy for her. You might read the entries in this book about Motivation and Giftedness, but if neither sounds like your child, your concern may actually be more with your child's teacher and her philosophy about homework than with your child.

In any case, your first step should be to talk with the teacher about the homework philosophy that guides the kind and frequency of homework she has assigned. With her, you can

Homework Problems Checklist

How often does your child:	Never	Sometimes	Often	Very Often
1. Fail to bring home assignments	0	1	2	3
2. Not know the exact assignment	0	1	2	3
3. Deny having a homework assignment	0	1	2	3
4. Refuse to do a homework assignment	0	1	2	3
5. Whine or complain about homework	0	1	2	3
6. Need constant reminders to begin	0	1	2	3
7. Put off doing homework to last minute	0	1	2	3
8. Need constant supervision/assistance	0	1	2	3
9. Daydream	0	1	2	3
10. Become easily distracted	0	1	2	3
11. Become easily frustrated	0	1	2	3
12. Fail to complete homework	0	1	2	3
13. Take excessive time to complete homework	0	1	2	3
14. Do messy work	0	1	2	3
15. Hurry and make careless mistakes	0	1	2	3
16. Become dissatisfied with work, perfectionistic	0	1	2	3
17. Forget/deliberately fail to return assignments	0	1	2	3
18. Complain that the work is boring	0	1	2	3
19. Argue with parent about homework	0	1	2	3
20. Report homework was done at school (parent not sure)	0	1	2	3

also determine if her expectations and yours are realistic for this child at this time. (See Part I for tips on how to talk constructively with a teacher.) If your concern is with your child, you can consider the solutions in the next section.

WHAT CAN I DO TO HELP?

First, it's important to understand what does not help. Homework is one of those issues that sometimes drives parents to do and say plenty of things they swore they never would. While there are lots of positive solutions to homework problems, it's hard to think of them in the heat of the moment. Being prepared is the best approach, but until you do feel more prepared to deal with homework issues, there are a couple of things you can think about.

First, psychologists have found that in

Summary Sheet for Homework Problems Checklist

What Item/Score	When Item/Score	Where Item/Score	How Item/Score	Why Item/Score
1	6	8	2	3
2	7	9	5	4
17	8	10	6	7
20	—	13	7	11
Total =	Total =	Total =	8	14
			13	15
			16	17
			Total =	18
				19
				Total =

Add the scores on the checklist for the items listed under each category. Divide by the number of items in each category and you will have an average for that category. Any category with an average greater than 2.00 is a problem category for your child.

most cases, punishing your child for not doing his homework does not get positive results as well as rewarding wanted behavior does. If you're used to disciplining for not doing homework by taking away things or privileges from your child, it might be a big transition for you to think about giving rewards for doing the homework instead. That transition may be made a little smoother if you take plenty of time reading this entry and thinking about it to let the new ideas become familiar. Then when you're ready, you can plan specifically which solutions you'll use and how you will implement them.

Second, psychologists have found that designing a plan that fits your child's specific needs is key to helping change her attitude toward homework. A group of psychologists writing in Behavioral Assessment developed a method to help you do that with their Homework Problems Checklist. Fill out the checklist shown in the box above to help iden-

tify which of five kinds of homework problems your student may be having.

When you have completed the checklist, use the summary sheet in the box above to arrive at a score.

Once you have identified the kind of problem your child has with homework, you can begin to address it. Five kinds of homework problems and their solutions are:

❏ *"What" and "How" Problems:* "What" problems are difficulties with knowing what homework is assigned and with organizing it effectively. "How" problems are difficulties in understanding instructions and assignments. (See Study Skills.) Ask the teacher:

- Are other students completing homework correctly?

- Does my child complete certain types of homework and not others?

- Are the completed portions correct?

- How long should my child spend on this homework?

Clearer instructions or slightly less difficult assignments may help. So will better record keeping on your child's part, follow-up of record keeping on your part, and supervision from you.

❏ *"Where" Problems:* These are difficulties with the environment in which your child does his homework. Is he sprawled on the living room floor surrounded by music and chatter as he works on algebra problems? Instead of letting him work wherever the spirit moves him, you can:

- Provide a special place to do homework. A desk, or even a lapboard, reserved for this purpose is fine.

- Make sure noise, toys, music, television, and food are not allowed in the work space.

- For younger children, make a Do Not Disturb sign to help make homework time a special time.

- Keep a homework survival kit stocked with pencils, paper, dictionary, and erasers to avoid interruptions.

❏ *"When" Problems:* These are scheduling problems. Finding time in a busy schedule can be just as difficult for some children as it is for their parents. If your child is sitting in the back seat of the car doing homework while you drive her from soccer practice to ballet, she might be overscheduled. With all the extracurricular activities available to children now, it's easy to do so much that homework is nearly squeezed out. You can address this problem in several ways:

- Provide a special time to do homework, just as you provide a special place.

- Check with the teacher to establish a reasonable amount of time to spend on homework, and make using all the allotted time a rule. On no-homework nights or on nights your student has correctly completed an assignment, remaining homework time can be used for independent reading or review.

- Consider building in some "free" time to your child's schedule, just as you do a gymnastics class or homework time. Everyone needs some space to play and daydream, too.

❏ *"Why" Problems:* These are problems with motivation (see Motivation), and arguably the most common source of homework troubles. Your understanding that the fundamental goal of homework is to teach responsibility helps, but offering rewards as motivation will help even more. (See Motivators, Appendix A). Choose rewards from the list that will work for you and use them with the following techniques to motivate your child.

For Grades 1–6:

❏ Write a surprise reward on a slip of paper and put it in a sealed envelope, which is opened when homework is complete.

❏ Play Beat the Buzzer. Specially designed for daydreamers who can turn a 10-minute assignment into an hour-and-a-half homework battle. Decide how long an assignment should take, set a timer, and if your child beats the buzzer, she gets the reward.

For All Grades

Try breaking it up. When an assignment seems overwhelming, divide it into manageable pieces and reward your student after each piece is successfully completed. It's not as overwhelming to learn 3 spelling words as it is to learn 20, and a small candy or two after every 3 words offers incentive to keep working. Or, a long report might not seem so daunting if your child has to concentrate on writing just a two-paragraph introduction one night followed by a small reward, and the first half of the body the second night, followed by another small reward.

For Middle and High School

Learning responsibility by doing a good job on your homework isn't nearly as attractive as hanging out with friends, so make a deal with your adolescent. Be sure you are clear about what you want your child to do—for example, you might want him to check homework for errors, turn it in on time, and review and correct mistakes on returned assignments. Then give your teenager the freedom to work within those standards. Agree not to harrass him about homework as long as his grades stay within an acceptable, defined range.

Improvement or remaining the same merit praise. Decline merits concern and discussion, but try to give your student a chance to handle it himself before you jump in. If necessary, you can go back to motivational rewards and a closer rein.

For children who are particularly resistant to doing homework, you might want to try a more elaborate plan. Here are the steps:

1 With your child, draw up a list if privileges or rewards she would like to earn. (See Responsibility.) Daily rewards might inlcude an extra half-hour of television, a special snack, the chance to stay up an extra half-hour before bed. Weekly rewards might be a trip to the mall or a fast food restaurant for lunch, or an hour at a local video arcade. Longer term rewards might be going to a movie with a friend, inviting a friend over for the night, or the chance to buy a small toy.

2 Now, again with your child, draw up a list of homework "jobs" for which she can earn points. Depending on your child's type of problem with homework (see checklist above), some might be:

- ❏ writing down homework assignments
- ❏ bringing home necessary homework materials
- ❏ completing (or starting) homework at a specified time
- ❏ completing homework with an acceptable standard of accuracy
- ❏ handing in homework done well and on time
- ❏ completing homework without nagging from you

3 Decide how many points each of the homework "jobs" can earn and how much each of the privileges or rewards will cost. To determine how much the rewards should cost, add up the number of points you feel your child will earn each day. Be sure that your child has about one-third of her points free to save up for special privileges.

4 Set up a notebook with five columns, one each for the date, the item, deposits (points she's earned from successful homework jobs completed), withdrawals (privilege points she's used), and the running balance.

5 Once a month or so, review the list of jobs and privileges and revise as necessary.

WHAT WILL THE PROFESSIONAL DO?

If none of these techniques works for your child, or if you see in her a persistent dread of homework or real difficulty completing assignments, she might need the kind of help a school psychologist can offer. Check with the teacher to see if she agrees.

The psychologist, the teacher, and you may collaborate to form a helping plan for your child by using homework in one of two ways:

1 Homework can be used as an *Intervention* through which targeted assignments help the child improve her grades and boost her sense of achievement. For example, testing had shown that Lisa, a quiet sixth grader, had low average abilities, but her grades kept slipping until they were well below those of the others in her class. Here's how her homework intervention worked:

❑ Lisa was given several weekly quizzes in math and reading by her teacher to serve as a baseline for measuring improvement.
❑ The teacher, working with the school psychologist and Lisa's parents, developed nightly math assignments geared to Lisa's ability.
❑ Lisa's parents set up guidelines at home for completing the assignments.

Weeks later, quizzes showed Lisa's math grades improving and reading staying the same. The teacher then designed a series of reading assignments to boost those grades. Eventually, Lisa and her parents were happy to see that the quizzes showed that Lisa's grades were up in both subjects.

If this seems a possibility for your student,

meet with the school psychologist and the teacher and ask:

❑ Is this type of homework appropriate for my child's achievement level?
❑ Is it closely tied to the curriculum?
❑ Are the directions so clear that the assignment is virtually foolproof?
❑ Will each assignment be reviewed in some meaningful way in the classroom?

2 Homework can also be used as a *task* for the child who needs extra help learning to complete homework or to work thoroughly. The teacher may give special directions and individualized assignments to your child, and the assignments are tracked by home notes between the teacher and parent. Home notes provide a clear record of what has been completed and when, and they also allow you to set up a reward system based on accurate information.

Homework and how to manage it may never be your favorite subject, any more than it is your child's. But remember that learning responsibility and independent work habits don't come easily to most of us. Your job is simply to provide the encouragement and atmosphere in which your child can work, and sometimes struggle, toward success.

See also:

❑ Motivation
❑ Responsibility
❑ Study Skills

Further Reading

Do-It-Yourself Homework Manual: A Sanity Saver for Parents. Write Dr. William Jenson, 327 MBH, Dept. of Educational Psychology, University of Utah, Salt Lalke City, UT. 84112

Rich, Dorothy. *Megaskills*. Boston: Houghton Mifflin, 1992.

Hahn, J. *Have You Done Your Homework? A Parent's Guide to Helping Teenagers Succeed in School.* New York: John Wiley, 1985.

Whitman, R. *Home Team: Over 60 Home Learning Tips from the American Federation of Teachers.* Washington, DC: American Federation of Teachers, 1984.

CHAPTER 24

Language Development and Disorders

"My daughter's kindergarten teacher says she's concerned Jolene has a language problem just because she can't seem to repeat rhymes in the right order. I don't see what she means; Jolene speaks clearly enough. What's the big deal about repeating a rhyme in the right order?"

Most people think of language development as the process of acquiring enough words to make up a working vocabulary. But while acquiring words is certainly a key part of the process, language development involves a whole range of communication skills both verbal and nonverbal. And language disorders don't necessarily mean a child has a speech problem.

Understanding how language development and subtle language disorders impact your child's academic experience can show you the best ways in which to be of help to a struggling child, paving the way to learning. While the school psychologist can be of help, your primary resource for questions about this complex area will be a speech-language pathologist.

WHAT WE KNOW NOW

Language development is a gradual, complex process toward both verbal and nonverbal communication that begins at birth, long before the first word is uttered. Your infant's first smile, then his babbling and cooing, even his early gestures are in the strictest sense, language, because they communicate meaning.

As your child grows and begins using words, he learns the fundamentals of spoken language. He learns:

❏ *semantics*, which is understanding meaning: the little round sweet things are "cookies."

❏ *syntax*, which is learning the correct order in which to say words so that they make a coherent sentence: saying "The cat is on the bed," instead of "The bed is on the cat."

❏ *pragmatics*, which is learning how to use language: to demand, ask, protest, joke; how to use it in a social context: how to enter a conversation, focus a topic, take turns speaking and ending a conversation.

For a summary of all the stages of normal language development, see the table below.

Language development may sound complex, and in a sense it is, but most children do all of this as a matter of course. For the 2 to 4 percent of children who do not (some estimate as many as 12 percent do not), a speech or language disorder can result. And those with speech or language disorders are six times more likely to have problems in reading.

It is difficult even for professionals to pinpoint why some children have speech or language problems and others don't. Several factors usually contribute. Of course, if early on—during the toddler years and even earlier—your child has been around people with good communication skills, he has most likely picked them up himself, because young chil-

Language Development by Age

Birth–10 months	Babbling, sounds
11–18 months	First words, intentional verbal language, imitate sounds
18–24 months	Building vocabulary, 2-word phrases
24–30 months	Average sentence about 3 1/2 words
30–36 months	Average sentence about 5 words
age 3–5	Can respond to variety of 2 step directions and some 3 step, learns to carry on conversation, asks and answers questions, vocabulary over 2000 words, sentences contain 8 or more words
grade k–3	Learning symbolic representation of language (letters, words, writing short sentences) understands time words like before, after, past, future, beginning to enjoy riddles, jokes
pre-adolescence gr. 4–6 age 9–12	Using reading to learn vocabulary and recognizes text as a source of information, pursues personal interest in reading more readily, Uses writing as means of communication, begins to be aware of listeners needs, formal language instruction such as composition, poetry, grammar; understands abstract language
adolescence gr. 7–12 age 12–19	Role of language in socialization, language arts through formal instruction, understands metaphors, proverbs, idioms

dren imitate what they hear. But some children are not around good communicators, and they pick that up, too.

Language disorders can also accompany or be indicative of other problems, such as ADHD (see ADHD) or learning disabilities (see Learning Disabilities). Testing and evaluation by your school psychologist and a speech-language pathologist can determine if this is the case for your child.

Speech and language problems typically fall into two categories:

■ *Receptive Language Disorders:* problems with listening and understanding. Children with these have difficulty with comprehension and meaning, vocabulary, grammatical constructions, and isolating sounds from background noise. All of these can have an impact on your child's memory span and her ability to follow directions and understand instructions.

■ Expressive Language Disorders: problems with speaking. Children with these have difficulty with vocabulary, semantics, finding the right word or grammatical form to use, organization of thoughts, and pronouncing sounds.

Stuttering is a third, less common, form of disorder, and—although many children normally go through a period of stuttering—if your child continues to stutter for more than about six months, talk to your speech-language pathologist or pediatrician.

WHEN SHOULD I BE CONCERNED?

If you know your child's language development during infancy and toddlerhood was significantly delayed—for example, she did not talk at all until age 2 or later—you should be aware of the possibility of a language problem surfacing during her early elementary years that may make it difficult for your child to learn to read, or much later, in middle school, when listening skills become so important as students take notes during lectures. While you don't have to jump to conclusions about your child's language abilities, it's good to be aware of the greater likelihood of problems with children whose early language development was significantly delayed.

During elementary school years, you should be concerned if your child:

❏ has difficulty repeating or making up rhymes,

❏ seems to lack the words to deal effectively with peers, clowning around or acting aggressively instead,

❏ doesn't talk as much as her friends, or has a vocabulary that seems significantly smaller than that of her friends. If you don't feel confident judging the size of your child's vocabulary, but you are concerned about it, ask your child's teacher for her opinion, too.

❏ has trouble following directions at school or at home,

❏ consistently has difficulty finding the right words to express herself, or talks around a word by describing color, size, etc., instead of using the word itself, saying for example, "The big gray thing," instead of elephant.

❏ consistently uses words like "stuff" or "things" instead of the correct word. Most children do this to some extent; you should only be concerned if it's a pervasive pattern for your child.

❏ speaks in a disorganized way, with words out of order in the sentence,

❏ has difficulty relating a sequence of events in the correct order.

You should also be concerned if your child's teacher lets you know that your child is generally having a hard time learning to read, comprehending what she reads, or writing simple stories.

Sometimes speech and language disorders prompt children to act out of anger easily, because they are frustrated or can't understand their peers, so you should be concerned if your child's teacher reports frequent anger. (See also Anger Control.)

You should be concerned if your child stutters for more than about six months. Young children often go through a period of stuttering that stops on its own. A persistent problem may require help from a professional.

You should not be concerned if your child does not make the sounds of the letters r, l, or w by school age. These are the last sounds to develop. If her inability to make these sounds persists beyond age 7, you should consult with the teacher or a speech-language pathologist.

You should be concerned if your child sounds nasal or hoarse even when she does not have a cold.

You should be concerned if your older child or adolescent suddenly begins having language difficulties when he has had no history of them, or shows a significant decrease in communication—well beyond normal adolescent reticence. It could be the result of a head injury or a hearing problem.

You should be concerned if your adolescent shows ongoing difficulties that stem from language problems, such as difficulties expressing complex ideas in writing, problems in decoding in reading (which of course will have an effect on academics in all subjects), problems in remembering material for tests, or problems with sequencing in which she has difficulty remembering the days of the week in the right order, for example.

WHAT CAN I DO TO HELP?

Since you talk to your child every day, the way in which you use language can be a good starting place for helping your child use language more effectively. You can:

❐ Say the names of objects, places, or people to help your child increase his vocabulary. Explain the word's meaning, and if possible, show him what you mean. For example, take your child outside and show him a puddle in the street and explain why the water stays there. If you give words context as well as meaning, it's easier for your child to remember them.

❐ Consistently use short, simple sentences and focus them on concrete objects or topics.

❐ Read to your child. Many parents stop or become too busy to read after the preschool years, but reading aloud is helpful for all children. Ask questions as you go along to check for comprehension, or stop to answer your child's questions about the story.

❐ Keep directions or instructions simple. Say "Shut the door," instead of "Can't you shut the door?" to avoid confusion.

❐ Avoid sarcasm or the use of words or phrases with multiple meanings like "pretty good," instead of "good, and "hand me the pencil," instead of "give me the pencil."

❐ Have your child repeat instructions or directions back to you to check for understanding.

❐ Encourage your child to write stories using a technique called *mapping* (see illustration below). Draw a large circle or a rectangle and write inside it the topic your child is to write about. Draw smaller rectangles attached by lines to the larger rectangle. Have your child (with your help if necessary) write one sentence of story details in each of the smaller rectangles. You can talk about or work with her on deciding which rectangles would come first, second, or third if she were telling the story.

In addition, you can praise your child when you see her doing a good job of getting her message across to someone else, using the correct words in the correct order. To reinforce that skill, make a game with her in which she has information you need—then help her relay the message to you in the correct order.

Children and adolescents with language problems often have difficulty organizing their thoughts as well as learning materials. You can also help your child learn organizational skills for school by:

❐ helping him arrange a binder with separate sections for each subject and a place to write assignments for that subject.

❐ working with him to develop a time budget for completion of assignments and study time. (See Homework and Study Skills.)

❐ teaching him the mapping technique described above for taking notes, or teaching him to outline his notes.

For any age child, talk with the child a lot; that's one of the best forms of practice for language difficulties. Ask your child what she did in school or over the weekend, or how she liked a particular movie and have her tell you about it in sequence. Using a computer to write stories will help her with spelling and with getting thoughts out. Your child can arrange and rearrange her thoughts once they are out. (See Reading—and Writing and 'Rithmetic.) Also, assign her writing tasks, such as corresponding with a pen pal or a relative.

WHAT WILL A PROFESSIONAL DO?

If you have concerns about your child's language abilities, first talk with his teacher about your concerns to see if the problems you see are occurring in the classroom. If they are, suggest that you, the teacher, and the school psychologist meet with a speech-language pathologist. The three professionals will want to observe your child in the classroom. If they share your concerns, they will suggest an evaluation of your child's speech and language skills. If they are not concerned and you are, in many states you can request that an evaluation be done.

In conducting an evaluation of your child's language skills, one of the first steps will be a thorough hearing evaluation (see Hearing), to rule out a hearing problem.

The speech-language pathologist will want to assess your child's oral (speaking) as well as receptive (listening) skills using techniques similar to those of a school psychologist: observation and question-and-answer evaluations.

Some of the things she'll be looking at are:

❏ sentence length and complexity
❏ word retrieval, or remembering and using the correct word
❏ word association, or being able to associate a word with many ideas
❏ articulation, or how your child pronounces words
❏ blending, or how well your child blends sounds to form words
❏ rhyming, producing or repeating rhymes
❏ a written sample to see how well the language a child uses translates to the written form

The school psychologist may want to give your child some IQ and academic-skills tests to determine your child's learning style and to see if this problem is interfering with your child's reading, writing, or spelling. She may also want to determine if emotional, social, or physical factors are interfering with your child's development by observing your child and interviewing you about your child's early language development, birth, and family history. She will want to know things such as when your child started talking or if there were any unusual circumstances during his birth or prenatally.

If the evaluation shows your child does have a language problem, the speech-language pathologist may work directly with him to improve or correct it. If the problem is seriously interfering with your child's academics, then a special education teacher may also work with your child alone, in a small group, or in the classroom. (See Special Education, in Part I). In some cases, the speech-language pathologist and special education teacher might serve as consultants to your child's teacher to implement a program to aid your child and to monitor your child's progress. Things they might specify that the teacher (or the other specialists) do with your child are:

❏ work on vocabulary development with a private dictionary of words your child is learning; defining and using those words verbally and in written form.
❏ work on grammar, so that your child understands how to change verb tenses from past to present, for example
❏ have your child tell or make up a story from a picture, to be sure he understands the concept of sequence
❏ have your child imitate the sounds the speech-language pathologist makes and the sentences she forms so your child hears and practices correct language

See also:

❏ ADHD
❏ Anger Control
❏ Hearing
❏ Homework

- ❐ Learning Disabilities
- ❐ Reading—and Writing and 'Rithmetic
- ❐ Special Education, in Part I
- ❐ Study Skills

Further Reading

Rich, Dorothy. *MegaSkills*. Boston: Houghton Mifflin, 1992.

FOR YOUNGER CHILDREN:

Topic:
DINOSAURS
(write a paragraph
for each question)

| How many different kinds are there? | What do they do? | Where do they live? | What do they eat? |

Concluding or
Summary Paragraph:
What have I learned
about dinosaurs?

FOR MIDDLE/HIGH SCHOOL CHILDREN:

**WHETHER OR NOT
TO CONTINUE THE
SPACE PROGRAM**

benefits basic science

costs too much

promotes U.S. pride

LIST POSITIVES AND NEGATIVES

PRO

CON

too risky

indirectly stimu-lates economy

no clear mission

Summarize statements
and your point of view

CHAPTER 25

Learning Disabilities

"We know Reed is very intelligent; he started talking when he was less than a year old, has always been curious, and figured out how to use the computer before he started school. But we've been suprised and disappointed to see how hard it's been for him to learn to read and to write. Now we're seeing him really turn off to school. He's only in the second grade and he says he hates learning."

The idea that a child could have a learning disability has been around since early in this century, and the first attempt at a definition came in the early 1960s. But rather than clearing up whatever lack of clarity there might have been about learning disabilities, that first definition opened up the whole idea to scrutiny and debate.

Since then, research and practical approaches to helping children who have learning disabilities has continued, every day giving professionals a better understanding of how to work with children who have them. That's good news for parents who have a child with a learning disability: While learning disabilities never go away, there are things you can do to help your child, and there are approaches professionals can take with your child to help even more.

WHAT WE KNOW NOW

A child is usually tested for—and diagnosed with—a learning disability when his academic achievement is significantly below what you would expect, based on his age and what you know about that child's educational background and level of intelligence. However, low achievement alone does not always mean a

child has a learning disability. If your child is not achieving up to his potential, for example, it could be because of low motivation, a lack in basic skills after frequent school moves when he was young, language or behavior problems, or another disability.

A learning disability can have an effect on your child's reading, spelling, math, and writing, or on such academic areas as social studies, science, or a foreign language. Usually, the learning disability reflects a problem with how the child processes information or with his ability to learn information. The problem can be with:

❏ memory
❏ organization
❏ the ability to pay attention or focus on a task
❏ the ability to rehearse and organize information in order to remember it
❏ the ability to retrieve information that has been learned
❏ the ability to understand some things in their proper sequence, for example, how events in a story must happen in a logical order

Having a learning disability can also mean a child has difficulty perceiving what he sees or hears, or that he has difficulty understanding written material or verbal presentations.

That's a wide range of problem areas. Current research is finding that categories of children with learning disabilities are just about as wide-ranging as there are learning disabilities. That's why most experts agree now there's no one way to "fix" them all. Each child needs to be treated differently.

We also see that in some school districts, there is an unfortunate tendency to label a child as having a learning disability without also looking at the classroom environment and the curriculum first, so that sometimes it seems that everybody has a learning disability of some kind. The more accurate way to arrive at who really has a learning disability is to look carefully at the child's learning ability, his learning style and how motivated he is, the curriculum used in his classroom, and the teacher's teaching style.

Even when a learning disability is accurately diagnosed, in most cases it is not possible to figure out why the child has the disability. Although the research is far from conclusive, some factors that seem to relate to learning disabilities are:

❑ genetic predisposition
❑ prenatal factors such as RH incompatibility, in utero exposure to diseases such as German measles, deficiencies in the mother's diet, and maternal drug-alcohol use
❑ events occurring during birth such as lack of oxygen to the baby, the effects of childbirth-related drugs on the baby, and injuries from forceps
❑ postnatal factors such as head injuries, strokes, tumors, or the ingestion of toxic substances—lead-based paint, for example.

WHEN SHOULD I BE CONCERNED?

You should be concerned when you see symptoms like those on the list below, most of which will show up in the first two or three years of school:

❑ has difficulty paying attention long enough to listen to stories and difficulty comprehending stories he hears
❑ has difficulty remembering details of stories read to him
❑ is unable to recite the alphabet or nursery rhymes in spite of practice
❑ can't remember his telephone number by the end of kindergarten
❑ has difficulty learning letter sounds or learning to write letters and numbers in first grade
❑ has a generally low frustration tolerance. Child typically gets mad and crumples up paper, cries, doesn't want to go to school, says he is dumb or stupid
❑ is a behavior problem in class; acts out to get attention
❑ doesn't finish class assignments
❑ constantly asks for help from parent or teacher
❑ seems to learn something one day and forgets it the next. For example, your child studies his spelling words and seems to know them at home but does poorly on the test and tells you he forgot the words. The same thing happens with reading: your child does well reading words with the short vowel *a*, for example, but has to be retaught the next week when words with that sound come up again.
❑ has difficulty remembering simple addition facts in second grade, and in third and fourth grade can't seem to memorize multiplication facts even with your help every night.

How to Help Your Child

IF YOUR CHILD:
Writes letters backwards,

TRY:
printing the alphabet on a large note card for him to keep with his school things. When he needs help with how to write a certain letter, he can consult the card. You can do the same thing with numbers if they are difficult for your child to write. (Reversing letters is normal until about age 7.)

IF YOUR CHILD:
Has trouble spelling correctly,

TRY:
dividing your child's spelling list into groups of five words, and working with him on only one small group a day. Here's how: have your child recite the words, write them from memory, then rewrite them after you've corrected for errors. If your child has a lot of trouble writing the spelling words, have him recite them instead.

IF YOUR CHILD:
Has trouble with math problems,

TRY:
practicing math facts with him for 15 minutes each night (for grades 1–3; 30 minutes for grades 4–6) using the steps listed above. Review old facts (or spelling words) before moving on to practice new ones. And, be sure you time your practice sessions so that you stop before your child gets frustrated.

IF YOUR CHILD:
Is having trouble learning to read,

TRY:
reading to her at home, up until even the fifth or sixth grade. For fourth-graders and older, if you read aloud to them their assignments in subjects such as science or social studies, and then have them read the assignments on their own, it can help your child keep up with the rest of the class in spite of reading problems.

❏ avoids or has a lot of difficulty writing stories or putting ideas on paper

❏ can answer questions aloud but when she tries to write the answers, they don't come out the same way

❏ has a good speaking vocabulary but uses an immature vocabulary when she writes because it's easier to avoid the longer words than it is to spell them.

❏ doesn't want to go to school

❏ says the schoolwork is too hard

WHAT CAN I DO TO HELP?

If you are concerned about your child's academic progress, first talk with your child's teacher; she may have the same concerns. And, she may be able to suggest some things you can do at home, like the ideas in the box above, to help your child.

Working with the teacher, the two of you should first compare work done at home with work done at school to see if there is a consistent pattern to the errors your child makes. Notice, for example, if your child does better when you are working with him individually at home, when he is working on his own at school, or working in a group at school. Knowing in which setting he does his best work will help you and the teacher better understand your child's learning style.

You'll also be looking for the kinds of mistakes we often see children with learning disabilities make in writing, spelling, and math. The previous box shows those problem areas and some ways you can help your child in each.

Children who have difficulty with these areas but who do not have a learning disability often respond well to the help. Children with learning disabilities can also benefit from these strategies, but they probably won't show steady improvement as would children without learning disabilities. As you're trying these, keep in mind that a child with learning disabilities will show much more frustration than a child without.

If these strategies don't help your child, and further evaluation shows that your child does have a learning disability, a special education teacher will give you similar techniques to use at home that are more specifically geared to your child's disability. (See What Will A Professional Do? below.)

You may also find that a computer is a big help to your child for writing his homework or other school projects. A computer can also help your child with spelling (using a spell-check program) and with other academic areas through educational games.

Be sure you include lots of encouragement and praise or rewards for effort as well as success, with any help program you may have with your child. It's also important to help your child learn about perserverance: that if he sticks with a tough problem, he can learn. Without some examples in his own life of success after effort, it's easy for a child to begin to feel that no matter what he does, he can't learn, which is a form of learned helplessness (see Dependency). It's also easy for a child to lose his motivation if his effort is never rewarded and he never succeeds. And, it's important that a child with a learning disability stay motivated because he almost always has to put in more effort than a child without a disability. (See Motivation.)

One more thing you can do to help your child is to provide him with other fun things to do that he can easily excel in, such as sports, music, or art. Don't use these as rewards for good grades or completed work, though; a child with learning disabilities needs to feel good about himself in areas other than academics.

WHAT WILL A PROFESSIONAL DO?

If you and your child's teacher have tried strategies like those listed above at home and at school, and you both feel your child has not made the progress you would have expected, or if you just believe your child has a learning disability, then it's time to meet with a multidisciplinary team to decide if a thorough evaluation of your child is needed. You and your child's teacher will meet with the team, which should include a school psychologist, the special education teacher, and other appropriate professionals such as the school social worker or the speech-language pathologist.

In this meeting, you'll talk about what has

been tried, what has worked, and what has not worked. If the team believes an evaluation is needed, information you contribute will be key to the process. For example, the team will want to know about your child's birth, medical history, developmental history (when your child began walking and talking), and about his disposition.

The purpose of the evaluation is threefold:

1 To determine if your child has a learning disability.
2 To determine what factors contribute to your child's learning problems, such as curriculum, teaching styles, or your child's self-concept and motivation.
3 To determine what kinds of interventions will help your child.

Professionals on the multidisciplinary team will do a variety of tests to determine your child's strengths and weaknesses. The tests listed below are all described in Appendix D, Samples from Tests and Assessments. They will evaluate or measure:

❏ your child's intelligence to get a general IQ, which will show what your child's abilities are, and what you can reasonably expect of him academically. They'll use a test such as the Stanford-Binet Intelligence Scale: Fourth Edition, or the Weschler Intelligence Scale for Children: Third Edition.
❏ how your child learns or processes information. These tests may show, for example, that your child has a visual memory problem, which means he has difficulty retaining what he sees. Consequently, it may be particularly hard for your child to learn letters or number facts by looking at them. You can see how this information is vital to designing strategies that will help your child learn more easily and

more efficiently. Tests they are likely to use are the Woodcock-Johnson Tests of Cognitive Abilities, Bloomer Learning Test, or Detroit Tests of Learning Aptitude.
❏ how much your child has learned so far. They will either develop tests based on the curriculum used in your child's classroom, or standardized tests such as the Reading Skills Diagnostic Test, Woodcock-Johnson Tests of Academic Achievement, Gray Oral Reading Test: third edition, Key Math Test—Revised, or the Kaufman Test of Educational Achievement. These tests should give a clear picture of the skills your child has and has not acquired. Children above third grade may also have tests of written language skills.

The school psychologist is also likely to interview your child to see how he feels about himself as a learner, and to understand the kinds of frustrations your child faces as a result of his difficulties. He may also ask your child to complete a self-report inventory such as the Piers-Harris Children's Self-Concept Scale, or have the teacher and you complete behavioral rating scales such as the Child Behavior Checklist and its Teacher Report Form.

Observing your child in the classroom to see how he does in that environment and with the teacher's instruction will also be important to the school psychologist and the special education teacher.

Once all this information has been collected, you will meet again with the multidisciplinary team to review the results and your child's performance and to come up with a plan to help him. Keep in mind that whatever strategies are used, it will be important for you and your child's teacher to monitor how they are working and adjust your approach as you go along. Your child might be able to tell you how different strategies are working for him, too.

The current trend is for whatever special help your child needs to be brought into his current classroom if possible, rather than taking him out of class to get help. In some cases, the special education teacher will work with your child's regular teacher so that she can provide the help your child needs. If it's not possible for the strategies you and the multi-disciplinary team have developed to be provided in the classroom, the special education teacher may have your child come out for a while each day, or several days a week, to work individually or in a small group. And sometimes it's necessary for your child to be in a separate special education class.

See also:

❏ Appendix D, Samples from Tests and Assessments
❏ Dependency
❏ Motivation

Further Reading

Bever, S. *Building a Child's Self Image: A Guide For Parents.* The Minnesota Association for Children and Adults with Learning Disabilities, 821 University Avenue, 494 North, St. Paul, MN 55105. 1982.

Bloom, J. *Help Me to Help My Child: A Sourcebook for Parents of Learning Disabled Children.* Boston: Little, Brown and Company, 1990.

Farnham-Diggory, S. *The Learning Disabled Child.* Cambridge, MA: Harvard University Press. 1992.

Greene, L. *Learning Disabilities and Your Child.* New York: Fawcett Columbine, 1987.

MacCracker, M. *Turnabout Children.* New York: Signet, 1986.

McBee Knox, J. *Learning Disabilities.* New York: Chelsea House Publishers, 1989.

Silver, L. *The Misunderstood Child: A Guide for Parents of Learning Disabled Children.* Boston: Little Brown and Company, 1992.

CHAPTER 26

Lying

"I just found out from his teacher that Leon hasn't turned in homework all week. He told me he didn't have any. I never thought that boy would lie to me like this."

"My daughter's friend Megan told her that another girl in their fifth grade class was spreading unkind rumors about my daughter Janie. Later, Janie found out that none of it was true—no one had spread rumors—and Megan had made up the whole thing so Janie would be mad at the other girl. Janie's upset and I don't know what to tell her about a friend who would lie like that."

When your child has lied to you, to a teacher, or school friend, the effect is somewhere between disappointing and devastating. It's important to deal with lying when it happens, but it's also important not to overreact and to understand that there are many kinds of lies, some more significant than others. What you do about your child's lying, and whether or not it is a problem will depend on the type of lie your child has told.

WHAT WE KNOW NOW

Preschool age children are famous for being excruciatingly truthful, saying and doing whatever strikes them at the moment. They will pipe up at a family gathering, for example, and inform everyone within earshot that Aunt Mae is fat, and they will be telling the truth.

As those young children mature socially, they learn that it is more socially acceptable to say nothing at all about Aunt Mae's size, or to deny that Aunt Mae is fat and say only she is big-boned. Adults are pleased when a child learns to temper her remarks like this. But in fact, the child has simply learned to become less honest. Sometimes the line between less

honest and lying isn't clear to children, and that's when adults step in to pull the lying child back inside the boundaries of social acceptability.

So learning about lying can be a complex feat for children. Learning about the types of lies and which are problems is almost equally complex for adults. There is a lot to understand about lying, and a good place to begin is with a clear definition: it is an intentional falsehood. There are also several kinds of lies:

- *Instrumental lying:* These are deliberate attempts to deceive another person in order to avoid blame, obtain a reward, or inflict harm.
- *Noninstrumental lying:* This includes two types: compulsive lying and wishful thinking. *Wishful thinking,* more common in younger children, is motivated by a child's desire that things be different. For example, a girl with no friends tells her classmates she has a very good friend who lives in a nearby town and they do fun things together all the time. The lie hurts no one and is a substitute for what the girl wishes were true.

With *compulsive lying,* a child is aware of his lying but not of his motive, and he lies all the time about everything without any obvious immediate or long-term gain. This actually involves an impulse control problem, similar to compulsive stealing, and little is known about its cause or treatment. Fortunately, this is relatively rare and not the type of problem your child is likely to have.

■ *Prosocial lying:* Even though these are still intentional lies, and thereby still wrong, these lies have positive motives behind them, such as avoiding hurting another's feelings. For example, at recess a child tells the class bully he doesn't know where another child is in order to keep that child from having to confront the bully. Or a sixth-grade girl tells her friend she likes her new haircut when she doesn't, to avoid hurting the other girl's feelings.

■ *Unintentional lying:* There are three types of unintentional lies:

1 *Fantasy,* in which (usually) a young child cannot distinguish fantasy from reality. If this continues beyond early elementary years, about fourth grade, it may be a problem.

2 *Unconscious defense,* in which a child can't admit to himself he did something wrong and unconsciously covers up to keep from having to admit it.

3 *Accidental falsehood,* in which a child makes a statement he thinks is true, but it is false because it was based on erroneous information.

The important thing to understand about your child's lying at school or at home is that it is complex and not necessarily a psychological problem in and of itself, although it may be an indication of other problems. (See for example Self-Esteem, Bullies and Victims, Friends, Perfectionism.) Recurring lies can affect your child's relationships with other children his age, and poor social adjustment can eventually undermine his academic achievement.

Understanding the context of the lie will give you direction as to what to do about it. And understanding how common lying is in children of all genders and ages may help to keep you from overreacting.

How children see lying and its consequences is linked to their moral development (see Cheating). For younger children, under about age 8, lying is more strictly defined as anything aside from the truth, and seen as "bad" no matter what the intention of the teller. Older children and adults tend to be more willing to define lies in terms of factual accuracy as well as intent. And all ages, down to about age 4, see lies with selfish intent as worse than other lies. Children as young as 4 clearly know the difference between the truth and a lie, and know that it is wrong to lie.

WHEN SHOULD I BE CONCERNED?

You'll need to stay calm and assess the nature of the lie and your child's pattern of lying before you become concerned.

To help assess your child's lie and to clarify your thinking, see the table below.

If the items you check off are mostly under A and infrequent, then your child's lying is not as much of a problem, and you can look to the next section for ways you can deal with the issue yourself. If the items are mostly under B, you can first try using the suggestions in the next section. If they aren't working for you, then you should think about contacting the school psychologist fairly soon for advice about the approach you are using to address the lying because its causes could be deeper than you could address alone.

WHAT CAN I DO TO HELP?

First, you will need to examine carefully how you handle falsehoods in your life.

> ## What Kind of Lie Was It . . . ?
>
> **A. Was the lie an attempt to . . .**
>
> avoid hurting another person?
> help another person?
> embellish a story?
>
> **B. Or was the lie . . .**
>
> intentional?
> an attempt to avoid blame for
> wrong-doing?
> an attempt to shift blame to an
> innocent person?
> an attempt to inflict harm?
> an attempt to get an undeserved
> reward?
> a repeated pattern?

Unfortunately, and sometimes embarrassingly, children simply repeat what they've heard at home in their actions at school.

For example, what do you tell your child when she's invited to a classmates' birthday party she doesn't want to attend? Do you encourage her to make up an excuse? Or do you work with her to figure out why she doesn't want to go and how to work that out within her own feelings and with the birthday girl?

Think about what you may have conciously or unconsciously taught your child about lying. If you want your child to stop lying, you will have to talk with him about the ways in which you may have handled the truth at times.

Then, you can use a problem-solving approach to your child's lying. You'll need to make a few notes in order to be very clear about what your child is, and is not, doing. Begin by:

❏ Listing behaviors you consider to be lying.

Write down specific incidents and exactly what was said and done. To do this easily, divide a sheet of paper into three vertical columns. In the center column, write your child's lie. In the left-hand column, write what happened right before the lie; in the right-hand column what happened as a result of the lie. This chart may help you to see patterns to your child's lying.

❏ Look back at the types of lies in the previous section and classify each lie based on those definitions.

❏ Then keep track of your child's lying over the next week or two, writing down each incident as in the first step.

During those weeks, tune in to your child's behavior, paying attention to things he does when you think he's lying, such as breaking eye contact. Check with teachers, siblings, or parents of your child's friends to verify the truth if you find he is lying. As you see patterns develop on your chart, think too about how you would rate your child in social skills compared to other children of the same age. Does it seem he just doesn't know how to behave with kids his own age but does fine with younger children? This can be a clue that your child simply hasn't yet learned the social skills he needs in his age group. (See Friends.)

If your chart shows that your child has more trouble with lying when he is around certain friends, limit his contact with those friends and involve him in other activities so that there is less opportunity to be with people you see as negative influences. This works well up to about age 14. If your child is older than this, while you should still try to exert a good influence on him, you may need to talk to the school psychologist about how to deal with your child's behavior.

Once you have a clear picture about how and why your child is lying, you can figure out how to handle it. Here are some ideas:

❏ For a young child whose lying is simply a matter of misinformation, provide her with the right information. Maybe this will mean a trip to the library together to find out what the moon is really made of, or looking through a few books at home to find the facts you need.

❏ For prosocial lying, you can brainstorm with your child a better way to have handled the situation. Use the example of saying you like a friend's haircut when you really don't. Then sit down with your child and make a list of other things she could say, even the silly things. You might come up with ideas that range from "No, I hate your haircut," and "It makes your face look really fat," to "I'm so used to the old style; it'll take some time for me to decide if I like this one," and "Honestly, I like the other style better, but don't go by my opinion; I don't always have the best taste."

Have a good laugh at the funny things on your list and discard the approaches that won't work. But talk with your child about the good ideas you came up with, and how to see the difference between hurtful truthfulness (it's not harmful to think your friend looks horrible in her new haircut), and the moral chipping away that even "harmless" prosocial lying can do.

❏ For unconscious defense lying, point out to your child that you understand why he lied, but that even though it's true he did something wrong and is trying to cover, now he's committed two blunders, not just one, and the punishment will have to double: one for the original deed, one for lying. Depending on the circumstances, the punishments should be carefully selected to reflect which is worse.

Ideally, if the lie is worse than the deed—spilling soda on the couch, for example—you can give a very minor punishment for the deed and a much stronger one for the lie. And of course you'll explain why to your child.

❏ Instrumental lying is the worst of these types of lying, so the punishments for this must be the most direct and the strongest. When you confront your child about this, you should:

❏ point out why what she did was wrong
❏ point out both the immediate and long-term consequences of her lie
❏ show your anger and disappointment
❏ mete out a significant punishment, such as the loss of a special privilege such as a planned skiing day or a canoe trip with dad

What if your child is caught in a lie and then comes up with the truth? Do you reward the truth or punish the lie? This is tricky because, although we do want our children to be truthful, we can't ignore the lie. But simply rewarding the truth can lead a child to work for rewards by telling the truth when he wants to, and lying the rest of the time. Punishing only the lie and not the misbehavior can motivate a child to become a more skillful liar so as not to get caught. And making a big deal about "getting at the truth" turns the parent into a grand inquisitor, giving the child lots of attention for lying, which may inadvertently reinforce lying.

In such cases, use as your guideline the idea that you want the rewards for lying to be lessened, and the rewards for telling the truth increased. For example, when your child lies to avoid punishment and is found out, she should get the original punishment plus punishment for lying. When she lies to avoid punishment but then admits to the lie, you can praise her for confessing (i.e., for not continuing to lie); however, the original misbehavior should still be punished.

Some negative consequences to consider using in teaching your child not to lie:

❒ standard techniques such as time out for younger children
❒ loss of privileges (see Appendix A, Motivators, for ideas)
❒ child takes the consequences at school, rather than a parent intervening to "save" the child. For example, your child should have to take the zero for not turning in homework, even though you are already concerned about his grades, and he should be punished in addition for lying to you about having turned in his homework.

WHAT WILL A PROFESSIONAL DO?

When a teacher or parent reports that a child lies, the school psychologist must figure out what type of lie the child is telling. Her actions will be based on the type of lie she identifies. For example, if the lie is:

❒ prosocial or accidental, no intervention is required.
❒ a fantasy that the child cannot tell from reality; if the child is older than about 6 or 7, the child may need a comprehensive psychological evaluation to determine why he is not able to tell the difference.
❒ an unconscious defense, no intervention is required if the child is less than 7 years old. If he is older, counseling may help him develop a more realistic self-concept.
❒ instrumental or noninstrumental lying, the psychologist will want to work with the child on changing this behavior.

In assessing a child's lying, the school psychologist will want to talk with the parents and the teacher. She will likely ask such questions as:

❒ *What behaviors do you identify as lying? How do you know it's a lie?*
❒ *How frequently does the child lie?* Parents and teachers may be asked to record the number of lies and statements they think are lies over a 7- to 12-day period.
❒ *What is the content and context of the child's lying?* The answer to this question will be critical in understanding your child's lying and figuring out the appropriate approach to take. Parents and teachers may be asked to write down, at least briefly, the circumstances leading up to each lie and the content of the lie. For example, a teacher might note that when one student brags to your child about academic accomplishments, your child is likely to follow with a lie.
❒ *Do other children view the child as having a problem with lying?* It is important to know if your child's behavior is affecting his relationships. The psychologist and/or the teacher may want to observe in the classroom and discuss with the teacher the children's relationships to see how the children view the one who is apparently lying.
❒ *What other problems does the child have?* Poor academic achievement, truancy, cheating, aggression, lack of friends, or social withdrawal are issues that may go along with lying, and the psychologist will be able to recommend a more effective approach for your child if she is aware of all problems. (See Friends, Anger Control.)
❒ *What prosocial behaviors does your child have or lack?* If, for example, your child has difficulty making friends at school, learning the social skills necessary to do so might make it unnecessary for her to lie about imaginary friends.

❏ *What socialization influences has your child had?* It is important that your child have the kind of role models that will help her learn and practice honesty.

Once the school psychologist knows the answers to these questions, she will likely respond in one of two ways:

1 Although serious lying is often the result of other problems, she will usually address this symptom directly, with a system of rewards and punishments focused on getting rid of this behavior.

2 She will also try to determine the overall reason for lying and address that need. Some of those reasons might be:

a a pattern of antisocial behavior, for which she would use techniques such as behavioral contracting, in which a child agrees with his parents to maintain certain behaviors in exchange for certain privileges. For example, an adolescent might get free time to himself in exchange for truthfulness.

b a pattern of wishful thinking, for which the psychologist might do some counseling with your child to help her develop a more realistic self-concept and to learn how to express her desires.

c a pattern of deficient social skills, for which the psychologist might recommend your child join a social skills group. Children often lie because they lack the social skills to be able to answer without lying. In social skills training, children are presented with lifelike situations involving the need to respond to an awkward situation where lying would be one way out. For example, the group could be presented with a situation where a child saw her friend steal from a classmate and then lied to the teacher to protect her friend. The children in the group could brainstorm and practice ways to deal with this that don't involve lying.

Although you won't be running a social skills class at home, in a sense what happens in your home is a generalized social skills class. The more your child sees you interacting with others in an open and honest fashion, the more your child will copy your behavior. The best skills your child can have to make it easier for her not to lie are: good verbal ability, self-confidence, and a feeling of being accepted for what she is. It also helps when you are consistent in how you treat her, and reasonable in your expectations for her.

See also:

❏ Appendix A, Motivators
❏ Appendix D, Samples from Tests and Assessments
❏ Assertiveness
❏ Cheating
❏ Friends
❏ Self-Esteem

CHAPTER 27

Motivation

"Molly is a nice, cooperative third grader. But she seems to be not at all interested in school; she's just not motivated to do her schoolwork and seems satisfied with average or low-average work. We know she's brighter than that, but we don't know how to motivate her to do better."

"Tyson always has been very self-motivated; even when he was in first or second grade, I never had to remind him about homework or chores. But lately, he only seems motivated to do the things he wants to do, and everything else falls by the wayside. How can we get him remotivated to do the things he needs to do on his own?"

Like the weather, motivation is one of those vitally important qualities we can define and we can talk about, but when it comes to actually doing something about it, no one knows where to start. Indeed, boosting their children's academic motivation is an elusive goal for many parents.

The good news is that even though it's not always easy, there are ways to understand and deal with your child's motivation that can help you to help him through some tough academic times.

WHAT WE KNOW NOW

Motivation is a tricky subject to get a handle on, even for psychologists and educators. No one understands fully how it operates, but we know there are lots of factors that influence a child's motivation.

A good place to start is to understand how most people define motivation: It's the willingness to expend a certain amount of effort to achieve a particular goal. Perhaps you wouldn't come up with exactly that definition, but whether you could define it or not, you could

probably say you know lack of motivation when you see it: It looks like boredom, procrastination, laziness, and careless habits and attitudes.

Many factors contribute to how motivated a child is. In school, the major factors affecting motivation are:

- Whether the task at hand is an elective one or a required one. Of course, required tasks usually involve lots of individual, tedious effort, such as learning math facts or memorizing French verbs. And of course, for many children, motivation can plummet when they are faced with long lists of required tasks, especially if those don't fit their particular interests.
- What kind of student the child is. Motivated children tend to be those with higher ability levels, encouraging and supportive parents, lots of previous success at learning, good self-esteem, good physical health, and balanced feelings about competitiveness and cooperation. The opposite qualities tend to lessen a child's academic motivation.
- The classroom atmosphere. For most tasks, a

competitive atmosphere in the classroom tends to lessen motivation for all but the most capable. Cooperative learning and individualized rewards tend to increase motivation for most children. (See Competition/Cooperation.)

■ Teacher's attitudes. Teachers who behave in a caring and helpful manner rather than having a more autocratic attitude seem to motivate more children. So do those who at least sometimes reward effort as well as success, and those who are able to match their expectations for the child's academic performance with the child's abilities. The teacher's personality also plays into motivation—obviously teachers who are enthusiastic, interesting, and pleasant are more motivating that those who are boring and ill-tempered.

■ Parent's attitudes. Your child is likely to be more motivated if, from the earliest ages, you have placed value on your child's efforts as well as successes, and if you actively value learning. For example, your child will know you value learning if he sees you continuing to learn: reading up on a topic that interests you, furthering your own education, showing curiosity about new ideas, and figuring out ways to find out more about them.

While psychologists don't agree on the underlying mechanisms of motivation, it might help you to know what some of their theories are as you decide how to deal with your child's motivation issues. These ideas can be useful in helping you identify your child's motivational style.

1 Some see motivation as primarily influenced by extrinsic factors, meaning that things outside a person determine how motivated the person is. According to this theory, a natural desire for things like good grades and praise, coupled with an equally natural desire to imi-tate those we admire or love are the foundations of motivation.

2 Some see motivation as primarily influenced by intrinsic factors—forces from inside a person. According to these theories, intrinsic motivation may mean:

❏ a person is inherently driven to "figure things out" (in other words, to learn).

❏ that although learning is a need we're born with, we only get around to satisfying it after other more important needs are met, such as needs for feeling safe, loved, or valued.

❏ everyone is born with the need to achieve. People born with high achievement needs have high goals and are thereby highly motivated to achieve them; those with low natural achievement needs still fear failure, so they shoot for very low or easy goals, or don't try at all if the task looks too difficult.

One thing most experts agree upon is that somehow everyone is motivated to do something. Although you may describe your child as "totally unmotivated" when it comes to school, in fact, he is motivated; it's just that his effort is not going into the things you want it to go into.

WHEN SHOULD I BE CONCERNED?

Lack of motivation turns up first as poor school achievement: Your child fails to turn in work or his work is sloppy and poorly thought out, and when the result is poorer grades, he doesn't much care. Although lack of motivation is not in itself a serious psychological problem, in the interest of your child's self-esteem (and his grades), you should be concerned when you start to see lower grades on homework and other assignments, and a careless attitude toward them.

WHAT CAN I DO TO HELP?

Carl's case study illustrates how parents can help their child become more academically motivated. At age 8, Carl loved science and computers. He was viewed by his parents and teachers as very bright, energetic, inquisitive, and verbal. He'd spend hours working on the computer, not just playing games, but on educational programs as well, including those meant to improve math and spelling.

While his parents were glad he was so willing to learn on the computer, they were dismayed by his grades. Even though Carl would happily spend hours spelling words correctly on the computer in order to win an educational game, he wouldn't spend 10 minutes on his spelling homework, and seemed satisfied with average spelling grades. All the time Carl spent on the computer was taking a toll on the rest of his schoolwork too, but Carl didn't really care; he just wasn't willing to stop working on his computer nor motivated to do his homework. He thought his parents were silly for worrying so much. After all, he could do the work if he wanted to. He just didn't want to.

That's the question Carl's parents were faced with: How do we make him want to do his schoolwork so he'll do a good job on it?

The school psychologist helped Carl's parents to see the question another way. He pointed out that Carl simply liked messing around on the computer better than he liked doing homework, and he was good at the computer (which, in turn, was like a reward every time he put finger to keyboard). Carl was motivated all right; he was motivated to work on the computer. The school psychologist further explained to Carl's parents that, in most people's lives, we work to balance what we like to do with what we have to do. So the real issue in Carl's lack of academic motivation was not to make him like school better or the computer less. The real issue was to have Carl learn that he had to bring his life back into balance—mixing activities he liked to do more equally with those he had to do.

Because his computer time was so rewarding to Carl, that was the perfect "motivator" to help him accomplish the things he didn't particularly want to. Carl's parents set up a simple incentive program for him: math and spelling homework completed and tests done at least at 85 percent accuracy or no computer time. As Carl got better at doing what he had to do, his parents were able to let Carl be in charge of his computer time, so long as he kept his grades at the agreed-upon level.

The bottom line here is that for children who are not academically motivated, you may not be able to significantly increase your child's motivation itself. While he still may not like it, you can be sure that he completes the school tasks he must do, and at a decent level of performance.

Techniques to be certain that happens are covered in other chapters, such as those on Homework and Study Skills. The Appendix on Motivators should also give you some ideas.

For some children, a little extra appeal using internal or external motivators is all they need. Some things you can do that might help your child become more motivated:

❑ Offer small rewards for effort along the way, as your child works on a long-term project, or for persistence, as she practices math facts faithfully every night.
❑ Use "speed" tasks to increase motivation, challenging your child to see how many animals she can name in a minute, how many

spelling words she can spell correctly in 3 minutes, how many correct math problems she can do in 4 minutes.

❑ Display your child's work at home. Your pride in his efforts is a great motivator.

❑ Make a work log for your child and keep track of small assignments that she's completed, giving points for on-time work, an exceptionally tidy paper, a creative drawing. The points accumulate to rewards, which come fairly quickly at first. Gradually increase your expectations as you withdraw your supervision. The ultimate goal is to make your child wait for a higher reward, which is the key to internal motivation: working hard toward a goal that is far off.

You can also think about some other aspects of motivation that will help you help your child:

❑ Make sure your child knows what she's supposed to do, both in class and in homework assignments. Confusion and uncertainty can kill anyone's motivation.

❑ Find out from school (your child's teacher or the principal) what your child's ability level is, to be sure your expectations of her are realistic.

❑ Carefully assess your role in helping your child become independent. Sometimes children who are unmotivated are also very dependent on their parents, especially when the parents have very high expectations of them and want things done perfectly—which usually means the parents' way, not the child's way. (See Perfectionism.) This decreases motivation because the child never learns how to accept responsibilty for herself or her work, and she knows it's not worth trying too hard because someone always comes in and corrects her work or tells her how to finish it. (See Dependency.)

❑ Be sure your child's basic needs are being met. Talk with him about any problems he may have related to school: with friends, teachers, assignments. When he comes home, allow him some time to play and to work off a full day's worth of school tasks before you require that he start homework or chores.

❑ If your child is feeling insecure or threatened personally, socially, or academically in school, talk with the teacher and the school psychologist about it to see what can be done. (See Fears, Bullies and Victims.)

WHAT A PROFESSIONAL WILL DO

If you are concerned about your child's motivation, you can talk with the school psychologist. He may give you ideas to try at home like those listed above.

If your child has a serious problem with motivation and it is consistently affecting your child's schoolwork, the school psychologist might call a multidisciplinary team meeting (see Special Education, in Part I). They'll discuss the problem and what has been tried to date. If it seems that nothing has worked for your child, the multidisciplinary team may request a psychological evaluation. (See Evaluation and Testing, in Part I.) Lack of motivation for school can indicate other personal problems such as depression, anxiety, stress, or learning problems, and the evaluation will try to determine which of these are contributing to your child's lack of motivation. (See Depression, Anxiety, Stress, Learning Disabilities.)

See also:

❑ Anxiety
❑ Competition/Cooperation
❑ Dependency
❑ Depression

Further Reading

Wlodkowski, R. J. *Eager to Learn: Helping Children Become Motivated and Love Learning.* San Francisco: Jossey-Bass, 1990.

Is Your Child at Risk for Dropping Out?

In most states, fewer than 75 percent of students who enroll in the ninth grade will go on to graduate from high school. Most experts agree that waiting until high school to address dropout problems is too late; the best dropout prevention programs begin in elementary school, when you show how much you value education by paying attention to your child's motivation.

Here are some reasons youngsters who have dropped out of high school give for leaving:

❒ A dislike for school; the opinion that school was boring and not relevant to their needs.

❒ Low academic achievement and poor grades.

❒ Poverty; a desire to work full-time; a need for money.

❒ Lack of belonging; a sense that nobody cared.

CHAPTER 28

Moving

"We know my husband is being transferred this year, and I'm afraid the move is going to be hard on the kids. We're trying to decide whether to move in the middle of the school year or wait and move during the summer. I don't know if it really makes a difference."

Increasingly, the United States is a nation of mobile families. Estimates are that, each year, about 8 million school children will move to new schools in new communities. Families move for a wide variety of reasons, from corporate transfers and military reassignments, to divorce, economic hardship, or immigration. For some children, a move will represent a welcome challenge or a new adventure. For others, it can be a frightening, disruptive change.

You can help smooth the way beforehand, or aid your child's adjustment after a move, by understanding how timing, temperament, developmental stages, and preparation can affect the way in which your child adjusts.

WHAT WE KNOW NOW

While moving school-age children to a new community is typically viewed as a negative experience, it's important to remember that for many children moving can be a positive change. As you plan your move, try to resist the temptation to assume that this change will inevitably be horrible or difficult for your child; there's no sense in setting up a self-fulfilling prophecy. Instead, base your assumptions and actions on how you've seen your child deal with change in the past and on what

he tells you now about his feelings regarding this move.

Overall, moving and the transitions it brings is often smoother for children in families who approach change positively and encourage them to explore new surroundings, develop flexible thinking skills ("How will I arrange my new room now that I don't have to share with my brother?"), and approach problems from a broad perspective ("How will I do things differently in my new school?"). Not surprisingly, children who already have social, athletic, and intellectual strengths are more likely to thrive on the challenge of a new setting and the prospect of finding and attaching to a new group of friends. And those who have the least personal resources to cope with change, those with minimal social, athletic, and intellectual skills, are more likely to have a hard time adjusting to a new situation.

Six more factors also have a strong impact on your child's adjustment to a move:

❏ *The reason your family is moving.* Children react differently to moving because of a divorce (see Divorce), compared to moving because of a corporate transfer, military reassignment, or other fundamentally positive reasons. The more positive the reason for a move, the smoother the adjustment in most cases.

❐ *Your family's socioeconomic status.* While moving may be stressful, children may feel it a little less if their family does not have financial difficulties in addition to the move.

❐ *Your child's academic abilities.* If you want to know how moving will affect your child's academics, look at how your child has always done in academics; studies have shown that's the best predictor. But keep in mind that the curriculum and the overall achievement level of the new school will have an effect on how well your child adjusts. For example, if you are moving from a high-powered academic community to one that is less so, your average student may look like an academic "star." The same is true for the opposite situation, though, and your academic star may struggle at a school where achievement and expectations are higher.

❐ *Your child's intellectual abilities.* Children do best with moves when they are reasonably adaptable in the way they think and respond to new situations, when they are flexible in the ways they approach challenges, and when they see new ways of doing things as enjoyable learning experiences. In addition, the more they are able to understand the reasons for the move, the better children are likely to adjust to the move.

❐ *The age of your child.* Relatively speaking, this is the least reliable factor to use in predicting how your child will do if you move. Children at any age may find it difficult to move, just as children at any age may find moving to be an exciting new challenge. Moving may be stressful for very young school-age children because it can interrupt the normal process of children separating from their parents and transferring their allegiance from home to school. At the other end of the spectrum, children over age 11 often find moving difficult because they are

relying increasingly on their peers in order to work towards independence from their parents, and leaving old friends to make new ones is hard.

❐ *The quality of your relationship with your child.* Supportive parenting is always important, but it is particularly necessary when you are about to move or have just moved to a new community and school. This is when you need to strengthen your family ties by spending extra time together as a family, and to be available for your young child as well as your adolescent to turn to you for help and support. A move means that the emotional support your children may have had outside your family will be gone, making family relationships that much more important. Adjusting socially in school is that much easier when your child has a stable home life. A stable foundation may also mean that adolescents will be less tempted to look for peer acceptance by experimenting with drugs and alcohol.

❐ *The frequency of your moves.* Children who have a "rest period" between moves do much better at adjusting than those who move constantly, because they at least have time to establish a network of friends. Experts agree that most children need between 6 and 18 months to recover their equilibrium after a move. Also, the more times a family moves, the more difficult a child may eventually find it to adjust to school. A recent study shows that children in families who moved three or more times are at greater risk for emotional, behavioral, and school problems than children who never moved. Those who only moved once or twice were not at significantly greater risk.

Not all moves involve huge geographical distances; sometimes it just means a move across town and a new school in the same district. For many children making this kind of move, the adjustment is much smaller because they won't face significant academic changes. For others, difficulties may arise because they don't really have to disconnect from old friendships, and sometimes that can get in the way of really becoming immersed in the new school and finding new friends. There's no reliable way to tell exactly how a short move like this will affect your child, but it may be helpful if you can place the emphasis on your child finding his place in the new school rather than strictly on maintaining old friendships.

WHEN SHOULD I BE CONCERNED?

Stress is part of life for everyone. Positive events such as graduations and vacations can be stressful, just as what we generally perceive as negative events can be. So even if you see your family's move as a positive thing, it may be stressful to your child.

A little stress handled with the help of a competent adult can teach a child about coping skills. But a lot of stress can take a toll on your child's emotional, physical, and academic life. You should be concerned if your child:

❏ shows serious academic difficulties in anticipation of a move, unlike those you've seen before. (See Stress, Depression.) It's easy to assume all the difficulties associated with moving will occur after the move, but many children (and their parents) feel the greatest stress before the move. You and your child might benefit from help from the school psychologist before you physically relocate.
❏ shows serious academic difficulties after a move.
❏ becomes unusually aggressive, or begins having temper tantrums not appropriate for his age. (See Anger Control.)

❏ is excessively fearful of things that never used to frighten him, (see Fears), or of school (see School Phobia).
❏ is uncharacteristically forgetful, impatient, withdrawn, or unfocused.
❏ seems generally physically run-down, and complains of frequent colds or flu, or phantom aches and pains, or shows significant weight gain or loss, or sleep interruptions.

Adolescents who are having difficulty adjusting academically or socially can easily become depressed (see Depression), which in turn can lead to low self-esteem (see Self-Esteem) and substance abuse.

And you should be concerned if your child is still having significant difficulties, academically or socially, after about 6 months at the new school.

WHAT CAN I DO TO HELP?

The timing of a move isn't always yours to determine, but if possible, consider the pros and cons of moving at different times of the year. For example:

❏ *For summer moves, the pros are:*

   ❏ You don't have to interrupt your child's academic year.
   ❏ You may have more time to complete the move, because you and your child won't have school activities taking you away from packing or settling into your new life.
   ❏ You and your child will have time to adjust to life in a new community before school starts by doing things like visiting the school.

❏ *For summer moves, the con is:*

   ❏ If there are not a lot of children living nearby, your child may have a hard time making new friends right away.

❏ For a school-year move, the pros are:

❏ Your child will immediately have a new peer group.

❏ A new student in a new school gets a lot of positive attention, with other children vying for his friendship.

❏ Your child might be thrilled to leave a less-than-perfect situation in a class where he doesn't like the teacher, kids pick on him, etc.

❏ For a school-year move, the con is:

❏ The sudden change in academic structure might be a difficult transition for some children.

As much as possible, prepare your child for his new school well before the day you move. (See the Getting Ready to Move checklist in the box below.) Discuss details of the move early and often, in a positive way, and write to the principal of the new school and to the main district office to get information about the school beforehand. When you arrive in your new community, visit the school with your youngster before his first day.

When you are moving in the middle of a school year, for your elementary-age child you can also:

❏ Ask the old school to send your child's health and academic records to the new school in plenty of time so that the new principal and teacher can be familiar with your child's needs before she arrives.

❏ Discuss the initial class placement with your child's new teacher before your child's first day to be sure it is appropriate.

❏ Request that the teacher or other playground staff observe your child during unstructured times such as lunch and recess when newcomers are most likely to feel—or to be—left out.

❏ Suggest that the teacher assign a classmate "buddy" to help your child become familiar with school rules and to help her to meet other children.

❏ Ask the teacher if she is comfortable not requiring your child to complete all assignments for the first week or two. Youngsters who are undergoing the stress of moving may find that a significant portion of their mental energy is going into feeling sad about friends they left, or anxious about gaining new ones.

❏ Keep in mind that teaching styles vary, and your child may take some time to adjust to the way they do things in her new school.

When you are moving during the summer, you can also use this checklist of things to do before you move:

❏ Contact the principal at your old school to arrange to have your child's health and academic records sent in time for the new school year.

❏ Discuss your child's class placement with the principal at the new school during the summer.

❏ Make time to visit the new school before school starts. Walk through the entire building so your child is familiar with the layout. Get to know the school secretary, who can be extremely helpful to you during the school year, and may be a welcome familiar face to your child too, once school starts. For a younger child, make more than one visit because their memory is not likely to be as good as that of an older child.

❏ Make an appointment with the principal to talk about your child's teacher and room assignment. Then you can show your child exactly where she will be in the building and how she'll get from there to the cafeteria, out to recess, to the bathrooms, and to the office.

❏ Check with the school secretary or principal

Getting Ready to Move

DOCUMENTS TO COLLECT AND SEND TO THE NEW SCHOOL

—— All basic school records such as grades, attendance, health, group achievement scores, notices of awards. These require your written permission to send and will not be sent automatically, so you must request that they be.

—— Special information in limited-access files such as counselor's summaries, special educational records, psychologist's reports. Because these records are confidential, you will have to fill out some special forms and permissions in order for these to be sent.

—— Comments you request from teachers to supplement report card grades, such as special teaching strategies or rewards that work well for your child.

WRITE TO NEW SCHOOL FOR INFORMATION—QUESTIONS TO ASK

—— Overall structure and philosophy of the school, and whether they have traditional or open classrooms. Ask also about class size, attendance and discipline policies, availability of extracurricular activities, sports programs, learning resources such as computer labs, whether they have shop or home economics facilities and before- or after-school child care.

—— The curriculum/book series your child will most likely be in; whether students are taught by a phonics or whole-language approach (see Reading—and Writing and 'Rithmetic), and whether inventive or traditional spelling is accepted. Check with current teacher about implications for your child if there are changes in these areas.

THINGS TO DO AT OLD SCHOOL

—— Collect names and addresses of classmates.

—— Arrange with teacher for a few special friends of your child to write a letter to your child she'll receive soon after arriving at her new town.

—— Be sure class has your new address.

—— Ask the teacher to write a short personal note to the new teacher pointing out your child's academic strengths.

THINGS TO DO AT HOME

—— Point out to your child that this is one of many school transitions they will need to make. Even if they never made a geographical move, they would change schools after elementary school, middle school, and again after high school.

—— Purchase a spiral notebook to be a diary. Encourage your young child to write or draw pictures documenting the move.

—— Give your older child a few blank cassette tapes. Encourage her to record special songs, or thoughts and feelings about changing schools.

If you use either of these last two ideas, you should monitor what your child writes or records. If her comments are either positive or ambivalent, that's normal. But if they are all negative, it's a sign she needs more support, and you should strongly consider discontinuing that activity until you have a chance to talk with the school psychologist.

Getting Ready to Move (cont.)

THINGS TO DO AT THE NEW SCHOOL

—— Meet with the new teacher(s) before your child begins school.

—— Ask that your young child have a "buddy" assigned.

—— For your older child, find out about youth groups or contacts for extracurricular activities and sports teams. Collect more than one or two, so he can make a choice of activities.

to see if there are any summer programs at the school your child could participate in.

❐ Follow up with the principal to be sure your child's records from the old school have arrived.

With all you have to do to prepare for a family move, the following checklist may help you to prepare you and your children to change schools:

All of these tips can help you and your child get ready for a move. But what do you do when you have moved, and your child isn't adjusting as well as you'd like? Here are some ideas you can try:

1 If your child seems depressed, withdrawn, or in general is refusing to get involved in her new school and keeps longing for the old school, you can:

a talk with her so she can express her feelings of depression, frustration, sadness over the move. But then remind her that there is no going back, so you'll all make the best of it. Remind her, too, that it's unrealistic for her to think that continuing to be sad will make you all move back to your previous home.

b offer to help your child connect with others by going with her to places like the local video arcade, or a community pool.

c model for her—that is, show her through your actions, how you've had to deal with similar issues: no old friends, everything feels

different, don't know where anything is in the grocery story so that it all takes more time, etc. Let her know what you're doing to deal with this.

It may be that only time will help your child adjust to your new home; don't rush the process. You may have to live with your child being a little down for up to six months. If you don't see any change in that amount of time, you might think about talking with the school psychologist. (See Depression.)

At school, you can talk with the teacher about making an effort to engage your child in classroom activities, such as telling about what life was like in the town you came from as part of a geography lesson, for example. You can also play up special skills your child has, such as ability on a musical instrument, in dance, or in sports, and be sure she gets involved in those, and that she gets recognition from classmates and teacher.

2 If your child is primarily angry, resentful, and acting out:

a you'll need to make the point, no doubt many times over, to her that the move is permanent, and her behavior will not cause a change.

b see Stress for a checklist to use with your child in helping her to see which strategies she is using, and which would work better.

c See the chapter on Anger Control

At school, they will no doubt try to be sympathetic to your child's plight as the new kid for a time. In addition, they may recommend short-term counseling with the school psychologist to help your child get in touch with the real source of her anger and ease the transition.

WHAT WILL A PROFESSIONAL DO?

In areas where there are a lot of children moving in and out of the district each year, some schools have on-going programs to help children adjust to moving. They meet weekly for a half-hour to an hour to discuss common problems about coping, and friendships are often forged among participants. Programs like Summer Visitation—which gives students a chance to tour the school building, meeting staff and faculty along with other new families—are extremely helpful, as are peer counseling programs that train students to help new students assimilate. Contact the school psychologist or the counseling office at the new school to see if they have ongoing programs such as these. Even without an ongoing program, your school psychologist may offer helpful tips on smoothing the way for your child that worked well for other children at this school, or he may be able to steer you to other community resources.

If not, and if your child's academic performance is suffering for more than about six months either during the period before a move or after a move, the school psychologist may be able to work with your child individu-ally, or develop a support group for new children. In addition, he can evaluate your child to see if other academic problems have developed, or with your child's teacher to develop classroom strategies to help your child work better within the classroom routine.

More specifically, depending on the symptoms your child is showing, the school psychologist might engage your child in short-term counseling about the move, encouraging her to talk about the feelings she has about moving, missing old friends, connecting with new ones, etc. The psychologist may also:

❏ help her evaluate the strategies she's using to cope

❏ help her to see that unproductive measures, such as anger, won't solve the problem and may worsen it

❏ try to figure out if there is another issue involved that must be specifically addressed—for example, if your child had a mild learning disability that went unrecognized at the previous school and is causing problems now; or if your child was mildly depressed before, and the move only made it more apparent.

See also:

❏ Anger Control
❏ Depression
❏ Divorce
❏ Fears
❏ School Phobia
❏ Self-Esteem

Further Reading

Nida, P. C. & Heller, W. M. *The Teenager's Survival Guide to Moving.* New York: Atheneum, 1985.

C H A P T E R   2 9

Nervous Habits

"Jerome is about to enter kindergarten and he still sucks his thumb sometimes. I'm worried that it's abnormal to still be doing that. But more than that, I'm worried that other kids will make fun of him if they see him doing it."

"Rita has always bitten her fingernails, but now that she's in high school, on some fingers they are almost completely gone. I've tried everything: from offering her money to quit, to offering her a manicure at the beauty shop each week. She says she can't stop because she does it unconsciously."

It's not unheard-of that a five-year-old still sucks his thumb. And certainly there are plenty of people who bite their fingernails, or pull their hair, grind their teeth, or have some other kind of habit such as pencil tapping, shoulder shrugging, or throat clearing.

These may or may not constitute a major problem for your child. But any one of them can be annoying for you to live with and, eventually, may be embarrassing for your child. Either of those is a good enough reason to figure out what to do about your child's nervous habits.

WHAT WE KNOW NOW

Nervous habits, or *maladaptive habits* as psychologists call them, are common. While only thumbsucking, nail biting, and tics are considered developmentally normal, or just a part of growing up for many children, the others are not generally thought of as serious problems. (For an exception, see box below on Tics and Tourette Syndrome.)

Thumbsucking often starts in infancy between about 4 and 10 months of age, peaks between 3 and 4 years of age, and usually disappears around the end of the fourth year.

About half of all children will suck their thumbs or fingers.

Nail biting can begin at about age 4, and it usually peaks around ages 10 to 13. Fifty to 60 percent of all children bite their nails at some time. After adolescence, the incidence falls off to about 10 to 20 percent, which continues through the adult years.

Surveys done by the American Psychiatric Association show that 12 to 24 percent of school children have a history of tics. What most of them have had is called a *mild transient tic disorder*, which lasts anywhere from a month to a year and usually disappears on its own. The most common transient tics are eye blinking and other kinds of facial tics such as lip biting.

The table below, developed by Bruce Pray, Jr., of the Kansas Unified School District and Jack J. Kramer of the University of Nebraska, shows six common nervous habits and their consequences.

The only one of these habits which could be considered abnormal at any age is hair pulling. If your child has been doing this for more than two weeks, you should get help from your family physician or from the school

Nervous Habits

HABIT	BEHAVIOR	CONSEQUENCE
Thumbsucking	Sucking finger(s)	Possible dental and/or thumb problems.
Nail biting/picking	Biting or picking at nails	Partial or complete absence of nails.
Hair pulling	Removing body hair by pulling, breaking or rubbing.	Damaged hair follicles, bald spots
Tooth grinding	Nonfunctional gnashing, grinding, clenching, or clicking of teeth	Abnormal wear to teeth, facial pain, loose teeth, dental problems
Motor tics	Recurrent, repetitive, rapid movements	No physical effect except over-strong muscle in affected area.
Self-destructive oral habits	Biting, chewing, sucking, licking or pushing of cheeks, tongue, lips, teeth, or palate.	Damage to soft mouth tissue, loose teeth, soreness, pain, swelling, dental problems.

psychologist because it can be an indication of a more serious problem and has more immediate and significant physical repercussions.

In almost all cases, nervous habits are the result of your child's struggling to deal with some kind of stressor. If it's possible to remove the stressor, then the habit often disappears. But it's not always possible to remove the stressor; your child will still have to take tests at school, 'for example, even though they make her nervous. Instead, you can focus on helping your child get rid of the habit with a technique called Habit Reversal, described in the next section, and then teach her how to deal with stress better. (See Stress.)

WHEN SHOULD I BE CONCERNED?

Consider the following questions as you decide whether your child's nervous habit is something to be concerned about, keeping in mind too, how common some of these habits are—not everyone has a problem just because they have a habit. Your primary criteria will be the degree of the medical, personal, and/or social problem your child's habit is causing. Try to consider together what you know about each of these items as you decide if your child's habit is a problem.

1 How chronic is the problem? If your child is "constantly" doing the habit and cannot seem to control it very well, you should be concerned. On the other hand, if your five-year old sucks her thumb only at night as she's falling asleep, you might not be concerned.

You should also be concerned if interrupting your child as she's doing the habit makes

What to Do Instead

NERVOUS HABIT	COMPETING EXERCISE
Thumbsucking	Clenching fists
Fingernail biting	Grasping objects
Eyelash plucking	Grasping objects
Head shaking, or jerking	Tense neck
Shoulder jerking	Depress shoulders

her angry or really upsets her, and she then immediately returns to the habit.

2 How serious or potentially serious are the physical problems the habit is causing? If the habit is creating physical problems, then you should be concerned: for example, with nail biting, if your child has made the skin around her nails bleed and there is a chance of infection and/or there is an infection; or with thumbsucking, if your child has sucked her thumb or finger so raw that there is a chance of infection, and/or there is an infection. You should also be concerned if the dentist tells you your child is developing a serious dental problem as a result of thumb or finger sucking.

3 How noticeable and serious are the social consequences of the habit? How much teasing does your child receive; how does your child respond to the teasing? You should be concerned if your child receives enough teasing to make her feel angry, withdrawn, frustrated, or embarrassed enough to tell you or her teacher about it.

WHAT CAN I DO TO HELP?

One of the most effective approaches was developed by N. H. Azrin and R. G. Nunn, which they wrote about in a book called *Habit Control in a Day*

(Simon & Schuster, 1977.) The method is called *Habit Reversal* and uses several specific steps to help your child break a nervous habit. Although it is fairly simple, a child must be about 6 or 7 years old before being able to participate in the plan. You should read through the plan first, then sit down with your child and spend some time going over the plan and deciding how you (and your child) will follow each of the steps. Be sure your child is willing to do this.

The steps for Habit Reversal are:

1 *Inconvenience Review:* List with your child the difficulties caused by the habit. Why would your child want to eliminate the habit? In which situations has the habit caused problems?

2 *Awareness Training/Habit Promoting Situations:* Noticing when a habit occurs and the situations in which it occurs are the first steps toward controlling the habit. You might make two charts with your child: one for you and one for her, to keep track of when and where you see her doing the habit, and when and where she realizes she's doing the habit. Compare charts after five days or a week.

3 *Competing Reaction:* This is key to habit reversal. In order to stop the habit, you and your child decide on something she will do when she catches herself doing the habit. It must be a behavior that can be maintained for several minutes without appearing unusual to others, does not interfere with normal activities, and increases self-awareness of the habit. The table above, developed by Azrin and Nunn, lists some ideas.

4 *Corrective and Preventive Reaction:* After learning the competing reaction, have your child use it to interrupt the habit or prevent its occurence in the first place.

5 *Associated Behavior:* Work with your child to identify the behavior that comes right before the habit, and use the competing reaction to stop this associated behavior. For example, perhaps you and your child noticed that she always brushed her hair back just before she put her thumb in her mouth—that's the associated behavior.

6 *Relaxation Training:* There are several relaxation methods to choose from. See Stress for an explanation of one.

7 *Social Support:* This support, encouragement, and praise for your child's efforts can come from you or a trusted buddy. (See Case Study I: Caitlin.)

8 *Practice:* Have your child practice the competing reaction daily until it becomes routine behavior. Also, have her rehearse the competing response while imagining the habit-promoting situations.

9 *Record:* Keep a daily record of the frequency of the habit so you and your child can see how much progress she's made.

WHAT WILL A PROFESSIONAL DO?

The school psychologist will help you set up a Habit Reversal plan like the one described above and in Caitlin's case study. He may also help you decide whether medical intervention

Case Study: Caitlin

Shortly after the beginning of the fourth grade, Caitlin inexplicably developed the habit of making a sound in class that her teacher described as somewhere between a snort and a grunt. She was a fairly heavy girl to begin with, and when her classmates began calling her "Miss Piggy," the teacher contacted the school psychologist and Caitlin's parents.

The school psychologist met with Caitlin and her parents, and they all agreed to follow the Habit Reversal plan. For the social support part of the plan, the school psychologist had Caitlin choose a "buddy" from her class to help her. The teacher changed the classroom seating plan so the buddy and Caitlin sat together. Then, every time the buddy heard Caitlin begin the sound, she would give her friend a secret "signal," so Caitlin could stop. The competing behavior Caitlin practiced was quiet, slow, rhythmic breathing through her mouth for about 10 seconds so she couldn't make the nasal sound.

Together, Caitlin and her buddy charted Caitlin's progress. In about three weeks, the sound-making was gone.

is necessary, and he may try to identify which stressors may be causing the problem.

In doing that, the school psychologist will likely interview you to see if there have been any recent changes in your home life, a special stress you may be dealing with, or medical factors in your child's life that may be

Tics and Tourette's Syndrome

Tics are a slight exception to other nervous habits because they are involuntary. A tic is a sudden, rapid, recurrent, stereotyped, and involuntary motor movement or vocalization. It is:

❑ experienced as irresistible, but can be suppressed by your child if he concentrates on doing so

❑ worsened during periods of stress; lessened or disappears when your child is very absorbed in some activity

❑ usually is markedly diminished or nonexistent during sleep.

Common forms of motor tics are eye blinking, neck jerking, coughing, and shoulder shrugging. Common vocal tics are throat clearing, grunting, sniffing, or snorting.

Some tics become very complex. Rather than being a simple sudden movement, they have several parts, as in certain facial gestures, grooming behaviors, or saying certain phrases over and over.

In addition to trying to help your child eliminate tics and other nervous habits, the school psychologist may assess a complex tic such as repeated hand washing to see if it is, rather, a compulsion, which is associated with anxiety.

Tourette's Syndrome is a neurological disorder characterized by multiple motor tics and one or more vocal tics that may occur together or separately. Because the location, frequency, complexity, and severity of the tics change over time, the syndrome is often difficult to diagnose. The tics can completely disappear and reappear later. Although this syndrome is seen in children, it usually doesn't develop until after the age of 5 or 6, and it can last a lifetime.

The kinds of tics associated with Tourette's Syndrome are:

❑ *Simple motor:* Eye blinking, facial twitching, tooth clicking, grimacing, shoulder shrugs, kicks.

❑ *Complex motor:* Sustained "looks," face/hand gestures, bending, throwing. These are more ritualistic and of longer duration than simple motor tics.

❑ *Simple phonic* (also called *vocal tics*): Barking, sniffing, throat clearing, spitting, grunting.

❑ *Complex phonic* (also called *vocal* or *verbal tics*): Syllables, words, phrases such as "How about it," repeating one's own or someone else's words, aggressive utterances, obscenities (which are actually exhibited by only a minority of people with Tourette's Syndrome).

Medication and behavior therapies are the approaches most often taken for children and adults with Tourette's Syndrome.

Case Study: Luke

Luke became extremely nervous about being on the school bus for the ride home after a fight on the bus between two other boys broke out right in front of him. Luke wasn't hurt, but the fight between two older and very much bigger boys was close enough to him that Luke's favorite lunch box was smashed in the melee.

Soon after that, Luke began twisting his hair out of nervousness, so much so that he actually began to pull out small amounts of hair. Others kids noticed this and began teasing him.

Luke's parents asked the school psychologist to intervene, and he met with Luke to thoroughly review the situation. Together they set up this competing response: whenever he noticed himself beginning to pull on his hair, he tightly squeezed his hands together and said to himself, "Ggggrrrrr" to express the anger he felt that the other boys drove him to this. Luke and the school psychologist rehearsed this together, and Luke and his parents did, too.

Then, in counseling, Luke was asked to pay close attention and describe, in great detail, what was going on in the bus when he had to use the technique. It required a lot of concentration to pay attention that closely, and that concentration interrupted the sequence of hair pulling. It also pointed out to Luke that often he began pulling when in fact there was nothing happening on the bus that could lead to another fight.

After about a month, Luke had stopped pulling on his hair and was no longer frightened of the trip home on the bus.

---

contributing. He may use some personality inventories to assess your child's degree of stress or anxiety, such as the Children's Manifest Anxiety Scale, or projective techniques such as the Roberts Apperception Tests for Children, figure drawings or sentence completion tasks. (See Appendix D, Samples from Tests and Assessments, Evaluation and Testing, in Part I.)

If you and your child are using the Habit Reversal plan, if necessary the school psychol-ogist will also help your child's teacher to participate, and perhaps train the teacher to use "cueing," as Caitlin's buddy did, to let your child know when he's doing the habit.

See also:

❏ Anxiety
❏ Appendix D, Samples from Tests and Assessments
❏ Evaluation and Testing, in Part I
❏ Stress

Further Reading

Heitler, S. *David Decided: No More Thumbsucking.* New York: Avon Books, 1993.

CHAPTER 30

Organization

"Tyrone's biggest challenge so far in middle school has been to remember his schedule. He's always had a hard time with directions and keeping times and dates in his head. But now that he's expected to be in a different room every hour of the day, he's really struggling."

A good part of being an effective student in school—and of being effective in life—requires that a person be able to organize things: books, assignments, class notes, types of information, and time, to name a few.

Children who have trouble with organization can be at a distinct disadvantage in school, with some having a serious enough problem to significantly affect their learning.

It's important for parents to understand what constitutes a problem, and what does not, when their child is disorganized. And it's important that parents see the difference between motivation and organization issues. For a child who can't organize well, it's not necessarily initially a matter of motivation, it's just that the child doesn't know where to begin, what to do next, and what to put where. For a child like this, the world can be unpredictable and confusing. A parent who understands can help that child learn to make sense of his confusing world.

WHAT WE KNOW NOW

When your child behaves in an organized manner, she is structuring and ordering objects, procedures, information, and communication in a meaningful way. For example, when she reads she organizes letters, sounds, and meanings into words and sentences that make sense. In math, she sees the pattern of a progression of numbers in order to predict the next number. And, in science, she sees that the tasks that make up an experiment must occur in a particular order to obtain the expected results.

She also shows an understanding of organization when she hangs her blouses in one area of her closet and her skirts in another, and when she puts books on the shelf and stuffed animals on the bed as she picks up her room.

An organized child sees an order or a pattern with relative ease. It makes sense to her that the stuffed animals go in one place and the skirts go in another. But to a child who has a problem with organization, that pattern isn't so apparent. For her, information—whether it's visual information about the state of her bedroom or whether it's the numbers on the page of her math assignment—defies sorting, categorizing, or classifying. And if she can't sort information and "put it away" in an appropriate place in her memory, she can't retrieve it for later use, the same as she would be unlikely to find her stuffed animal easily if she put it on a hanger in her closet instead of on the bed.

Exactly why some children have a problem with organization isn't clear to psychologists, but research has offered some clues. Lack of organization skills may be related to:

❒ *Language development*—especially conceptual skills—because organization, like language, is actually an intellectual way of classifying things. (See Language Development.)

❒ *A child's level of anxiety*, which can compound organization problems as well as be a result of it. (See Anxiety.)

❒ *A lack of good role models.* Children rarely invent their methods of organizing. They are more likely to have incorporated strategies and techniques they've seen teachers and parents use.

❒ *A lack of structure.* Most children need at least some degree of structure at home in order to achieve an understanding of order, predictability, and routine. Structure contributes to a feeling of security and stability, which also help in the development of organization.

❒ *Other psychological problems.* Disorganized thinking, in a mild form, can be an indication that your child is under unusual stress, is depressed, has ADHD, or has a motivation problem. (See Stress, Depression, ADHD, or Motivation.) In more extreme, and rare, cases disorganized thinking can be a sign of serious psychologocial problems such as organic brain disorders or schizophrenia.

WHEN SHOULD I BE CONCERNED?

A high degree of organization is a big deal to some parents, and not such a big deal to others, depending on personal habits, preferences, values, and resulting expectations. Think about your expectations for your child and then about your child's temperament. For some children, a high level of organization will never be a priority because it is not in their nature for it

to be. Try to examine if your concern for your child's level of organization is the result of a personality difference between the two of you, or a real problem for your child.

Lack of organization is a problem for a child if the disorganization threatens the child's effective progress in school. Disorganization on several levels—from personal tidiness to inability to think through the steps of a report—should be pronounced, extensive, and enduring before you become concerned. Ask yourself:

❒ Does the disorganization cause significant problems in all academic areas? If only in one area, there is likely another issue at work rather than a pervasive disorganization problem. (See Language Development, Reading—and Writing and 'Rithmetic, Study Skills.)

❒ Is promotion to the next grade in jeopardy? (See Grade Retention.)

❒ Is your youngster showing signs of disorganization even outside of school because of an inability to keep in mind schedules, routines, and the correct order of basic tasks?

If you can answer yes to two out of three of these questions, you should be concerned about your child's ability to organize.

Be careful though, about jumping to conclusions. Disorganization may be difficult to identify for at least two reasons: it can be the result of other factors such as depression, which may be more important to address first, and it can look like other problems, such as a motivation problem, for which it is often mistaken. (See Motivation, Depression.)

There are academic and social behaviors that are often shared by children who have a problem with organization. Some of these behaviors are that the students:

❒ keep an extremely messy workspace

❑ lose school books, assignments, homework papers regularly

❑ have a hard time sustaining attention in class

❑ have a hard time recalling the daily schedule or weekly routine

❑ depend on others for structure and cues

❑ manage their time poorly

❑ have difficulty following the sequence of events in a story

❑ seem clumsy or generally confused

❑ turn in spatially disorganized paperwork, having trouble keeping numbers in a column or keeping words from running into one another or floating out of order.

In language and academics, they may also:

❑ have a hard time finding the right word to express themselves

❑ tell stories or jokes in the wrong sequence

❑ be unable to make a point when talking with others

❑ have difficulty following directions in sequence

❑ have difficulty in using references such as the dictionary or telephone book because they can't discern the order in which items are likely to appear in them

You can also go over your child's development to see if she has had a history of disorganization that you might not have labeled that way, but which has since shown up in school. Go over this checklist to spark your thinking:

▪ Can your young child get dressed with clothes put on the right way? (For preschoolers, it's normal to get clothes switched around).

▪ Did your child naturally fall into feeding and sleeping routines in infancy?

▪ Did your child have at least a few words he could speak by age 2?

▪ Was your child's motor development in learning to walk relatively smooth?

▪ Did your child learn to ride a bicycle without training wheels before age 6? Was it a particularly arduous task?

▪ Does your child have a sense of time and how long things last? Is there a sense of the order of the day's events or the weekly routine? Does your child anticipate meals, chores, bedtime, etc.?

If you answer No to about half of these questions, you should be concerned about your child's level of organization.

In the face of all this, if you are still uncertain whether to be concerned about your child's level of disorganization, it never hurts to schedule a consultation with the school psychologist.

WHAT CAN I DO TO HELP?

Now that you've looked so closely at whether or not your child has an organization problem, you should have some idea of where her organizational skills fall short. Your overall approach will be to help her create systems, strategies, routines, and checklists to bridge those gaps.

By doing this, you will also be defining further the nature and the extent of your child's problem with organization. The information you gain from doing this and the activities in this section will be helpful not only to you, but to the teacher and the school psychologist who can use it to help further refine these activities to fit your child.

Use these guidelines to decide where to start. If your child is an adolescent, do this in conjunction with him. For a younger child, include her in as much of the process as is possible and reasonable. Think and talk about:

❏ which area of disorganization is most upsetting to your child, to the teacher, and to you

❏ which area interferes most with daily living

❏ which area interferes most with academic objectives

❏ which area would be easiest to tackle first so that the rewards for organizing come quickly

Suppose you and your child decide that working on a term paper or report is the most pressing need. Write down and work with him on the following steps to organizing a task. They apply to everything from preparing for a report to applying for a driver's license.

STEPS TO ORGANIZING A TASK

1 Brainstorm all the steps you think you'll need to complete the task.
2 Write them down.
3 Put them in the order you think they'll need to be in.
4 Choose the step that seems to come first.
5 Compare each other step with that one, one at a time, to find which comes second, and so on.

This task organizer is helpful because it allows the youngster to compare one step at a time with one other step so as to put the steps in the correct order, instead of seeing a whole group of steps and not knowing where to start.

For example, if your youngster was assigned to choose a Native American tribe and describe their daily life, here's how the steps might work out:

1 Brainstorm. The order will be random, for example:

❏ get books

❏ go to the public library

❏ pick one aspect to start with

❏ determine how long the paper has to be

❏ go to the school library

❏ choose a tribe

❏ find picture to go with report

❏ get some good typing paper

❏ find out if pictures are needed for report

2 Write these down.
3 Put them in order. You can start by simply assigning a number to each as you review the list, like this:

❏ get books (3)

❏ go to the public library (1)

❏ pick one aspect to start with (2)

4 Choose steps and compare them. At first glance, your child might think heading off to the libary is the first step. Once he's been through the whole list, he might find that being sure about all the assignment entails should come first. You don't have to know the order of the steps to begin with; it's ok to change your mind and reorder them many times until the order seems workable. Also point out to your child how this same method can work for other organizing tasks in addition to the one at hand.

Once that method seems clear to your child, you can use the following method for other kinds of projects, such as cooking or science lab projects.

ORGANIZING TO ACCOMPLISH A PROJECT

1 Read the directions.
2 List all supplies and materials mentioned in the directions, then gather them to your work area.

3 *Gather* all the utensils and tools needed to handle those supplies and materials.

4 *Preplan* the procedure, using Steps to Organizing a Task.

Another way to help your child is to help him organize his belongings so that he's not living in chaos. Have him make an organizational "blueprint" or plan for his desk at school and for his room at home. Have your child draw a map of his desk from a bird's-eye view, then work with him on listing all the items that need to be in the desk, containers that could hold them individually, and where the items and containers will go. Some teachers will do a plan like this as a class project for all the students, and each child can keep the plan inside a notebook or taped to the inside of the desk lid as a clean-up guide.

You can do the same at home with a map of your child's room. Label baskets, bins, shelves, or crates you use so your child can easily figure out where things go.

Other ideas you can encourage and explain to your child as they come up are:

- Break big jobs into small segments. Take any task one small step at a time to help see which step should come first, and to make accomplishing it easier. For example, if the task you've assigned your child is to clean his room, breaking it down might mean starting with just one area, such as his desk. Help him develop a plan: put everything on the desk onto his bed temporarily; open and clean the desk (or clean out drawers and top of desk), rearrange needed items on and in desk, get rid of or store elsewhere other items until the bed is clear. You can translate this method to school tasks.
- Categorize and sort items or ideas to help organize them. In picking up his room, for example, encourage your child to think of dealing cards, and pick up one item from the pile on the floor, and then "deal" it into the appropriate bin or basket. The same can be done with sorting class notes: "deal" them into appropriate category piles for lab notes, study notes, lecture notes, etc.
- Developing routines helps your child relate the parts (activities in a daily schedule) to the whole (an entire week). Talk about how the pieces make up the whole. Write down the daily routine on a large family calendar as a reminder. Then ask your child to fit changes in the routine (birthday parties, soccer games, dentist appointments) into their proper place on the family calendar. Not only will this help your child organize the changes that come up, but as your child becomes more aware of routines, he can develop a greater sense of structure and predictability.
- Provide opportunities for decision making to encourage self-reliance and self-confidence in your child's understanding of his ability to organize himself. Have your young child choose one of two options of how she will spend an hour's free time after school; an older child could be given more options. Have her estimate how long each activity will take, or time an activity with a kitchen timer to help her develop a sense of the passage of time and how she uses and can plan her time.
- Use checklists. For adolescents (and certainly many adults), checklists are one way to be sure you haven't forgotten something, or that you are completing tasks in the proper order. You can make a checklist for your younger child, too, perhaps of schoolbag items she always seems to forget. For young nonreaders, you can make a picture list, drawing such items as a toothbrush and a bed to be sure she remembers things she needs to do before

school—without so much reminding from you.

Some rules of thumb to impress upon your child as you work with her on organizing any kind of task are:

- Approach any job systematically, noting the steps needed to finish, and then not moving from one step to the next until that step is finished.
- Always take a step, no matter how small, toward making progress. Sometimes youngsters with organization problems get stuck on one step because they're unsure of what comes next. Assure your child that even a tiny step can help bring her closer to finishing the task.
- Never leave a task without first figuring out and writing down the step that comes next. It will make it easier to come back to the task.
- If your child can't figure out what the next step needs to be, have her figure out instead what information she needs in order to determine the next step, and write that down.

WHAT WILL A PROFESSIONAL DO?

For most children with mild organization problems, the school psychologist can be available to you and your child's teacher to help with organizational ideas like those in the previous section to use at home and in the classroom.

If disorganization has seriously affected your child's academics, you or the teacher can request an assessment from the school psychologist. She may want to look over the standard intellectual and academic achievement tests most schools give. While these don't measure organization directly, they require organization of ideas to complete well. She will also most likely want to interview you and your child,

---

What's for Dinner?

One fun way to help your child learn about organized thinking is to enlist his help in planning family dinners once in a while, using the task organizing methods in this section. Start by asking, "What do you want to eat this week?" and brainstorm with your child which dishes sound good, given family tastes, nutrition, the weather, your budget, etc. Then:

❏ Put the dishes in order for each day of the week, figuring out which days are too busy for complicated meals.
❏ Check recipes for each dish; compare ingredients with what you have.
❏ Make a list of what you need.
❏ Then, take him grocery shopping with you.
❏ Adapt the process to fit your needs, and point out to your child along the way how this is similar to planning a school report or a science project.
You can involve him in the cooking of some of the meals, too, using the steps in Organizing to Accomplish a Project.

---

observe your child in the classroom, and gather from the teacher impressions of your child's ability to organize thoughts and material.

The school psychologist will work with this information to understand the nature of your child's organization problems and to rule out other factors, such as depression or motivation issues, as explained earlier.

Once she has a clear understanding of the level of your child's organization problems and their cause, she can devise activities for your child like those explained under What Can I Do To Help?

If the interventions proposed by the school psychologist do not seem to be working, even after several sincere attempts, she may recommend a much more complete evaluation to understand the problem more fully. In some cases, the disorganization may be a sign of a more serious problem. A correct diag-nosis means that an effective intervention can be planned.

See also:

❏ Depression
❏ Learning Disabilities
❏ Motivation
❏ Stress
❏ Study Skills

C H A P T E R   3 1

Perfectionism

"I'm finally at my wit's end with Marsha. I can't take another night and morning of her going over and over her homework, changing things, erasing, redoing, wanting a better pencil or pen, better paper to write on, you name it. And after all the effort she puts into her homework, she always complains that she's done an awful job!"

"Curt is driving both us and his teacher crazy. Nothing is ever good enough; there's a problem with everything he does. To hear him talk, he's flunking out. But, in fact, he's getting straight A's! He says the grades mean nothing, that the standards aren't high enough at this school."

Most parents want their children to try hard and to be careful with their school work, to turn in tidy, accurate papers, even to get that perfect score on the spelling test.

But when a child's concern with doing well in school goes from effort to a compulsion for doing everything perfectly, the behavior can be not only hard to live with, but frustrating and—in some cases—destructive for your child.

Understanding perfectionism and how it gets started can help you keep your child's school efforts in proper perspective.

WHAT WE KNOW NOW

Perfectionism is sometimes honored in our culture as an admirable attribute. People who have their perfectionist tendencies in perspective derive a very real sense of pleasure from a job done perfectly, even if the effort to do that has been enormous. And, perfectionists with perspective know when to say when: they are able to be less than perfect if they see the situation just will not permit the time or the effort

to do a job exactly the way they might like to.

On the other hand, out-of-control perfectionists will pursue excellence to an unhealthy extreme. They strive toward unrealistic goals and measure their entire worth in terms of how perfectly they meet the standards they assign themselves.

Children who are perfectionists often seem bothered by not meeting their own standards in their schoolwork. They can seem somewhat glum and lacking in spontaneity, and sometimes appear to be carrying around a big personal burden, most likely because, in a sense, they are. Their tendency to be meticulously organized, wanting things always to be a particular way, and their skepticism of everything can make life itself a burden. Jamie, for example, would come home from a school field trip to the art museum complaining that the trip wasn't worth messing up a whole day's schedule for: some of the pictures weren't hung straight, the lights didn't hit them for the best effect, and the bus was late picking the class up from the museum. For Jamie, as for many children who are perfectionistic, routine and a rigid attitude about how things ought to be done are hallmarks of their personalities.

While a wide range of factors can contribute to a child's becoming perfectionistic, we know many characteristics that these children can share. Children who act like perfectionists are often:

❑ very bright
❑ very rigid and black-and-white in their thinking. For example, only straight A's on a report card are acceptable; one B means failure.
❑ plagued by self-criticism and by setting unreasonably high standards for themselves.
❑ persistently and recurrently dissatisfied with themselves, which results in an unrelenting feeling of distress. This can show up in a number of ways. For some youngsters it comes out as an eating disorder, anorexia nervosa; for others, it eventually can result in alcoholism. Other signs of perfectionist's distress can be depression, inability to study, procrastination and performance anxiety, or physical symptoms—often abdominal problems such as ulcerative colitis.
❑ likely to set up a no-win situation for themselves by setting goals so high that they cannot possibly succeed
❑ frustrated by their constant need to achieve perfection and their inability to do so
❑ unable to fully appreciate their accomplishments even when they do succeed
❑ likely to approach most tasks as if their entire self worth depended on it.
❑ either working too hard at a task or doing the opposite: not trying at all or procrastinating because they are afraid they won't do it perfectly.
❑ seem happy when things they like are as they want them to be. They may spend a lot of time creating their world the way they want it to be—for example, arranging their model car collection or their doll collection properly. You might not see them be upset in general unless something disrupts the orderliness they like.

In the extreme, children who have become perfectionistic are also often quite serious for their age and very much into their schoolwork or a hobby. They are likely to be almost obsessive over these: arranging, rearranging, always trying to make their work or their hobby efforts better, yet always dissatisfied with the results. These traits may be more obvious to you than to the teacher because of your child's ability to complain more about his "shortcomings" at home.

As with many issues, there is a range of behavior for people who are perfectionistic. They may range from those who simply like more tidiness and predictability in their lives to those who are extremely inflexible and rigid in their thinking. A child who has lost perspective on perfectionist tendencies often is living a painful, anxious life. (See Case Study: Peter).

WHEN SHOULD I BE CONCERNED?

The two main criteria for deciding whether or not your child's perfectionist tendencies are a concern are:

1 Does your child's perfectionism interfere with her functioning?
2 Does your child's perfectionism produce a great degree of personal difficulty for your child?

Both of these are judgment calls on your part: there is no single standard against which to measure your child's behavior to decide whether or not it's a problem. Keeping that in mind, you can use the following examples to help decide if you should be concerned:

Case Study: Peter

When the school nurse sent a note home about Peter's fingernails, his mom knew it was time to talk to the school psychologist. Peter had bitten his nails so far down that the nurse had noticed and was concerned about the torn, bleeding skin around them becoming infected. Then the teacher called Peter's mom. She had already mentioned at parent-teacher conferences that although Peter's school work was exemplary, he seemed tense, never relaxing and having the kind of spontaneous fun other kids did.

Now the teacher had told Peter's mom that after he had made a few simple errors on a test which resulted in a score of 88, Peter had become extremely upset in class, turned bright red, and began hyperventilating.

After an evaluation by the school psychologist and interviews with Peter's family, it was clear where Peter's perfectionist tendencies had come from. Peter's brother and father both had serious psychological problems, and once the father had to be hospitalized briefly. The strain in the family of trying to maintain some kind of normalcy against a background of upheaval had been more than Peter could cope with, both within himself and within his family. He wanted to keep everything "perfect" so that his dad wouldn't get "sick" again and so his brother wouldn't act out more of his emotional problems.

- You should be concerned if, for example, your child has completed a science project that everyone says is excellent, but your child is reluctant to show it at the science fair, or refuses to show it, because she says it's lousy.
- You should be concerned if your child won't try out for a school team because he knows he won't be the best player.
- You should be concerned if your child regularly berates herself for getting a 98 on a test instead of 100.
- You should be concerned if your child can't or won't work with classmates on projects because their work doesn't measure up to his standards.
- You should be concerned if your child regularly procrastinates because she's afraid she can't do a perfect job on the task she's putting off.
- You should be concerned if your child seems depressed or anxious a lot of the time over how well he is doing at school.

WHAT CAN I DO TO HELP?

Children don't "catch" perfectionism the way they catch a virus. As with many issues that affect your child, children learn perfectionism from those around them. Of course, society teaches our children plenty about perfectionism by offering unrealistic role models (excruciatingly thin fashion models, extraordinarily talented sports stars, etc.). But the strongest influence on children comes from the people closest to them.

Consequently, the first thing you can do to help your child is to examine your own expectations of your child, your parenting style, and how you go about accomplishing tasks in your own life. Do you consider yourself to be very demanding or perfectionistic? Do you criticise a less-than-perfect outcome on your own work? If you would describe yourself as a perfectionist, you might consider talking with the school psychologist for a referral to outside counseling, to get some ideas about how to ease up on yourself so that you can help your child do the same. (See Competition and Cooperation, Anxiety, Depression.)

Research has shown that parents of many children who show perfectionist tendencies share a similar parenting style, characterized by:

❑ low tolerance for less-than-perfect behavior or accomplishment from your child

❑ inconsistent approval or nonapproval of your child's behavior

❑ a perception on the part of your child that love and approval is contingent on perfect behavior or accomplishment

❑ a relationship that's not very physically comforting

It's not easy to face some of these things in oneself as a parent. But if you can, you may be able to help your child live a less painful life.

Your best bet will be to look for things you can do with your child that he can't make into competitive activities. For example, going for a hike with him, or going sight-seeing in your own town can provide good chances to talk with your child in a noncompetitive setting. If your child manages to bring perfectionism to any activity you try (on a hike, for example, obsessively reading the map, figuring out how long it takes to go a certain distance, evaluating the condition of the trail, etc.), you will need help from the school pscyhologist or an outside counselor in dealing with this.

Other activities you can try are:

- Set generally lower, or at least clear, reasonable academic expectations for your child.
- Provide very structured situations for your child, with clearly defined expectations that are not too difficult, in order to put limits on what your child can do. For example, when your child has an assignment to do a report on a country in Africa, check with the teacher about the amount of research she expects. Then talk with your child about how many reference books it's reasonable to consult before writing the report so that he doesn't try to find every book on Africa in the library. You might tell him, for example, that one encyclopedia, one almanac, and one book specifically on that country's history is all he's allowed to use.
- Check with the teacher about setting time limits on your child's study efforts so that she can stop going over and over the material in an effort to be perfect. Set a timer for the agreed upon time and place it in your child's view so she can learn to pace herself.
- Try some activities with your child that do not require perfect performance or are hard to measure as being perfect or not. Go for a walk or a hike, draw pictures together, write stories together. Stay away from board games and card games.
- Encourage your child to relax, and plan relaxing time with him during which you do nothing in particular: window shop at the mall or go to the beach.
- Model, or demonstrate, nonperfectionist self-talk. For example, you can say, "I really wanted my quarterly report at work to be perfect, and I thought about staying up all night to work on it. But I know that finishing by 5 P.M. and coming home was more important. And I did a good job on the report." You can also ask

him to use positive self-talk like: "It might be better to get an A+, but I'll still be a good person and a good student if I get a B."

WHAT WILL A PROFESSIONAL DO?

The school psychologist will probably serve as a consultant for parents and the teacher if a child is referred for problems with perfectionism. He will most likely:

❏ interview the parents and the teacher
❏ and observe the child in the classroom

He'll also probably design some activities to fit your child's situation, like those listed above that are structured to keep your child from working obsessively. However, in most cases, the psychologist will do some counseling with you and your child to get at the underlying reasons that the child is behaving this way, or refer you to an outside psychologist who could do the same.

If the school psychologist does any testing of your child, he will likely use personality testing to better understand your child's motives for this behavior, having your child complete self-report inventories to gain insight about her self-esteem, and having you fill out personality rating scales about your child to get your view and understanding of her. (See Evaluation and Testing, Part I, Appendix D, Samples from Tests and Assessments.)

See also:

❏ Anxiety
❏ Appendix D, Samples from Tests and Assessments
❏ Competition and Cooperation
❏ Depression
❏ Evaluation and Testing, in Part I

Further Reading

Smith, A. W. *Overcoming Perfectionism: The Key to Balanced Recovery*. Deerfield Beach, FL: Health Communications, 1990.

CHAPTER 32

Reading—and Writing and 'Rithmetic

"Gina loves school and does very well in math and science, but she hates reading. She's only in third grade and already she's telling me she wishes she could skip reading class because she doesn't need it anyway to do well in math. How can I turn her on to reading?"

Most adults would agree that in our culture, reading well is the key ingredient to becoming educated. In spite of the popularity of computers and video games, the ability to gain information from the written word remains the single most important factor in academic achievement in all subjects, not just language arts.

Unfortunately, not all children want to believe that. If you have a child who doesn't like reading, or who doesn't do well in reading, there are strategies you can use to be sure she learns the basics she needs, and to translate those into math and writing skills.

WHAT WE KNOW NOW

If your child has a reading problem, she's certainly not alone. It has been estimated that about 10 to 15 percent of school-age children will have a reading problem. That fact translates to about 2 to 4 children in most elementary school classes. And, the National Institute of Education reports that about 13 percent of 17-year-old high school graduates are functionally illiterate, which means that while they may be able to decipher some words, they are incapable of using these minimal skills to complete real-life tasks such as filling out job applications.

Obviously, the ability to read and comprehend is key to almost everything we do in our culture—from academic endeavors to job searches—so that it is vital for your child to learn to read well, even if reading is not her favorite subject. The written word is used to explain every subject—favorites as well as those she'd rather avoid. (See The Second "R"—Writing, The Third "R"—'Rithmetic boxes below.)

If you're concerned about your child's reading progress, it's important first to understand that all children pass through certain stages as they learn to read, and the stages occur in a specific developmental order. Once you know what those stages are, you'll know if it's unreasonable to expect your child to be able to accomplish certain Stage 4 tasks when her age and development show that she's appropriately in Stage 1. The box below, developed by Gerald Spadafore, shows a range of ages during which you can expect your child to accomplish each of the different reading stages.

There are four basic approaches to teaching reading. Although they are not mutually exclusive, most districts choose to emphasize one method, perhaps also incorporating a few principles from one or more of the others.

Stages of Reading Development

	Age	Grade
STAGE 1: PRE-READING		
Focus is on speaking skills and understanding words	2–5	
preschool development of visual and hearing skills,	2–6	pre–1st
and development of social maturity in attention span and curiosity.	4–7	pre–2nd
STAGE 2: BEGINNING READING		
Focus is on decoding, or naming letters, understanding letter sounds, blending and sight reading. Also learning to understand and discuss what has been read.	6–7	pre–2nd
STAGE 3: BASIC READING		
Focus is on more advanced decoding to figure out new words, on reading paragraphs, word lists, working on reading speed and accuracy, silent and oral reading.	6–9	1st–4th
Also on listening comprehension, including understanding both literal and inferred meanings, and evaluating what's been read.	6–11	1st–6th
Silent comprehension comes a little later,	8–11	3rd–6th
as does work on vocabulary skills including meanings, root words, prefixes and suffixes.	8–13	3rd–8th
STAGE 4: APPLIED READING		
Children develop:		
Reading in special interest areas	6–17	1st–12th
Attitudes toward reading	6–9	1st–4th
Ability to read to solve problems	9–17	4th–12th
Ability to read for pleasure	6–17	1st–12th
Ability to read for fact finding	11–17	6th–12th
Ability to read assigned materials	8–17	3rd–12th
A motivation to learn through reading	11–17	6th–12th
A broad vocabulary through reading	11–17	6th–12th

That's because in most cases, the school district purchases a reading curriculum, complete with reading books and work books, which of course follows a particular philosophy. Or, in the case of some whole language approaches, the district may not purchase textbooks at all, and instead use library or other books, student stories, or one of the published whole language curricula that has been developed in recent years. If you want to see the curriculum your school uses, check with the teacher, who may have a copy you could borrow. Some districts place copies of their entire curriculum in the public library; others will have copies available at the superintendent's office or principals' offices. See Part I, Know Your School, for information about who makes curriculum decisions.

The four approaches to reading instruction are:

1 *Sight Words.* This approach stresses visual skills and teaches children to recall simple whole words through repetition and practice, as in reading books with passages like: "See Dick. See Dick run. See Dick run fast." Generally, before reading a story, children memorize key words that are then repeated throughout a passage. As they learn more key words, they are able to read more complicated material on the basis of their expanded vocabulary.

2 *Phonics.* Stressing listening skills, a phonics approach teaches individual letter sounds, and then how to blend the sounds to form new words. Children who master phonics skills are able to figure out unfamiliar words, which greatly enhances their reading ability.

3 *Linguistics.* This is similar to the phonics approach, but linguistics uses a system that groups letters to form word families, like cat, nat, sat, mat. A child's reading vocabulary is expanded by learning letter sounds and blends, and then relating like-sounding words.

4 *Psycholinguistics.* Also known as the *whole-language approach.* This one emphasizes allowing children to use their own language to predict the sequence of events within a story. Children are initially taught how to read songs and stories they are familiar with, like Humpty Dumpty, to increase the relevancy of their reading by allowing them to relate reading to past experiences—learning the poem or the song. Reading mistakes are not often corrected unless they drastically alter the content of the story. The close relationship between reading and language makes this an appealing approach to some.

WHOLE LANGUAGE OR PHONICS?

The big controversy you've no doubt heard about in reading instruction is between a phonics approach and a whole-language approach. The trend for many years has been towards the whole-language approach, which proponents say integrates all the language skills of reading, writing, telling, and listening. However, more recent studies show that children who do well with whole-language reading are those who have developed personal phonic skills—in other words, those who have figured out for themselves the relationship between letter sounds and words in order to help them decode new words. Those who do not, critics say, see each new word as a blank, guessing what the word is based on story context, or asking the teacher.

Research shows that for the first two years of school, using the phonics approach in which most of the letters in children's readers correspond with the sounds they are being taught, is critical to effective reading instruction. Two examples of basal readers that accomplish this are the Reading Mastery series published by Science Research Associates and the basal readers published by Allyn & Bacon. Others that adapt well to a phonics approach but are classified as linguistic readers are published by Merrill, Open Court, Palo Alto, SRA, and Scribner.

What this means to you, is if your child is having difficulty and she is in a curriculum that excludes phonics, the problem could be with the curriculum, not necessarily with your child. Many educators are finding that an approach combining phonics with whole language works best. If you suspect there is a problem with the curriculum, talk with your child's teacher about using other methods to supplement what she does in the classroom. If she says that it is not possible to include phonics instruction in your child's program, then you may want to consider hiring a reading tutor to teach your child phonics. (See Know Your School's Personnel, in Part I, for how curriculum decisions are made.)

We also know that reading problems can be can be the result of such things as vision or memory processing problems, lack of exposure to books, lack of motivation, or anxiety. (See Learning Disabilities, Vision, Hearing, Motivation, Anxiety.)

WHEN SHOULD I BE CONCERNED?

Since reading is the fundamental skill that can predict how well your child does in all other subjects, it's worthwhile for you to keep close tabs on your child's progress as she learns to read. Of course, you need to be sure your expectations coincide with what is developmentally appropriate (see box, above), and you need to be in touch with the teacher about what skills she is covering and how she is teaching reading, and about your child's progress.

You should be concerned if your child:

❏ does not seem to be making progress in reading
❏ avoids reading
❏ regularly complains that reading is too hard
❏ notices that other children are reading significantly better than she is
❏ seems to learn words one day and forget them the next day or the next week
❏ has difficulty following a story when you read to him, and can't answer basic questions you ask about the story
❏ seems to read significantly slower than others his age

❏ regularly reports she can't remember what she reads

WHAT CAN I DO TO HELP?

First, you can work with the teacher, or on your own, to rule out:

- *Vision problems.* Sometimes the simple vision screenings done at school don't pick up more subtle kinds of vision problems which can be affecting your child's ability to read. If your child has never had a thorough eye exam, and she is having reading problems, this would be a good time to schedule one. (See Vision.)
- *Hearing problems.* If your child is having a hard time distinguishing sounds of different letters or doesn't seem to be learning sounds, have a hearing evaluation done. (See Hearing.) Next, talk to the teacher about your concerns. She may have similar concerns, or she may be able to tell you that some children just take more time learning certain skills than others. If she does have similar concerns, ask what you can do at home to support the skills she is teaching. Ask, too, if your school has a reading consultant who may be able to offer some ideas you and the teacher could use to help your child. (See What Will A Professional Do? below.)

Many teachers will tell you that rather than pressure a first- or second-grade child about their reading, the best thing to do is simply to read to them at home. (This is true all through elementary school as well. Children learn a great deal about reading from being read to.) Have your child choose a book, then talk for a minute or two about the book and what the title and cover tell you the story will be about, and give your child a purpose for reading the story. For example, you could say, "Let's find out what happens after. . . ." After reading the story, ask your child what did happen after . . . , who the main characters were, which was his favorite and why, and what the characters did that made key events occur. In other words, read and talk about books that are of interest to your child. As with many issues, your child will ultimately emulate what you do. If you approach reading with enthusiasm and curiosity, your child is more likely to do so too. If you read to get information or for pleasure, that sets a standard for your child. If these things have not been part of your life and you see your child struggling with reading, it's a good idea to re-evaluate your own attitudes and make the adjustments you can in order to help your child.

An approach to reading with your child is outlined below. Gear your efforts to your child's interests, but aim for 5 to 15 minutes a day of reading time, in a comfortable spot away from television, radio, people, and other distractions. Then:

1 Have your child choose a book. Talk about the title and the cover as described above. Ask if she knows of other books by the same author. Flip through the pages and look at and talk about the pictures. Ask your child what she expects might happen during the story.

2 If your child wants to, try taking turns reading, switching the reader after each sentence, paragraph, or page.

3 When your child comes to a word she doesn't know, allow about five seconds for her to figure it out. If she gets it, praise her immediately. If she doesn't, tell her the word.

4 Stop at a logical place when your time is up. When you start reading the next day, talk for a minute first about what was happening in the story when you stopped.

5 Talk about the book when you finish it. Were

your predictions about it correct? It's fine if they weren't. What did you and your child like best about the story? About the characters? What bothered you or surprised you? How did this book compare to others by the same author?

6 Rereading the book is fine if your child wants to. Practice is confidence-building.

7 Your child may want to read certain books with you, no matter how well she has learned to read. That's fine. The whole idea is to make reading an enjoyable, shared learning experience.

Whether you use this approach or another method, it might be fun to keep a record with your child of books you (or she) has read, with a few comments next to each title about the book, or about how well your child did reading the book.

Another way to get your child tuned in to reading is to be sure she is reading things that interest her. For some children, reading material that is not of specific interest to them is boring enough to make them not try hard. In the box below, you'll find lists of questions for different age groups that may guide you in helping your child pinpoint some interest areas from which she can pull her reading material. You can ask these questions of your child and simply have a conversation about them. Or, if it fits your family (or if a teacher is using these in a classroom), you can ask your child to take a few mintues to write an answer to each question and then talk about what reading material might be right for her.

WHAT WILL A PROFESSIONAL DO?

If, in spite of activities like those listed above involving you, your child's teacher, and the reading consultant, your child still has signifi-

What Are You Interested In?

(Developed by Gerald Spadafore, Idaho State University)

For Grades 1–3:

❏ What is your favorite game?

❏ If you could get someone to read out loud to you, what kind of story would you choose?

❏ What kind of TV programs do you enjoy the most?

❏ What kind of stories do you enjoy reading?

❏ Do you have a library card?

❏ What kind of comic books do you enjoy reading?

❏ What do you enjoy doing the most outside of school?

❏ What kind of activities do you do for recreation?

❏ If you could choose to do anything you wanted to do, what would it be?

❏ What are your interests?

For Grades 4–6:

❏ How much time do you spend reading school-related materials?

❏ How much time do you spend reading material of your choice?

❏ Do you read the newspaper on a regular basis? If *yes*, what sections are you most interested in?

❏ What kind of TV programs do you enjoy the most?

❏ Do you have a library card?

❏ What kind of books do you enjoy reading the most?

❏ What do you enjoy doing the most outside of school?

❏ What kind of activities do you do for recreation?

❏ If you could choose to do anything you wanted to do, what would it be?

❏ What are your interests?

For Secondary Students:

❏ If you had to solve a problem, how much reading would you be likely to do?

❏ Do you subscribe to or read a magazine on a regular basis? If *yes*, what kind of magazine?

❏ Do you read the newspaper on a regular basis? If *yes*, which sections are of most interest to you?

❏ How many library books do you read during an average month?

❏ What kind of TV programs do you enjoy the most?

❏ What kind of movies do you enjoy the most?

❏ What kind of activities do you do for recreation?

❏ If you could choose to do anything you wanted to do, what would it be?

❏ What things really interest you?

cant difficulty with reading, you (or the teacher) can refer your child for a multidisciplinary team meeting where testing might be recommended to find the source of the problem and to pinpoint other strategies or techniques that might work better.

Several specialists may be involved, depending on how your school is staffed:

❏ A special education teacher may do academic testing or other testing to see how your child learns in reading, as well as in other areas such as math, to determine if the problem is specific to reading or more generalized.

❏ The school psychologist may test for general IQ with a test such as the WISC-III (see Appendix D for sample questions, or Standardized Tests, in Part I). She may also do some brief academic testing using tools such as the Weschsler Individual Achievement Test, which evaluates reading, spelling, and math achievement, or using other tests that could show how your child learns.

❏ The speech-language pathologist may do some other testing to see how your child learns and remembers what he hears in class.

Based on the test results, it might be useful for your child to:

❏ have additional reading instruction in a small group or individually from the teacher or a reading consultant.

❏ receive some special education services if tests show she has a learning disability. (See Learning Disabilities.)

❏ receive special services if tests show that he has a language problem. (See Language Development, Hearing.)

❏ use a different curriculum either within the classroom as supplemental exercises, or in a different class.

MORE IDEAS FOR WRITING PRACTICE

❏ Draw a large circle and have your child write the story topic inside. Write story details in smaller circles attached to the big one by lines. Talk with your child about which small circles

The Second "R"— Writing

YOUR CHILD CAN PLAN TO WRITE WELL

Good writing grows out of good reading. Reading well and about a broad range of topics gives your child practice in understanding the written word, as well as examples of how other people have shaped words into stories or accessible information. Even beginning readers can learn to write stories. There are many ways to teach writing, but one of the simplest is to use the step-by-step process described below. Before you start, be sure to tell your child a couple of key ideas about writing:

- Writing is a process, not a problem-solving technique; even experienced authors write, and rewrite, and rewrite again before they are satisfied with their work. Writing is not something you do once.
- There is no right or wrong way to write a story. Of course, a certain amount of common sense must be used to be sure a story is understandable to the reader, but beyond that you can encourage your child to take her own direction with her stories. There are many techniques and activities you can do to help your child with writing. One developed by

should come first, second, third, etc.

❏ Encourage your child to write letters to relatives or a pen pal.

❏ Take pictures on vacation and have your child write something about each. You can put these in an album or send them to friends and relatives.

❏ Make a personal spelling dictionary for your child. Glue or tape small alphabet tabs every few pages on a little notebook. When your child asks the meaning of a word or how to spell it, add it to her notebook.

❏ Take turns writing four- or five-sentence stories. The writer cuts the story apart, sentence by sentence, and the reader has to rearrange it in the right order.

❏ Display your child's stories as you do her artwork. Put up rough drafts she's worked hard on, too.

❏ Have your child talk her story into a tape recorder if she has a hard time getting started. She can write from her own tape.

❏ Encourage your child to write in a diary or journal.

❏ Try sharing a daily 10-minute writing time with your child. This can be story writing, journal writing, or whatever strikes your fancy.

Give your child story starters, an intriguing first line like: "The day I won the lottery I . . .", "I wish I knew about . . .", or "When I am a grandparent, I will . . ."

See also:

❏ Anxiety
❏ Hearing
❏ Know Your School's Personnel, in Part I
❏ Language Development
❏ Learning Disabilities
❏ Motivation
❏ Standardized Tests, in Part I
❏ Vision

The Third "R"—'Rithmetic

MATH ANXIETY . . . MATH ANXIETY: A SPECIAL TERM FOR A SPECIAL PROBLEM

Plenty of children would rather read a story than work a math problem. Others would happily face columns of numbers rather than be confronted with a few lines of poetry. Everyone has their preferences and their special abilities.

But some children seem to go beyond those to build for themselves an aversion to numbers and math at an early age. Perhaps they've come to believe spoken and unspoken messages ("Girls are good readers; boys are better at math."). Or perhaps they've had trouble grasping math concepts and ended up feeling like a stranger in a strange land of incomprehensible numbers.

Math anxiety is what it's called. And it's not too different from other kinds of anxiety (see Anxiety, Self-Esteem). One of the key ingredients in anxiety of any kind is discomfort with the unknown or unexpected. So, the more you do to help your child feel friendlier towards numbers, the less anxiety she may have about math.

1. Point out to your child that like words and reading, numbers and math are all around us, and we use them every day. Set the table and count how many forks you need for your family. Have your young child help measure ingredients for a recipe. Have your older child double a recipe for you. Let your child check your groceries against the receipt. Tell her to slice the pizza into halves, then fourths; ask how many fourths in a half. Measure or weigh each family member: who is biggest? who is nearest half the size of the biggest? You get the picture: these friendly numbers are with us every day, helping us describe things and figure things out.

2. Point out to your child how closely reading and math are associated. Have her circle key words in word problems. Talk about how if you couldn't read well, you couldn't figure out word problems. And, of course, compare word problems to the kind of real-life situations listed above that require math knowledge.

3. If you are helping your child with math homework, figure out with her how long you can work before you or she becomes frustrated. If that amount of time is 10 minutes, then plan to work on homework in slightly less than 10-minute chunks, so that you and she stop before frustration sets in.

4. Be liberal and supportive with your praise for every success, even if it's just figuring out the next step in a problem, not the whole problem. Your child's sincere effort and good attitude will count for a lot in her overall success with math.

5. Of course, if you can buy computer math games, appealing math workbooks, or make up flashcard games for learning math facts, all the better.

6. When you're working with your child on math facts, break up the material into manageable segments, practice until your child has mastered that bit, but always stop before she becomes frustrated. Just 5 to 15 minutes a night for first- through third-graders is enough; 15 to 30 minutes a night for fourth- through sixth-graders.

C H A P T E R   3 3

Responsibility

"Jimmy isn't a bad kid, but I can't seem to get him to take full responsibility for his work at school. He's always missing some assignment, or blowing a big test, or clowning around in class. Then I have to go to school to try to patch things up with the teacher. It's the same at home: I expect him to do certain things, and he rarely 'remembers.' I'm always finishing his chores for him."

Raising a child to be a responsible adult is a goal most parents share. School seems to be the perfect setting in which children can learn responsibility. But a sense of responsibility doesn't always come easily to children, and sooner or later, many parents hear a report from school of their child's irresponsible behavior. Or perhaps it's just that you feel at your wit's end when your child forgets to bring his book bag to school with him for the umpteenth time.

Understanding how much responsibility is enough at different developmental stages will help you evaluate whether or not your child is on target for her age. And knowing this, you can use appropriate means to nurture your child's growing sense of responsibility.

WHAT WE KNOW NOW

Before talking about how to help your child be responsible, you'll need to think clearly about what responsibility means. We think of it as respect for the rights of others and personal accountability for one's actions. Responsible children use their own resources, confidence, and judgment to make decisions, act independently, consider the effects of their actions, and meet their own needs without interfering with the rights of others.

For most children, from preschool through high school, there is a slow but steady increase in expectations and demands at home and at school for responsible behavior. No matter what your child's age, learning to become responsible means showing acceptable behavior in three areas:

1 Following rules
2 Using good judgment
3 Showing respect and courtesy for others and their property

That's what responsibility is. What it is not, is learning to conform, and it's important to see the difference between the two. The fact that your child can pack items into her schoolbag in the same manner you told her to, for example, does not mean she has learned to handle her school items responsibly; it only means she has learned to conform to your idea of how these items should be handled.

As every parent knows, children don't spring from the womb as responsible beings. In fact, we start our lives in exquisitely irresponsible fashion: we have no responsibility for meeting our most basic needs other than to alert someone else to take care of them. Growth and maturity mean learning responsibility bit by bit. Preschoolers are expected to

What Can You Expect?

AGE	WHAT THEY WANT	WHAT THEY CAN DO
Grades K–3	A little social independence	See cause and effect Respond to competition Have some maturity in judgment of right and wrong.
Grades 3–6	Social independence Peer recognition	Can predict how someone will feel as the result of their actions. Begin process of gaining independence from family. Tests limits. Conceptualize far-reaching moral implications of social acts Can sustain effort on task over several days More mature response to competition—accepting defeat somewhat gracefully, not blaming, playing within rules, improved sense of fairness.
Grades 7–12	Solidified independence	Explore personal values Awareness of long-term life planning Awareness of gender role definition

be responsible for their behavior toward other children and are given consequences when they hit a playmate, for example. Intermediate school-age children are expected to responsibly balance work and play time so that they finish their homework each night. And adolescents are expected to use new-won privileges such as driving themselves to school, in a responsible manner or face consequences, too.

Teaching responsibility to our children also has a lot to do with how we were taught as children. Families that are run more as a dictatorship than a democracy don't often teach responsibility well because parents hold the reins so tightly there's no opportunity for a child to be responsible for something; that's adult territory. By the same token, families in which anything goes really don't teach responsibilty well, either, especially if the parents aren't behaving in a responsible manner. The most workable scenario occurs in more democratic families where parents are the leaders, but are also willing to share responsiblity for such tasks as care of the household and each other.

That's a key point about teaching reponsibility: you have to be willing to give responsibility in order to teach it. Responsibility cannot be taught by lecturing your child about it. Your child learns by being given responsibility and by reaping the rewards or suffering the consequences of how he handles it. As a parent, you must be willing to stand back and let that happen, which means you have to surrender some of your ideas of how things "ought" to be done, or how you want things to turn out, in favor of letting your child figure out some things for himself. And you must allow him to be responsible for his errors: If he forgets his school bag after agreeing to be responsible for it without your reminders, you're not teaching responsibility if you take the bag to school for him when he forgets it anyway. You must allow him to bear the consequences for being irresponsible, to take the zeros on the homework he didn't have with him.

Learning to be responsible is like many skills: the more you practice, the better you'll be. For your child, the more practice he gets with being responsible at home, the better he's likely to handle responsibility at school. You can be sure your child has an opportunity to practice being responsible by letting him contribute to the running of the household, remember belongings, structure time, plan activities, and demonstrate preferences in clothing and food.

Of course you'll want to start small, by first having your child be responsible for little things, so that if he doesn't handle it well the repercussions won't be enormous. As a rule of thumb, you should always give responsibility in accordance with your child's developmental level. The checklist below will give you some idea of where your child may be developmentally at different ages. Specific tasks you can expect at different ages are listed in the next section, When Should I Be Concerned?

WHEN SHOULD I BE CONCERNED?

Helping a child learn to be responsible at home and at school is not usually a smooth process, so try not to let yourself become concerned just because it feels as though you are always battling over this issue with your child. That's a fairly typical feeling, and one that seems to go along with what is often one of the less pleasant tasks of parenthood.

You can become concerned if you suspect your child is more than a little off track with the amount of responsibility normally to be expected of someone her age. To get more of an idea of what you should be able to expect at different ages, go over this checklist:

Does My Kindergarten Through Third-Grade Child . . .

❏ Often follow the rules of group games?
❏ Express anger without hitting most of the time?
❏ Remember to attend to personal belongings (brings home gloves, books, etc.) with little reminding?
❏ Complete simple chores independently, like clearing the table or putting belongings away?
❏ Care for his own hygiene and dressing needs?

Does My Fourth-Grade Through Sixth-Grade Child . . .

❏ Complete school assignments independently?
❏ Organize personal time to fit in homework, play, etc.?
❏ Help with household chores daily?
❏ Respect personal property of others?

Does My Seventh- Through Twelfth-Grade Youngster . . .

❏ Evaluate and respond on their own when extra help is needed around the house?

❏ Follow curfew rules, let parent know change in plans, etc.?

❏ Work independently on school projects, developing long-term career interests?

❏ Respect personal rights of others?

If you feel your child is consistently irresponsible in any one of these areas (by age), you have reason to be concerned.

If you are concerned, use these guidelines to further evaluate your child's behavior:

■ *How often is my child's lack of responsibility a problem?* A pattern of behavior that shows lack of responsibility is a problem. If your child has only an occasional lapse, forgetting an assignment once in a while or ignoring chores when their schedule gets overloaded, it's worth reminding him about, but it is normal, not a big problem.

■ *How does your child act when lapses are brought to his attention?* If the behavior changes promptly, you needn't become overly concerned.

■ *How disruptive is your child's lack of responsibility to his class?* If you have reports from the teacher that your child's lack of attention to classroom rules is disruptive to the class several times a week, it's time to be concerned.

If you are concerned about your child's level of responsiblity, think too about exactly what your expectations are of him, how far off the mark his behavior actually is, and in what ways. Think about:

❏ What are my expectations of my child?

❏ What are my child's teacher's expectations of my child?

❏ How different than each of these is my child's behavior?

❏ Does the behavior violate the rights of others?

❏ Is my child actually capable of the expected behavior?

❏ Do I give my child opportunities to be responsible that are appropriate to his age and development?

WHAT CAN I DO TO HELP?

As with many behaviors we want to teach our children, we are the models our children follow. If your child sees you being responsible about keeping appointments, finishing necessary chores before relaxing, and holding schoolwork and school projects in high regard, she will eventually learn a lot about the basics of responsiblity because she sees responsible behavior every day. On the other hand, without an appropriate model of behavior for your child, you will be fighting an uphill battle in teaching her responsibility.

You can also help your child by communicating with her clearly about exactly what it is you expect of her and about your rules concerning responsible behavior. You should tell your child the reason for your rules so that she understands why it's important to be responsible. And often, when a child knows and understands why they are required to do certain chores, she can feel good about being a helpful part of the family or about being able to behave independently. See the box below for how to organize a responsibility chart.

What kinds of responsibilities should you give to your child? Everyone has different abilities and expectations, but it is reasonable to ask your third- to sixth-grade child to:

On a daily basis:

❏ keep track of her school materials and be sure she takes them with her each day.

❏ make her bed each morning

❏ put out her own school clothes each night

❏ set her own alarm; get up when it rings

❏ have her lunch or lunch money ready the night before

My Responsibility Chart

RESPONSIBILITIES	DAY OF WEEK	NO. OF POINTS

1.
2.
etc.

HERE'S HOW IT WORKS:

Decide which things you want your child to become more responsible about. Start with just a few items, and add no more than one a week if your child is doing well. Have a maximum of 10 items at any one time.

After your child has been successful carrying out a responsibility for four consecutive weeks, you can remove it from the chart, so long as she continues to fulfill that responsibility.

Your child earns points for completing each responsibility each day of the week. Total points at the end of the week earn a reward. Use ideas from Appendix A, Motivators.

❏ care for a pet (e.g., walk the dog each day after school)

❏ practice a musical instrument for 30 mintues each day (or dance lessons or sports practice)

❏ complete homework accurately, neatly, and without nagging

On a weekly basis:

❏ strip the bed and place linens in the clothes hamper

❏ vacuum and dust her room

❏ help out with a household chore, such as shopping for and putting away groceries

❏ carry out the family trash/recycling

For younger children, be sure you teach them how to do the chores you expect of them. Also, be sure that they are physically big enough to do them (tall enough to reach the controls on the washing machine, for example, or strong enough to carry out the recycling). For older children, you can add some chores that take more skill, for example, ironing or mowing the lawn.

Give your child opportunities to be responsible by letting him set goals, make choices, solve problems. At home, this can mean setting household maintenance goals and chores (keeping his own room and one common area such as the living room clean each week; for a younger child, picking up newspapers for the recycling bin; for an older child, washing and folding laundry), and then entering into an agreement with you about how and when these can be done. This kind of agreement can include details about the quality of the finished job, for which the child can earn more points on the Responsibility Chart. See box on quality control.

Give your child a range of acceptable options to choose from in terms of time management, television viewing, free-time activities, clothing and food selection. See the checklists above for some age-appropriate ideas.

One question parents always have is

whether they should pay their children for chores they do. There's no one answer for this, because values and lifestyles are so different from family to family. If you can't afford to pay your children at all, then don't worry about it. Children still have a responsibility to contribute to the smooth running of the household. If you want to pay your children somehow, keep these ideas in mind:

❏ You could pay your child only for one-shot chores (painting the fence), or "over and above the call of duty" chores (washing the kitchen floor without being asked when she knew you were expecting company), which your child completes in addition to a reasonable regular list of responsibilities. Having this apply only to specific, time-limited chores will keep your child from expecting to be paid for every chore.

❏ You could simply give your child a weekly allowance that is a completely separate issue from chores. By giving your elementary-age child money for lunch, for example, you are again offering valuable lessons about responsibility. As your child gets older, the amount of money can increase, but so must the expectations about what it will be used for—for example, not only for school lunches, but for school supplies, clothing, cosmetics, etc.

Perhaps the most important thing you can do to help your child become more responsible is to let her experience the effect of her own actions. Natural and logical consequences for both responsible and irresponsible behavior are the best teachers of all. The schoolbag left at school means a zero in homework the next day. Poor planning for study time for a test means a lower grade. But both can mean an important lesson learned.

Keep in mind that allowing your child to

Quality Control

Quality-control agreements aren't for everyone. But we find that they are sometimes necessary when a child is particularly stubborn about fulfilling his responsibilities, and splits hairs: yes, he cleaned his room, but in order to do so, he threw everything into the closet because your orginial agreement with him said nothing about cleaning the closet.

To address this problem, you can add a quality-control point system to the responsibility chart. For example, if the chore is cleaning his bedroom, and it's done as expected, your child would get four points; if it's clean and the closet is tidied too, he would earn six points; if the room is clean but you had to nag him to do it or the dirty clothes are on the floor of the closet, he gets just one point.

Quality control should be a short-term addition to a responsibility chart, both because it's a lot of work to administer, and because if you and your child are at that kind of stand-off all the time, there are likely to be other negative factors at work in your relationship that may need to be addressed by a third party, like the school psychologist or an outside counselor.

reap what he has sown won't always have the results you want, especially if your child has an underlying psychological problem that may be causing the lack of responsible behavior in the first place. In fact, if the natural consequences approach really doesn't work with your child, it may be a clue that you need to look deeper for the source of your child's irresponsibility, or ask your school psychologist about it.

There are a few behaviors for which there are no natural consequences, such as when your eighth-grader stays out past his curfew. Curfews are arbitrarily established, and you can just as arbitrarily set the consequences for them. The key is in telling your child ahead of time what the rule is and what the consequence for breaking it will be. A blown curfew could mean an earlier curfew next week, no going out at all next week, no taking the car out next week, etc.

You should also know that no parent can anticipate everything. When your child does something unexpected that's not acceptable to you, you don't need to feel obligated to decide on a course of action immediately. Instead, you should

❐ tell your child how disappointed you are (or concerned, or angry)
❐ tell your child there will be consequences for their actions,
❐ but that you will not give the consequences in the heat of anger.

Then, you can decide on an appropriate consequence and impose it, within a day or two.

WHAT WILL A PROFESSIONAL DO?

This is an area in which the school psychologist is more likely to consult with the parent or the teacher, or both, than to do an assessment of your child.

The school psychologist will:

❐ Try to identify the specific problem behaviors your child has. Often, parents or teachers use the term *irresponsible* too loosely.
❐ Look at the reasonableness of expectations for your child
❐ Think about what might be the motivation behind your child's irresponsible behavior
❐ Look at the intensity, persistence, and effects of your child's behavior
❐ Examine what opportunities your child might—or might not—have for responsible behavior

Any plan developed by him will most likely be based on setting up a school and/or a home chart of responsibilities and expectations that lead to consequences or rewards in both places. Most special programs in schools for children with behavioral problems are structured this way. Some consequences the school might provide are: staying after school, losing recess privileges, not earning a field trip.

Sometimes it's the teacher or classroom setting that's the root of the problem for your child. In that case, the school psychologist may consult with the teacher to see if changing the way she teaches or manages the class will increase the likelihood of responsible behavior in your child.

See also:

❐ Dependency
❐ Motivation

Further Reading

Berry, J. *Let's Talk About Being Lazy*. Peter Pan Industries. 1982.

Clemes, H. & Bean, R. *How to Teach Children Responsibility*. New York: Putnam, 1990.

Eyre, L. & Eyre, R. *Teaching Children Responsibility*. New York: Ballantine Books, 1985.

Lott, L. & Intner, R. *The Family That Works Together*. Rocklin, CA: Prima Publishing, 1994.

Phillips, C. & Williams, L. *A Positive Steps Approach: A Parent's Guide to Teaching Youths to be Responsible for Today!* Fort Worth, TX: The Summit Group. 1993.

CHAPTER 34

School Discipline

"Darien's behavior had gotten out of hand at school so many times that when the counselor called me at work to say my son was being sent home for fighting, we agreed that Darien would walk the three miles home from school and call me when he got home. Other times I had rushed to school to take him home or to deal with the problem. This time Darien paid the price, not me."

Most parents don't need statistics to prove to them that school discipline is a real concern. The news media is full of reports of violence, disruption, and frightened or frustrated students and teachers.

As with many emotionally charged issues, there can be a lot of finger-pointing between parents and school administrators when people address school discipline. In fact, school discipline problems have roots in both places. But so do the solutions. A healthy collaboration between home efforts and school efforts can make school discipline problems an issue of the past.

WHAT WE KNOW NOW

If your child has gotten in trouble at school enough times that you are making a point to find out more about effective school discipline, it might be a relief for you to remember that you are not alone. Almost every kid, at one time or another, is found to have been fighting, swearing, talking without permission, stealing, lying, teasing, tardy, truant, or simply refusing to follow the rules. A certain amount of even rather serious varieties of these behaviors are a normal part of growing up for most children. In one study, over 60 percent of ado-

lescents admitted to having taken part in serious antisocial behaviors at some point—vandalism, arson, aggressive acts, and drug abuse.

But while some antisocial behavior is a normal part of growing up, so too should be discipline. At home and at school, children need the structure and boundaries that effective discipline can provide. At school in particular, there cannot be an effective learning environment without discipline. Studies have shown that students show greater gains in academic achievement, and have more favorable perceptions of the classroom, in classes where little time is spent in disciplinary encounters. In those classrooms, discipline enhances an academic focus rather than stealing the show.

Most education professionals agree that the traits that ensure academic success are not purely a strong intellect or even unbridled enthusiasm. Rather, they are positive attitude, cooperation, and motivation. When you think about it, those are the same traits that foreshadow success in the post-school days world too: Simply being smart or being a good test-taker doesn't mean a student is going to be successful in business, for example, after graduation. Real-world success also requires an ability to focus one's efforts—in other words, be self-disciplined—and get along with and respect others in a work environment.

There is a strong correlation between overall school adjustment and adjustment later in life. For the majority of children, how they adapt to school with all its rules and requirements is a reasonably accurate predictor of how they will do later. That's a good reason for paying close attention to discipline problems as soon as they develop, rather than waiting to see if your child will "grow out of it." As with many issues, the earlier you can address frequent or serious discipline problems, the better chance you will have of helping your child to develop new, more constructive behaviors.

Most school personnel strongly rely on you and your home environment to have provided your child with a basic understanding of discipline before he reaches school age. They generally assume your child comes to school with at least a willingness to follow the rules and enough self-control to allow him to do that most of the time.

If that is not the case, school personnel also agree that the classroom is not the best place to begin to teach a child about discipline for a number of reasons, not the least of which is that there are a couple dozen other children in the classroom whose days will be disrupted while one child learns how to follow the rules. In addition, schools operate under many constraints when it comes to disciplining children. If it was ever actually true, the old saw about some tough teacher "whipping the kid into shape," is an idea whose time has passed.

So while discipline is fundamentally a parenting task that first takes place outside of school, it can become a serious school issue if it hasn't taken place before a child reaches school age, or if the parents' approach and expectations for the child are significantly dif-

ferent from those of school personnel. That's why mutual effort, cooperaton and collaboration between home and school are vital.

Most schools will have a two-pronged approach to discipline problems, which focus on:

1 Instruction designed to teach appropriate conduct or to prevent disciplinary problems, and
2 Actions used to correct, punish, or control disciplinary problems when they do occur.

Most discipline techniques used to accomplish these things can be grouped under one of three goals:

1 To prevent misbehavior and to develop self-discipline
2 To correct misbehavior
3 To treat chronically disruptive or "at-risk" students.

WHEN SHOULD I BE CONCERNED?

You should be concerned if your child's discipline problems begin very early in his school career, in preschool or kindergarten for example, and if they are frequent and/or serious— for instance, frequently, blatantly disobeying or talking back to the teacher, teasing or bullying (see Bullies and Victims), or inappropriate language.

Deciding which kinds of behavior are serious is a subjective process, and you'll need to account for your child's maturity as you do this. For example, you and your child's teacher will need to talk about whether this discipline problem is the result of your child's being unable to follow the rules (because he lacks maturity) or simply unwilling to follow the rules.

In deciding when to be concerned, you

will also have to take into account the standards of your particular school. Behaviors that one school tolerates may be unthinkable at another school. There is no single standard to which all schools, or even the majority of schools, will conform. But as a guideline, you should be concerned if your child:

❐ receives comments on his report card indicating that his attitude, behavior, and/or effort are low

❐ reports that he is frequently sent to a quiet corner of the classroom

❐ brings home teacher's notes expressing concern about your child's behavior

❐ is referred to the principal for misbehavior

❐ is excluded from school activities like recess or a movie because of his behavior

❐ continues to misbehave even after being disciplined, which results in action that is the next step up from exclusion, such as demerits, suspension, and, in extreme cases, expulsion from school

WHAT CAN I DO TO HELP?

Although children can and should be held responsible for their own behavior, or misbehavior, it's important for parents to understand what part they play in how their children act. Taking some time and thought to analyze your behavior toward your child is the first step toward getting your child's behavior at home and at school back on track.

Psychologist Michael Valentine, writing in NASP's book, *Home-School Collaboration: Enhancing Children's Academic and Social Competence* (1992), has developed guidelines for parents and schools for dealing with school discipline problems. He suggests parents look at two aspects of their own behavior first. Think about:

1 *What you believe your child is capable of doing.* Sometimes the bottom line on children's behavior problems is a parent's or teacher's belief that the child is incapable of behaving in the ways the school is asking. For example, it's sometimes easy to attribute a child's misbehavior to a developmental stage ("terrible twos"), or to make other excuses for inappropriate behavior such as "boys will be boys," thinking your child can't help himself, he's bored, he's "just like his Dad," his friends make him do things he shouldn't, it's because of the divorce. If a parent or teacher believes your child is incapable of the behavior, it's a sure bet your child will live down to that expectation.

Think carefully about your child, his developmental level, and what is being asked of him. Valentine suggests one way to decide if your child is capable of the behavior is to ask yourself if your child has ever done the behavior, even once. If he has, then he is capable of the behavior.

2 *What you tell your child in between the lines you speak.* Valentine has found that in most cases, when children act inappropriately, adults do not give clear, direct, specific, and concrete messages to children to stop the inappropriate behavior and start doing what the adults want them to do. Here are some examples Valentine offers of vague, indirect communication that can actually reinforce your child's inappropriate behavior:

a *Ignoring the behavior.* Many adults think that ignoring inappropriate behavior will make it go away. But Valentine says this sends the message to your child that you silently condone his behavior and don't mind if he keeps on acting inappropriately.

b *Actually encouraging inappropriate behavior.* Statements like "I'd like to see you try it. . . ",

"Go for it. . . ", "Why don't you save that up and do it for your father so he can see what I put up with. . . " do not tell the child to stop the behavior immediately. They imply instead that the inappropriate behavior is all right if the child does it someplace else or under different circumstances.

c *Demanding honesty.* If your child is suspected of stealing another child's notebook at school, and your focus is on demanding he tell you the truth about the incident, the unspoken message is that what's important is truth-telling, not that your child should not steal. Truth-telling is important, but not the only issue here. (See Lying.)

d *Being concerned.* When your first-grader kicks her six-year old friend and she is urged to say she's sorry, the emphasis is on being concerned about the other person, not on stopping the behavior.

e *Making an effort to change.* "Try to get to class on time," you call to your son as he heads out the door. You've just told him that trying to do the right thing is more important than doing it.

f *Thinking about the behavior.* "Think twice before you do that again," tells your child that it's OK to do it, so long as he thinks about it beforehand.

g *Don't get caught.* "Don't you ever let me catch you doing that again." It's OK to do it, so long as you don't get caught.

h *Abstract, meaningless directions.* "Grow up" means nothing specific to most youngsters. So does "You're not working up to your potential," and "If you respected me, you wouldn't do that."

i *Statements of fact.* "I see you forgot your homework again," may certainly be an accurate observation about your child, but it doesn't tell her anything about what you want her to do.

j *Questions.* Statements such as, "How many times have I told you. . . ?" and "Why are you fighting?" do nothing to tell your child the behavior you'd rather see.

k *Threats.* "If you don't do these 10 problems, you're staying after school," implies to your child that he has a choice, which further implies that either choice is all right with you.

l *Wishes, Wants, and Shoulds.* "I wish you'd sit still in class," or "You should sit still," simply lets your child know your preference. Neither statement is a clear message to sit still.

While some of these vague statements may work with some children, they rarely work with really difficult children.

In any case, you can help your child most by giving clear, direct messages that tell him specifically what is to be done, and by working with your child's teacher to be sure she is doing that too. For example, instead of telling your child "Get to work," the teacher can say, "Sit in your seat now, and stay there until I tell you to get up. While you are there, do these 10 problems neatly and correctly. Have them finished in 15 minutes. Start now and do nothing else until they are finished."

In order to be able to give your child such direct messages, you must first believe that:

❐ It is reasonable to tell your child and expect your child to do the specific behavior.
❐ Your child is capable of the behavior.
❐ Your child has no choice but to do the behavior.

Valentine explains that clear objective statements given to your child in a context of love and respect do not constitute a hostile approach to discipline, but rather they are an effective way of guiding your child to do what he must.

Every parent knows that children don't always do what you tell them, even when you are trying to be clear and direct. But Valentine points out that most parents will admit that children usually comply when they have told them the 10th time or so, when the parent "really means it." Coincidentally, the 10th time is often when parents stop the vague messages and say, in no uncertain terms: "Do it now."

For those times when even clear messages don't seem to be getting through to your child, Valentine suggests nonhostile, nonpunishing backup techniques you devise to fit your situation, based on two principles:

1 A clear focus on the behavior you want, and only on that behavior. For example, your child did not complete the 10 math problems. Your focus (or the teacher's) should be on his completing the problems; not on staying after school or writing 100 sentences about doing homework.

2 Communicating as clearly as possible to your child that he must do the goal behavior—there is no way out. You can say, "Because I love you and care about you, I will not hurt you, belittle you, or punish you, but you will do the goal behavior. I expect you to be successful, and I will not allow you to do anything other than be successful."

It's important that your child understand that success is the only option. The choice is not, for example, "Would you like to be successful (i.e., go to school), or fail (i.e., drop out of school)?" The choice is, "Would you like to be successful on your own?" or "Would you like us to help you be successful until you get the message you can be successful on your own?"

Helping your child be successful means

that you, with your child, put in the time and energy to:

❏ identify the goal behavior
❏ give direction to make the goal behavior happen
❏ be consistent in giving the direction
❏ monitor the behavior
❏ follow through to be sure the behavior is achieved.

WHAT WILL A PROFESSIONAL DO?

The school psychologist will most likely focus first on clearly identifying the nature of your child's discipline problem. She'll try to assess both your child's maturity level and whether your child has the skills she needs to get along. She'll also talk to your child, to you, the teacher, and the principal—if she has been involved—to determine the full scope of the problem.

Intertwined with basic discipline issues may be factors such as:

❏ the child's lack of self-discipline,
❏ the teacher's inadequate classroom management
❏ the school's tolerance level for some problematic or developmentally expected but annoying behavior
❏ the school's lack of preventive programs and/or discipline-related policies.

In-class observations and a second round of interviews will help the psychologist gain a deeper understanding of the problem, and she can then recommend a course of action, most likely using one of the methods described above or something similar.

A key part of working with the school psychologist on your child's discipline problems will be close collaboration between the program designed for school and the program she gives you for home use. One will not work without the other. The psychologist is likely to devise a program similar to what's described in What Can I Do to Help?

If you and the psychologist diligently work at a course of action and still see no positive results in your child, and if your child's academics are suffering as a result, the psychologist may recommend that the school's multidisciplinary team conduct a more thorough review of your child's behavior, and possibly recommend an evaluation. They will use a variety of testing and evaluation tools (see Testing and Evaluation, in Part I) to rule out the possibility of contributing problems such as learning problems (See Learning Disabilities), lack of ability, or a social or emotional adjustment problem.

See also:

❏ Anger Control
❏ Learning Disabilities
❏ Evaluation and Testing, in Part I

Case Study: Ross

(This is an example of how essential parent support is. Without parent support, school efforts are usually ineffective.)

Ross, a fifth-grader, was referred to the school psychologist quite often because of misbehavior in class. He'd pass notes, talk in class, and get up and walk around when the teacher was talking, refuse to do assignments or tear up his paper before the teacher could collect it. He was physically larger than most of the children, and because of his size he could manipulate and intimidate others into disobeying the teacher.

Ross was very dependent on his mother, and she was very supportive of him. Unfortunately, her support often translated into her not following at home the agreed-upon discipline standards we'd set up at school.

Ross' behavior deteriorated over time despite many meetings between the school psychologists, the teacher, and his mother. He had been tested and was in a special education class, but even with special attention, Ross' behavior and his schoolwork continued on a downward spiral.

Finally, after a particularly bad day for him in school—he'd had several in-class time-outs and been sent to the principal's office more than once—his parents were called and asked to come take him home because he couldn't be controlled at school. His mother picked him up and took him to a toy store where she allowed him to pick a toy "because he had such a bad day and needed a lift."

It was the opposite of the message we'd hoped she give him.

Getting Your Child to Do What You Want

Use this checklist as you formulate a plan for changing your child's behavior. Have I:

❏ Decided on the specific behavior of my child's I wish to change, and made sure he is capable of that behavior?

❏ Discussed the issue with my partner and have his/her support on the change and the method?

❏ Discussed the plan with the teacher?

❏ Developed a clear and specific goal statement I can tell my child: "Go to school each day. Do all your homework every day."

❏ Broken the goal into manageable units: "Do these 10 math problems neatly and correctly within the next 15 minutes; then I'll check them with you."

❏ Committed to put my time and energy toward monitoring the behavior? If my child is not successful, then it is a clear message to me I need to give him more help and guidance to be sure he is successful.

❏ Gotten rid of excuses I've made for his behavior so that I can send a clear message about what is acceptable and what is not?

❏ Developed a plan to counter my child's likely reaction to these efforts?

❏ Made sure I'm not using vague communication with my child?

REMEMBER THE BOTTOM LINE:

I am giving my child a clear, specific, concrete, direct message and following up on my words to tell my child that I love him so much that I will not allow him to be unsuccessful, that he must do this behavior, and that there is no way out of doing what is requested.

Further Reading

Canter, L. & Canter, M. *Assertive Discipline for Parents.* New York: Harper & Row, 1988.

Glasser, W. *Control Theory in The Classroom.* New York: Harper & Row Publishers, 1986.

C H A P T E R 3 5

School Phobia

"This morning I couldn't find Leslie when it was time to go to school. We searched the house from top to bottom and finally found her hiding in the basement. She's always been such a good girl, and we've had a close relationship, I can't believe she's acting this way about first grade."

"Every morning I think the whole neighborhood knows when Tim and I arrive at school—his screams can been heard for blocks around, I'm sure. I have to peel his fingers off my arms and force him into his third-grade classroom. I'm in tears myself by the time I leave. What could be so terrifying about third grade?"

School phobia doesn't occur in many children, but when it occurs in yours, it can be upsetting to you too, and it can feel as though you're looking at a dead-end academic life for your child before it really gets started.

The study of children's anxieties and fears is not nearly as developed as the study of adult fears, and because school phobia is relatively uncommon (it occurs in only about 2 percent of the school population), many educators may not be familiar with effective approaches.

But you can gain some peace of mind, and help your child, if you understand what school phobia is and how to work with the school psychologist to ease your child's way toward a good, productive school experience.

WHAT WE KNOW NOW

Defining school phobia is difficult. You would think from the term *school phobia* that your child is simply afraid of school or something there. While that may contribute to his feelings, school phobia actually has more to do with separation anxiety—the anxiety many children

normally feel when they begin to separate from their parents and develop their own lives in the world. (See Anxiety.) That's why many psychology textbooks and professional journals now use the term *school refusal* or *school-induced anxiety* rather than *school phobia*. Although many children experience separation anxiety at some time in their lives, few develop school phobia, and it's not clear exactly what pushes a disconcerting and uncomfortable anxiety over the line to become a paralyzing problem.

While school phobia is not purely a fear of school, you cannot completely rule out the possibility that your child is, indeed, afraid of something at school. In some cases, what's labeled school phobia is a combination of real fear and separation anxiety.

Unraveling how a child develops school phobia leads back to that child's home life. Sometimes the child with school phobia is the one who has been so accepted, and feels so accomplished at home, that when he goes to school he feels threatened by the other children and how competent they are, by school tasks, by the responsibility of sharing, and all that comes with getting along with a classroom full of children.

Other times, it may be the child who has spent weeks recovering at home from an illness or an accident who has enormous difficulty getting back to the relatively unprotected status of a child in a classroom.

There are probably as many ways to develop school phobia as there are children, but one important point to remember is that there is no particular personality type that is more likely than others to develop school phobia. It shows up in both genders with equal frequency, without regard for birth order. It does tend to occur more commonly in children between the ages of 6 and 10, although it has been known to occur in both older and younger children. In any case, it's important to see that school phobia is a behavior that grows out of a constellation of situations in a child's life, without regard for gender, age, birth order, or other personality characteristics.

Some of those situations that can make some children more vulnerable to developing school phobia are:

❑ a lack of social skills that has resulted in being teased, being ignored, or fighting at school
❑ a major life change for the child or for her family, such a moving (see Moving), a serious illness of her own, or the serious illness or death of a parent or sibling
❑ an unstable or stressful home life as the result of divorce (see Divorce), financial problems, the remarriage of a parent, or the arrival of a new sibling.

If refusal to go to school occurs for the first time when your child is an adolescent, it may either be a sign that there is something else seriously troubling your youngster, or that something at school genuinely frightens or threatens him. Even though school phobia involves anxiety more than fear, being frightened can worsen the anxiety. If you think your child is frightened at school, some things to look for no matter what your child's age, are:

❑ an insensitive, demanding teacher or other adult at school
❑ inappropriate educational placement—usually being placed in a situation which your child perceives as too demanding.
❑ difficulty with, or fear of, a particular activity—recess, oral reading (see Assertiveness and Shyness, Anxiety), giving reports in front of the class, or physical education.
❑ physical threats or actions by others in school or on the way to school (see Bullies and Victims).
❑ an upsetting school environment in which there is extremely poor morale, violence, unpredictability.

School phobia is different on several counts from truancy, or simply not attending school. The checklist in the box below can help you determine if your child is simply truant, or if she has developed school phobia. Check the behaviors that best describe your child.

If you checked numbers 2, 4, 6, 7, 9, and 11 as behaviors typical of your child, it is more likely your child has developed school phobia than that she is simply being truant. As you can see from the checklist, truants are more likely to be poor students who avoid school but don't want to be home, who may engage in antisocial behaviors when they miss school, and who skip or are late for school intermittently without their parents knowing it.

Children with school phobias, on the other hand, tend to be those who are good students (or were before they missed too much

Truancy or Phobia?

MY CHILD:

❏ is absent intermittently

❏ complains frequently of a stomachache or a headache as a reason to stay home, but isn't really sick

❏ hangs out with people I find unacceptable when he misses school

❏ seems anxious even when he stays home from school

❏ doesn't seem to care about academics, isn't really interested in school

❏ is absent for days or weeks at a time

❏ doesn't seem to feel guilty about missing school

❏ misses school, and I don't find out until after the fact

❏ was a good student when he was attending school regularly

❏ is frequently tardy when he does go to school

❏ has been extremely anxious or has had panic attacks at school

school), who prefer to be at home with their parents, and who miss school for larger chunks of time.

WHEN SHOULD I BE CONCERNED?

In addition to paying attention to the kinds of behaviors described above, you should be concerned if your child:

❏ seems increasingly passive, withdrawn, shy or fearful about participating in school activities

❏ is more frequently fighting, crying, or seeking attention at school

❏ seems to be torn between wanting to stay home, but at the same time being extremely anxious about missing schoolwork

❏ frequently asks the teacher for permission to leave class, especially to go to the school nurse

You should of course be concerned if your child has developed a pattern of crying, screaming, claims of illness, or refusal to go to school, all of which disappear after you agree to let him stay home with you.

Other behaviors that should concern you are:

❏ generally anxious behavior

❏ frequent physical complaints with no medical basis

❏ depression, or what looks like depression (see Depression)

❏ behaviors that indicate your child feels inferior (see Self-Esteem)

❏ perfectionistic tendencies (see Perfectionism)

❏ highly self-critical comments

As with many issues affecting children, it's always a good idea to examine our own roles as parents to understand how we may be involved in our child's issues. You should be concerned if you are thinking of giving in, or have given in to your child's behaviors and demands, and feel that it might be easier for him just to stay home with you. You should also be concerned if you:

❏ feel happier or less worried when your child is home with you

❏ would characterize your attachment to your child as unusually strong

❏ honestly would describe yourself as a protective parent (see Dependency)

❏ know your family is struggling with emotional problems, financial problems or other issues.

WHAT CAN I DO TO HELP?

One of the most helpful things you can do for your child is to clearly understand your own view of your relationship with her and how you feel about her attending school, in order to understand how your child developed school phobia.

Some things to think about:

- How do you feel about your child leaving home? Are you worried what will happen to her at school? Do you lack confidence in the school personnel's ability to protect your child or to treat her with kindness? Most children are adept at picking up unspoken signals from parents, inferring for example that if you don't like her school, you will be happy if she doesn't want to go there.
- What kind of memories do you have of your school days? If you had unpleasant experiences at your child's age, you may unwittingly be magnifying, misinterpreting, or distorting things that happen to her.
- How do you feel about your child's teacher? Strained or poor communication and major disagreements can produce an atmosphere of "us against them" for your child. (See Parent-Teacher Communication, in Part I.)
- How does your family or how do your friends see your child's school? Negative comments can inadvertently play into a child's existing concerns or anxieties.

You can help alleviate some of your child's anxieties (and perhaps your own) about health by taking her for a medical exam to rule out the possibility that she is actually ill.

Because school phobia can be difficult to deal with, particularly if you feel you have some part in your child's issues with school, it's a good idea to talk with the school psychologist both about ways you can help your child and ways you can adjust your own thinking.

WHAT WILL A PROFESSIONAL DO?

You should talk to the school psychologist as soon as you recognize some of the signs that your child may be developing school phobia. Experience has shown that the sooner the problem is addressed, the more likely it is to be worked out. Experience has also shown that children whose school phobia is never addressed have increasingly complicated and serious problems, from learning delays, to an inability to establish friendships with peers, and perhaps even to panic attacks at the thought of leaving the house.

In deciding if your child has school phobia, the school psychologist will probably first talk with you and your child to see what has been going on, and to discern if there is some real fear involved. She will probably also want to talk with the teacher, again, to figure out if the live pet snake in the classroom for example, has anything to do with your child not wanting to go to school. The school psychologist can also explain school phobia to the teacher if she hasn't seen it before, and can act as a liason between you and the teacher. Many teachers simply take a "get tough" attitude and want to force a child to come to school without recognizing the complexity of the problem. Forcing school attendence may get your child to school, but won't address the basic anxieties that made him want to stay away in the first place.

The overall approach of a school psychologist, working with the teacher and you, will be to develop a plan that centers on getting your child back to school. Often this means having your child come to school for a short time each day, for example, being rewarded for those times, and then slowly lengthening the time spent at school. The case study about James shows how a child with school phobia was slowly reintroduced to school.

While there are many reasonable variations on a plan like this that a school could use, there are other approaches most schools will almost certainly not use. Your child's school psychologist and administration will probably not go along with:

❏ using long-term homebound tutoring. Tutoring can work well for school phobia, but always as a way to get a child back in school.

❏ ignoring the problem. School phobia is a potentially serious problem, and there are laws in every state about school attendance that, if ignored, result in the school's seeking help from a state social service agency.

See also:

❏ Anxiety
❏ Assertiveness and Shyness
❏ Bullies
❏ Dependency
❏ Depression
❏ Fears
❏ Moving
❏ Perfectionism
❏ Self-Esteem
❏ Divorce/Single Parents

Case Study: James and School Phobia

James seemed fine as a first-grader. He liked school and did well, had plenty of friends, and seldom had to be reprimanded for talking or rambunctious behavior. Over the summer his grandfather died. James had spent every summer fishing and hiking with Pops since he was a toddler, and he missed his Pops terribly. James' mother was also very upset at her father's sudden death, and by the end of the summer she was quite depressed.

When school started, James was at first happy to see his friends and his new teacher. But within a few weeks, he complained of so many headaches and upset stomachs (he even threw up one morning) that his mom was letting him stay home more and more often. She felt she hardly had the energy to make him go to school anyway, and it was pleasant to have him around the house. Once the before-school tantrum was over, James spent the day reading or helping her around the kitchen.

But she knew he had to go to school, and the principal kept calling. Finally, James' mom consulted with the school psychologist. After talking at length with her and with James, and after a medical exam to be sure James wasn't really ill, she told her James had developed school phobia. But the psychologist also said she had a plan to get James happily back to school. The school hired a tutor, and she and the school psychologist met with James and his mom and dad at their home to present the plan:

Week 1: The tutor meets with James at

Case Study: James and School Phobia (cont.)

home to deliver his lessons, get acquainted, and to develop a rapport.

Week 2: The tutor and James' mom come with him to school for tutoring in the classroom after everyone else has left for the day. (In less severe cases, the tutor might work with the child in a nonclassroom setting—such as a conference room or a quiet section of the library—at school during this week).

Week 3: James' mom no longer joins him during tutoring sessions.

Weeks 4–8: The tutor slowly increases the number of hours she works with James at school, with the goal being to work with him at school during normal school hours. For example, at first she would work with James from 3–4 P.M., the next week she would work with him from 2–4 P.M., then 12–3 P.M., etc.

Weeks 9–12: James spends a little time each day in the classroom, gradually increasing the time.

Weeks 12–15: The tutor works with James less and less as he is able to work on his own or in the classroom, until the tutor is no longer needed.

To go along with the school plan, the school psychologist also worked with James' mom and dad on ways they could handle any difficulties he might have with the plan, using a system of rewards for the behavior they wanted and punishments for noncooperation. James' mom was also encouraged to receive personal counseling so that she could resolve her feelings about her father's death, and help James in ways that were constructive for him.

Self-Esteem

"Lisa does extremely well in sports; she's always been the best player on any team. It's not quite the same for her academically, but she's definitely better than average. However, to hear her talk, you'd think she was a complete loser. She seems to focus on what she can't do, or on what she doesn't do as well, rather than on her best qualities. I think that attitude hurts her, academically."

Self-esteem is a term every parent runs into just about from the day their child is born. Instilling, protecting, and developing their child's self-esteem is at the top of the list of essential parenting skills because we know that a strong sense of self-esteem is critical for everything from successful social relationships to your child's ability to learn.

When your child gets to school, interest in her self-esteem goes into overdrive, and for the most part, with good reason. A healthy sense of self-esteem is crucial to many aspects of her further development, not the least of which is learning. But while everyone seems to be aware of the importance of self-esteem, not everyone agrees on exactly what it means. You'll be more able to help your child with self-esteem issues once you see the issue clearly yourself.

WHAT WE KNOW NOW

In defining self-esteem, most experts agree on drawing a distinction between it and self-concept, even though the two terms are often—though incorrectly—used almost interchangeably. Self-concept is a person's perception of herself, including her attitude, feelings, and knowledge about all her traits: her abilities, skills, appearance, and social acceptability.

Self-esteem, on the other hand, is her evaluation of those traits and the degree to which she can accept and approve of them. To understand the difference between the two, take for example a youngster who accurately describes herself as a good student who is intellectually capable (that's her self-concept), but who nevertheless doesn't think much of herself (that's self-esteem) because she doesn't have as much ability in sports as she would like in order to fit in with the "jocks" at school, whom she admires.

So a child's self-concept can be positive, but if the abilities she has aren't the ones she wants (or aren't the ones her parents want), she can still have low self-esteem or feel badly enough about herself to affect her academic performance or her social relationships. And, self-esteem is so subjective a personal evaluation that it may not make sense to anyone else, as in the case of the third-grade boy who is devastated when he gets a B on his report card because to him, only perfect A's are acceptable.

Current research shows that while all children's self-esteem during puberty, roughly between grades four and ten, is somewhat fragile, it is particularly so for girls, presumably because of cultural pressures to play a supporting rather than a leading role, and because of cultural messages that she is not, in fact "good enough" since she now needs makeup and dieting to win approval. A 1991 American Association of University Women report on a study of 3,000 children in grades four through ten showed that while a majority of elementary school children stated they were "happy the way I am," eight years later, less than one-third of the girls retained that degree of self-esteem compared to nearly half the boys. Both Hispanic and African-American girls in the study started with higher self-esteem than Caucasian girls. By high school, Hispanic girls' self-esteem had declined in school achievement, confidence in their abilities and talents, and in other areas such as appearance and family relationships. African-American girls in the study retained their self-esteem, but by high school had lost their positive feelings about teachers and schoolwork. Caucasian girls, even though they started out with lower self-esteem than either Hispanics or African Americans, declined in self-esteem farther and faster in all areas than either of the other two groups.

It's hard to imagine how children get to the point of judging themselves so harshly. We do know that self-esteem develops gradually beginning the day your child is born. Initially, very young children have self-concepts only, because they aren't capable yet of evaluating themselves. Their self-concept depends on what they are told about themselves—"Aren't you pretty!" or "Can't you ever do anything right?"

As kids mature, they begin to evaluate their own self-worth, forming self-esteem, and they begin to add other sources to do this, primarily teachers and their peers. Since school is such an important source of input, you need to really listen to what your child says about school, not just hearing what he does in school, but also how he feels about what happens in school.

Self-esteem continues to develop until it becomes fairly stable by about age 10, just in time for adolescence to put it to the test. Clearly, the strongest influence on a child's self-esteem is parents, since children spend their early years soaking up what adults around them think of them, and then to a large degree, reflecting in their actions what they have heard. The next greatest influence on the formation of your child's self-esteem are your child's teachers. And last, contrary to popular wisdom, are his peers.

Children with a healthy sense of self-esteem should feel relatively capable in both academic and nonacademic areas. They should:

❐ show a reasonable amount of confidence in attempting tasks,
❐ generally like school, and
❐ look and seem relatively happy and optimistic about school and friends.

Children whose self-esteem is hurting tend to:

❐ have lower academic achievement,
❐ experience less social success (see Friends),
❐ be more prone to depression (see Depression),
❐ be more likely to be influenced by peer pressure to indulge in drugs and alcohol (See Drug Abuse),
❐ withdraw and generally be more anxious (see Anxiety),
❐ lack confidence, and
❐ be consistently hard on themselves, easily turning inward with negative thoughts and feelings about themselves.

Girls with low self-esteem tend to be self-critical, viewing themselves as "not smart enough" or "not good enough" for academic achievement or their dream career. During puberty, girls with low self-esteem also often:

❑ fear success,
❑ lack assertiveness, and
❑ feel victimized.

In addition, girls with low self-esteem may show it through eating disorders, substance abuse, dropping out of school, depression, poor academic performance, and limited consideration of job opportunities.

WHEN SHOULD I BE CONCERNED?

As with many behavior issues, you should be concerned any time you feel uncomfortable or worried over your child's behavior, particularly when you see a significant negative change you can't explain or didn't anticipate. Review the list of poor self-esteem characteristics above to see if the description fits your child. You can also listen to what your child says about herself. Self-deprecating talk is, of course, a strong clue to low self-esteem. But so can be continuous comments that are hypercritical of others.

You should also be concerned if your child:

❑ shows serious lack of confidence in one or more significant areas, such as school and learning or peer relationships
❑ begins to verbally or physically bully others
❑ withdraws from social contact she used to enjoy
❑ is reluctant to try new things
❑ overdoes attempts to draw attention to herself or brags constantly
❑ is generally pessimistic regarding herself and her ability to exert an influence on people and events that concern her
❑ seems to consistently think you don't love her or prize her as much as she thinks you should

And you should be concerned if your child's teacher expresses her concern about your child's self-esteem because of behavior she sees in the classroom.

WHAT CAN I DO TO HELP?

A generally positive home life with definite boundaries and clearly expressed love forms the foundation from which children learn to have high personal as well as academic self-esteem. If you feel some of these factors are missing from your family, you can contact the school psychologist for help. (See What Will a Professional Do?, below.)

But if you feel that stronger effort on your part might shore up a temporarily lagging academic self-esteem in your youngster, there are some things you can do on your own.

■ Examine your academic expectations for your child. Are they realistic given your child's abilites, or do they have more to do with what you need for her to accomplish?
■ Emphasize to your child what she does right in school more than subjects she has problems with. A low grade in English should not overshadow all her work and success in Social Studies.
■ Encourage your child to continue trying even when she doesn't meet with success, with comments like "I'm glad you enjoy learning," or "I'm proud of how hard you work."
■ Recognize improvement, as well as successes.

Studies have shown that girls who like math and science in school are more likely to aspire to professional careers than those who don't, so you might consider looking for ways to enhance your daughter's experience with these subjects. You can:

- Ask the teacher if at least part of the math or science curriculum in their class could be taught in a relaxed, cooperative, group atmosphere that tends to make the subjects more accessible to all, including girls.
- Talk with your daughter at home about what she's doing in physics or chemistry classes, and relate those to things that happen in everyday life. If you are not familiar enough with these subjects to do this, talk with the teacher about incorporating "real world" examples into class lectures.
- Help your child's elementary, middle, or high school teacher find scientists or mathematicians of both genders to visit and speak to the class, to help reduce the negative and intimidating stereotypes about people in these fields.

Another way studies have shown girls can avoid the perilous personal and academic self-esteem drops of puberty is for them to be involved in sports. (See Competition.) Girls in these studies who participated in some kind of sport tended to have above average levels of self-esteem and less depression.

WHAT WILL A PROFESSIONAL DO?

If it seems your child's academic performance is being affected by low self-esteem, the school psychologist may want to do a full assessment. This kind of assessment will focus on what your child's skills are compared with the perceptions she has, her teachers have, and you have of her. If your major concern is for your child's academic performance, then the focus of testing will be on intelligence and achieve-ment. But if your sense is that your child's low self-esteem and resulting poor social development is affecting academics, testing will focus on personality and emotional factors.

In either case, the school psychologist will need maximum cooperation from you so that she can honestly evaluate the difference between "reality" and your child's view of things. Consequently, in the interview, you and your partner can expect very straightforward questions that may seem quite personal. Remember though, that as a professional, your school psychologist maintains strict confidentiality.

Some of the tests you or your child may be asked to complete are instruments such as the Child Behavior Checklist, the Social Skills Rating System, or the Personality Inventory for Children. (See Evaluation and Testing, in Part I).

The school psychologist's assessment of your child should do two things:

1 Confirm if your child has a self-esteem problem.
2 Add more detail about the nature and severity of your child's self-esteem problems.

The assessment should show, for example, which of these areas (could be one or more) your child feels bad about:

❐ academic performance or capabilities
❐ physical appearance or traits
❐ behavior
❐ physical abilities regarding sports
❐ relationships with peers

The nature of the problem will pinpoint one or more of these areas, and the severity will show if almost all areas are involved or if only one or two are involved, but very intensely. This information will give the school psychologist the direction to pursue in working with your child, focusing on classroom and teacher for academic problems for example, or counseling for relationship problems.

The psychologist may also talk with you about expectations for your child. The seat of many children's self-esteem problems lies in a mismatch between parental expectations and a child's true ability in a specific area.

See also:

❐ Anxiety
❐ Depression
❐ Friends
❐ Evaluation and Testing, in Part I

Further Reading

Clemes, H. & Bean, R. *How To Raise Teenagers' Self-Esteem.* New York: Price Stern Sloan. 1990.

Fuller, C. *365 Ways to Build Your Child's Self-Esteem.* Colorado Springs, CO: Piñon Press, 1994.

Glenn, H. & Nelsen, J. *Raising Self-Reliant Children in a Self-Indulgent World.* Rocklin, CA: Prima Publishing & Communications, 1987.

Helmstetter, S. *Predictive Parenting: What to Say When You Talk to Your Kids.* New York: Pocket Books, 1989.

Loomans, D. & Loomans, J. *Full Esteem Ahead: 100 Ways to Build Self-Esteem in Children and Adults.* Tiburon, CA: H. J. Kramer, Inc., 1994.

Phillips, D. & Bernstein, F. *How To Give Your Child a Great Self-Image.* New York: Plume, 1989.

CHAPTER 37

Stress

"Reggie has claimed to have a headache so bad he can't do his homework three times this week. We even went to the doctor and there doesn't seem to be anything physically wrong with him. But the headaches go on and the homework never gets done."

"Tyesa is 15 now, and instead of seeming more mature about school and responsibility, all we hear about is how 'stressed-out' she is. What could possibly be so stressful for her?"

Stress is one of those words that's become a part of many people's daily vocabulary over the last 10 years or so. It has certainly become part of most people's lives—children and adults alike.

However, ask your child if she felt stressed at school today, and if she's younger than about 8 she probably won't know what you're talking about. That doesn't mean she doesn't feel stressed; it just means the concept and the ability to explain complex feelings and reactions may still be beyond her.

That's why your understanding of what those stresses are likely to be, and how to help your child learn to cope with them, will be a great help to her.

WHAT WE KNOW NOW

To a child, stress could be defined as the result of an event that leaves her feeling bad or upset. On the other hand, an adolescent may define stress as the basic demands of life coming at him from teachers and parents, or as anything he classifies as a hassle.

Both of these ideas, though very different, are legitimate definitions because stress is ultimately seen through the eyes of the beholder. What your child considers stressful is con-

nected to her temperament: some children have a low threshold for challenges and changes, and they feel stressed or uncomfortable at the slightest pressure. Others seem to be able to weather a lot before they feel overwhelmed. We are all born with a particular temperament: it's the fundamental way we approach the world, and it's extremely difficult to change it. While you'll want to teach your child ways to cope with stress at school and at home, it's helpful if you can do that with regard for your child's particular temperament.

Generally, stress is experienced in three stages: alarm, resistance, and exhaustion. For example, your child is sitting in class and finds out there will be a pop quiz and she hasn't studied. Her first reaction is alarm, during which her heart rate and breathing increase and her mind races thinking of how she will make it through this quiz. In the second stage, resistance, the body attempts to slow down and return to normal functioning. But now your child is taking the quiz, and she can't slow down. She's still pumped up, struggling for the answers and chewing her pencil. By the time the quiz is over, she's probably in the third stage, exhaustion, when she says to herself, "Whew," takes a deep breath and begins to focus her attention on something else—even though she may feel drained.

Most preteen children will not then come home from school and tell you directly how stressful their day was because of the unexpected quiz. This is partly because they don't yet have the conceptual ability to label what they felt as stress. Instead, you will have to be alert to the signs of stress such as your child criticizing the teacher, complaining about being treated unfairly, and other similar signs discussed later.

A key point for parents to understand is that not only do *stressors*—things that cause stress—change with your child's age, but things that are stressors for children are usually very different from things that adults normally identify as stressors. For example, things like having the right cartoon character lunch box or the right label on his clothing may be a big deal to your child, but seem like a small annoyance to you. Even so, that doesn't negate what a big deal it is to your child. There are also stressors about things parents can't change, and those are likely to involve something you did such as working long hours, or perhaps something you didn't do, such as not volunteer in your child's classroom when most of the other parents did. It may be hard to face the source of your child's stress when the source is you, even when what you're doing may ultimately be for the best. For example, one of the most prevalent stressors for children of all ages is parents who divorce. Younger children find it stressful because they are naturally still egocentric in the way they see the world, and they blame themselves for problems their parents are having. Older children get disgusted with fighting and bitterness. They know it's not their fault, but they feel the stress anyway.

Often, the younger the child, the less able he is to cope with stress because he simply hasn't yet learned how. While older children and adolescents can certainly still feel stressed, they tend not to become overwhelmed as easily because they have figured out how to handle it by talking about it, by solving problems, or by using other techniques they may have learned. At any age, when a child successfully copes with a stressful situation, it can feel like a real victory, and it often results in a higher level of confidence and competence for that child, so there's value in teaching coping techniques to your child, and then letting him use them in his own way to adapt to stress in positive ways.

While specific stressors may differ for different children, stress is usually the result of:

❏ something new and unfamiliar
❏ not knowing what to expect in a situation
❏ a situation with an element of unpredictablity or suspense
❏ an expectation of an unpleasant outcome
❏ all major developmental hurdles, such as separation from parents for daycare, going to school, school performance, relationships with friends at school.

Studies of adolescents have shown that academic stress for them comes primarily from four sources:

❏ Parents and their expectations
❏ Friends and their expectations (see Friends)
❏ The importance of school (see Anxiety, Grades, Competition)
❏ Fear of failure (see Fears)

From these lists, you can see that, in many cases, stress is just part of life and necessary changes. Your job as a parent is not to remove all stressors from your child's life, but to help him learn how to cope with the stressful situations that no one can change.

WHEN SHOULD I BE CONCERNED?

Younger children especially may not be able to report clearly to you or to a teacher that they are feeling stressed. Look for clues in the kind of language they use to describe events. Words that may indicate your child is feeling particularly stressed are words, such as: *sad, worried, scared, angry, disgusted*; or concepts they may be acting out, such as seeming overwhelmed, helpless, hopeless, fearful, nervous, disappointed, or guilty. Keep in mind that as children grow, they are more able to explain how they feel conceptually, so that the words may change, but the idea is the same.

Often physical symptoms are the first way in which stress is noticeable. A younger child might suddenly begin wetting or soiling themselves, or have sleep problems. Older children may report headaches, abdominal pain, fatigue, or vague physical symptoms that make it impossible for them to go to school, finish homework, or attend activities. And children of any age tend to escalate or exaggerate these symptoms until someone finally gives them the attention they're looking for.

If any of these symptoms appear in your child, and you think they do indicate stress, you should be concerned because they also indicate that your child is not coping well with the stress and could use some help, either from you or from a professional.

WHAT CAN I DO TO HELP?

The first thing to do is to listen carefully to your child, noting behavior changes like those listed above that might mean your child is having a problem with stress. Most children won't directly tell you they're feeling stressed; most don't really know the meaning of the word until about fourth grade. If your child either won't talk about, say, an upcoming gymnastics competition with you, or she brushes off your questions and you feel sure she's feeling pretty stressed about it, what can you do? We have three good ways to help you know when it's time to help your child deal with stress:

1 Talk to another source. Try the coach or her teacher or, perhaps, parents of your child's best friends, and ask if they have noticed any behavior changes or signs of stress in your child. Seeing if their observations coincide with your own can give you some direction.

2 You can take your child at her word when she says everything is fine, even if you are quite sure she is having a problem with stress. But then you must hold her accountable for schoolwork and gymnastics practice as usual. If your child then says she can't do it all, you can revisit the subject of stress. You can use the same process if your child gives an illogical reason for why she's behaving differently. If you hold her accountable to her reasoning as well as her actions, the stress topic will come up again. In either case, you can repeat the process until you and your child have come to some understanding or resolution about her behavior.

3 A child younger than about 8 who seems to be agreeing with you when you ask if she's feeling stressed, probably is just echoing whatever you say. Children of this age don't really know or understand what might be wrong, even though they might indeed be feeling stressed. In this case, an inability to explain themselves is not really a problem, but developmentally appropriate for children under age 8. That's where your common sense has to take over, and you take your best guess at what's going on with your child, adjusting your actions with her as you figure out how she's feeling.

If you are concerned that your child may need help coping with stress, you can begin teaching him ways to deal with it. A starting point is to talk with him about how you handle stress. Three points are most important:

1 Model for your child: show him, through your actions, how you cope with a stressful situation. Talk with him if you can while you are feeling stressed, or explain how you coped with something stressful in the past. Tell him how it made you feel (frightened, pressured), and how you resolved the situation. Part of modeling is showing not only how you handled stress well, but what happened when you've handled it badly.

2 Talk about how you handled stress badly, acknowledging your mistakes, showing your child how you learned from them instead of denying that things were your fault and remaining upset over them.

3 Set realistic goals (as opposed to overly high goals) for yourself and for your child. For example, when in an attempt to keep old friends while making new ones during his first year in middle school, your youngster finds he has overcommitted by joining two youth groups—an intramural soccer team and the band—you can help him ease the stress by showing him how to prioritize. Talk about how you've had to make some tough choices yourself: for instance, the time you gave up the art class you loved because juggling work deadlines, family responsibilities, and the class were giving you ulcers. Then sit down with him and have him list all his commitments. By going over the list and discussing the reasons for each choice and its importance in terms of priority (schoolwork comes first) and really listening to the reasons he gives when he resists dropping an activity ("But I won't ever see Chris if I'm not in the band!"), you can help him to prioritize the list and see that dropping something is the only way to reduce the stress.

Once your child is in a stressful situation, you can use the checklist in the following box to help him work out what to do about it and to shed some light (for him and you) on how he usually goes about coping. The list includes both effective and ineffective ways of dealing with stress. If he chooses mostly ineffective methods (wishful thinking, for example), you can talk with him about how that works compared to how he thinks other methods, such as problem solving, might work and what has happened for you when you have tried different methods. This list is best for children who are over the age of 7. Children younger than that are more likely to want magical solutions and really believe the kindergarten teacher could be replaced by Mary Poppins.

If you are aware of your child's stress over a family situation, it might also be a good idea to talk with the teacher about it. She may have already noticed that your child has had a hard time concentrating or has missed the deadline for a report. Although the teacher won't be able to do much to alleviate the stress, you can throw light on your child's behavior without making excuses.

Conversely, if you think a school problem is the source of your child's stress, you should ask the teacher what she thinks is going on with your child. Between the two of you, you should have a pretty complete picture of your child's life, which will help in figuring out what may be stressful for him.

Other things you can do to understand and help your child cope with stress:

■ *Listen.* Listen to the way your child describes a stressful event. Sometimes you can help him take a blown-out-of-proportion worry and give him some perspective. For example, in a discussion with your first-grader about getting

What to Do . . . What to Do. . . ?

(Developed by Anthony Paolitto and Kathy Jaret, school psychologists)

PROBLEM SOLVE:

❑ Get information about problem
❑ Think of different solutions
❑ Make a plan and follow it

SEEK SUPPORT:

❑ Talk to someone about it
❑ Get help or advice

FOCUS ON THE POSITIVE:

❑ Hope for the best
❑ Look at the bright side
❑ Realize I'm growing, changing, learning because of this

REDUCE TENSION:

❑ Take a rest
❑ Exercise

WISHFUL THINKING:

❑ Wish it was over
❑ Daydream as an escape
❑ Hope for a miracle
❑ Wish you could feel different

BLAME MYSELF:

❑ Criticize myself because it happened
❑ Convince myself it's my fault

DENY IT:

❑ Try to forget the whole thing
❑ Wait to see what happens
❑ Avoid being with people
❑ Keep it all to myself

on the wrong bus to come home from school, you can listen to his description, discuss the event, and compare it to other events to help him see that one event does not make someone a good or bad person.

■ Remember that school life and friends are of prime importance to your child. Your child may be fine at home, but can still find it difficult to adjust to expectations of peers at school, for example. Talk about school with your child and help him to see positive things he is involved in there.

■ Encourage your child to connect to others in ways that are comfortable for him. For some children that means sports; for others it means a less competitive activity, such as 4H clubs or after-school science or crafts classes.

■ For children who tend to be overachievers and keep taking on more obligations, you can use the example above to help your child prioritize and to keep him from setting unrealistic goals for himself. You can also strive to accept and reward your child for less than perfect performances. (See Perfectionism.)

■ Help them find new coping behaviors. Preteens and teens tend to withdraw into their bedrooms or watch television excessively in the face of stress; their approach is typically indirect and inactive. Encourage them to try more direct and active approaches they might be interested in, such as making some of their own decisions, developing new friendships, and working hard to achieve a goal.

■ See if stress stems from other issues. See for example, topics on Anxiety, Fears, Lying, Self-Esteem, Shyness, Bullies and Victims.

WHAT WILL A PROFESSIONAL DO?

If your child's stress level is significantly affecting his academic achievement, the school psychologist will most likely want to do an assessment. This assessment will focus on six primary factors:

1 *Your child's age and developmental stage.* She will likely review your child's school records and interview you and the teacher for this information.

2 *Your child's intellectual level.* Generally, higher cognitive ability may give a child more coping capacity. The psychologist will probably look at existing school IQ and achievement data on your child and may also do an individual assessment of your child's intellectual functioning.

3 *Your child's temperament.* She should observe your child and interview you, the teacher, and your child to discern personality characteristics such as your child's flexibility, persistence, and the intensity with which she responds to different levels of stimuli.

4 *Your level of support for your child,* which the psychologist will determine through interviews with you.

5 *Your methods of coping with stress.* What you do is a model that your child will follow, so it's critical for the psychologist to understand what is normal for you to do in stressful situations. She will determine this through interviews with you.

6 *Your child's relationships with friends* and with others who influence her. The psychologist will gather this information through observing your child, teacher reports and self-reporting inventories. (See Appendix D, Samples from Tests and Assessments).

Some schools have stress reduction groups, particularly for children whose parents are divorced. (See Divorce.) These emphasize recognizing problems and problem solving skills.

The school psychologist and the teacher can also implement one or both of two types of strategies often used to help children cope with stress. They are:

1 *Direct Methods:* Talking with the child about the stressful situation and his reactions to it. The psychologist would most likely use a checklist like the one in the section above to help your child determine how he works with stress, and how he might change that. The goal of this kind of counseling is to help the child to think differently about the stressor so that it's not so overwhelming to him.

2 *Indirect Methods:* Working in a group (a special group or an entire classroom) on the issues children find stressful. This uses some of the direct methods along with peer support to help children learn to cope with stress.

See also:

❏ Appendix D, Samples from Tests and Assessments
❏ Anxiety
❏ Competition
❏ Expectations, in Part I
❏ Fears
❏ Friends
❏ Grades
❏ Divorce/Single Parents

Further Reading

Cohen, D. & Cohen, S. *Teenage Stress.* New York: Laurel Leaf Books, 1992.

C H A P T E R 3 8

Study Skills

"It seems that Juanita spends hours sitting at her desk with her books open, but her grades sure don't look like she studies much. I try to help, but I'm not sure what to do. She's bright, I know that, but all her studying doesn't seem to do much for her."

There's an interesting paradox in most schools. Educators share a goal of guiding their students towards becoming independent learners. They agree that every student needs to know how to study in order to do so. Even students know they need study skills and they worry they won't have them when they really need them. Studies have shown that a significant portion of ninth-graders anticipate a "big problem" with improving study skills to fit high school demands, and nearly half reported they felt a great deal of pressure to get good grades (read: study effectively) in high school.

But research has shown that study skills are not necessarily naturally acquired nor specifically taught in school, although the need for study skills is becoming more clearly recognized. As a result, more and more schools are including study skills as a part of their curriculum.

If your child is struggling with how to study, you don't have to stand by and hope he picks it up. And if your child is just starting out in school, it's probably best not to assume he will be taught the study techniques he needs. Once you understand which are the key study skills, you can guide your child toward figuring out the techniques that work best for him in acquiring those skills.

WHAT WE KNOW NOW

Beginning in about third grade, when children have trouble with academics, it is often study skills—their lack, misuse, or poor development—that are at least part of the problem. For a few students, a closer look reveals a legitimate learning disorder (see Learning Disabilities), a problem with how they view their studies (see Anxiety), or lack of motivation (see Motivation). But for most, ineffective studying is a simpler issue, involving the learning and application of a few specific skills.

While good study skills usually do lead to higher grades, they do more than that for your child. Children are likely to increase their feelings of competence and confidence as they learn how to study more effectively. Children who know how to study also tend to approach their school work with a positive attitude, rather than feeling negative or anxious, because they feel capable of accomplishing academic goals.

Study skills are basic learning tools, and the more adept your child is with his tools, the more successful a learner he will be. No matter what your child's age, he will need good study skills to move through the four stages of learning. These stages are:

❏ Taking in information from books, lectures

or presentations. To do this well, your child must be able to listen and read.

❐ Organizing information. Your child will need to know how to underline, take notes, make lists, or be able to ask himself questions about the material.

❐ Practicing or rehearsing the organized material, which requires some kind of review or discussion by your child.

❐ Recalling and/or applying the information. This means that your child needs skills in test taking and in writing or preparing reports.

There is no simple, single formula for acquiring or improving these skills that applies to all children, so that your job will be to help your child discover how he learns best and then help him work out a study system that fits those needs.

In doing this, you can use some of the techniques suggested below in What Can I Do to Help?, or see the section titled Homework. But no matter what techniques you use, there a few basic rules you'll need to follow:

■ *Establish a study routine.* Decide with your young child, or ask your older child, to pick a place, find a time, and arrange a space for studying. Be sure all three fit into your family routine so that you and your child will be able to stick to the routine a major part of the time.

■ *Make sure study surroundings allow your child to concentrate.* Some children actually do study well with quiet background music. Others need total silence. Agree with your child ahead of time that he won't be interrupted during the designated time with telephone calls or visiting friends.

■ *Keep track of assignments.* For younger children, this may mean using a system of folders: one color for material to take home, another color

for assignments to bring back to school. For older children, go over with them at the beginning of the school year how to write down assignments in a notebook or other organizer. There they will note dates that assignments are due, and schedule time for studying before a test, for researching and writing before a report is due. These skills, which are really time management skills, are discussed later in What Can I Do to Help?

WHEN SHOULD I BE CONCERNED?

Figuring out when a child needs help learning to study is fairly straightforward. But keep in mind that it's a good idea to teach these skills to your child before he is having a problem, because it is likely he won't be taught them specifically at school.

You should be concerned when:

❐ You receive calls or notes from the teacher questioning if your child is really studying.

❐ Your child complains he doesn't understand the material even though he spends time with his books open . . . studying. (See Motivation.)

❐ He picks up on less relevant points rather than main points.

❐ Your child is spending noticeably less time, or noticeably more time, studying than are his classmates, and he is not necessarily achieving great results.

❐ Your child's grades are not reflective of the time you've seen him put into studying.

❐ You notice when you help your child study that he has a disorganized approach. (See Organization, Homework.)

❐ Your child simply tells you he doesn't know how to study or that he needs help learning to study.

WHAT CAN I DO TO HELP?

Your first step in helping your child learn to study is to talk about why he has to study in the first place. As with many issues that bridge school and home, you will no doubt address it in conversation hundreds of times while your child is of school age. The focus of your talks with your child on this issue should be that everyone has to practice in order to become proficient, no matter what the skill: kicking soccer goals, playing the piano, sketching horses, or learning history facts. Studying is just a formalized way of practicing for school.

It helps young children to become familiar with the most basic study tools they have— their books. You can walk them through the parts of a book to remind them of the sources they have for finding information. Sometimes just remembering to refer to the index, a glossary, chapter headings, chapter summaries, or the table of contents is a great help.

Earlier in this section you read about the four stages of learning your child needs to reach while he studies: acquiring, organizing, rehearsing, and recalling and applying information. The study strategies listed below can help him with each of those stages. He will pick up these strategies best if you explain to him how to use them, then show him on one or two strategies, then guide him as he practices what you have explained. Choose a time when neither of you feels rushed or in a panic about an upcoming test.

Study strategies to try when your child is:

- *Acquiring Information:* When your child reads to get information, it helps some children to think of their reading like a sports practice:

  ❑ He has to warm up, or get ready to read.

To do this, he should check out the chapter title, subtitles in the chapter, pictures, graphs, and captions, and the questions listed at the end of the chapter. Then read the first and the last paragraph.

❑ He has to apply effort as he reads. Some people call this *active reading.* That means your child should jot down notes (see the section below on notetaking), pick out the most important ideas and restate them in his own words, and think of questions he has about the material.

❑ *He has to cool down.* When your child finishes a part of a chapter, encourage him to stop for a minute to think of and write down what question the teacher might have on a test from that part.

There are several methods educators have come up with to help children with acquiring information, and each has its own ways of describing how to acquire information. One of the most popular is called *SQ3R*, which stands for:

❑ *Survey:* Quickly scan the reading assignment

❑ *Question:* Make up questions by turning headings into *who, what, where, how,* and *why* questions.

❑ *Read:* Read to answer the questions you made up.

❑ *Recite:* When you are finished, try to answer your questions without looking at the book or the notes you took.

❑ *Review:* Immediately review the lesson to organize ideas and to help you remember it.

Other methods are similar to SQ3R. Some of them are:

❑ *T-SQUARE:* Take the Textbook, Survey,

Question, Underline, Answer, Review, and Expand.

❑ *REAP*: Read, Encode, or put into own language, Annotate by writing notes, and Ponder to process or think about the message.

❑ *PQ4R*: Preview, Question, Read, Reflect, Recite, and Review.

You can tailor any of these to fit your child and his language, using these steps as a guide.

■ *Organizing and Rehearsing Information.* A system of notetaking can be very helpful for your child as he reaches the upper elementary grades, middle school, and high school. Here are the basics for a notetaking system that is like outlining:

❑ As he reads, your child should write down the most important idea from each paragraph or small group of paragraphs, remembering that the first sentence of a paragraph is usually the topic sentence.

❑ Indent and briefly list important details in his own words, using symbols (+ or = or &), and abbreviations.

❑ Indent again and list subordinate details.

When your child has finished taking notes, have him go over them to be sure what he has written is accurate and makes sense to him. Then have him write one question he thinks he might find on a test about that material in the margin next to each section of his notes. The questions can help him study later.

Once your child has practiced using this technique while he is reading, it should become easier for him to use it to take notes during class lectures. He can practice listening for and writing down main ideas, then abbreviating and rewording details.

To use his notes to study for a test, he could try the RCRC technique:

❑ Read a main idea or small section of notes.

❑ Cover the section with his hand.

❑ Recite what he read.

❑ Check to see if he was right.

Another way for an older child to study from a textbook or review for a test is to write a summary of the material. The steps to do that are:

❑ Skim the material.

❑ List key points.

❑ Look over the key points and combine those which are related into single statements.

❑ Cross out the least important statements.

❑ Combine more single statements and refine them until you have a summary that is clear, accurate, complete, and brief.

Sometimes the organizing task means organizing materials as much as organizing ideas. For a younger child, show him how to use two pocket folders to organize his work. One is for in-class use and one is for take-home work. The in-class folder could have pockets labeled "paper" and "work;" the take-home folder could have pockets labeled "leave at home" and "bring back to school."

For an older child with a notebook, have him label each divider with the name of a subject, then label one more divider "extra paper," and another divider "take home" for finished work or notices for parents.

Assignment books or calendars can be helpful for teaching time management to children, beginning in about the third grade. Of course your child should record when assignments are due and when certain events or activities are scheduled. But you can also guide him in planning to read a certain number of pages in a textbook each night, or in estimat-

H = *Heading* Includes first and last name, date, subject and a page number if needed.

O = *Organized* Write on the front side of the paper, save a left and right margin, use good spacing between words, about one finger width.

W = *Written neatly* Write words and numbers on the lines, erasing neatly.

Study Skills Teachers Look For

Effective studying begins with classroom behavior and continues home with each child. If you are concerned about your child's study skills and you are scheduled to talk with her teacher, use this list when you meet to guide your conversation. In a survey of more than 200 middle school teachers, 85 percent agreed that these school behaviors could help set your child up for study skills success.

In reviewing study skills, ask the teacher whether your child:

❐ Asks for help when needed.
❐ Listens during lectures or discussions.
❐ Attends class regularly.
❐ Comes to class with the proper materials.
❐ Utilizes independent work time in class effectively.
❐ Is ready to work at the beginning of class.
❐ Turns work in on time.
❐ Socializes only at appropriate times.
❐ Prepares for tests.

ing how long it will take him to review his notes for a test, or in planning how far ahead of the due date he should start collecting rocks for his science fair geology project.

Another aspect of organization is turning in papers that look neat and are easy for the teacher to read. Use the HOW method described in the box above so your young child knows what a neat paper should look like.

- *Recalling and Applying Information* for test and report writing. These are the concrete reasons your child needs strong study habits. You can help your child with test taking by teaching him to:

❐ Anticipate what will be on the test by using the notetaking and summary writing methods described above.
❐ Study and memorize by using the RCRC method described above.
❐ Respond to specific test formats, such as multiple choice and true-false.

For any test format, your child should learn to:

❐ Read the questions carefully.
❐ Note if "all of the above" or "none of the above" is a choice.

❐ Go through the test methodically, answering those questions he is sure of.
❐ Make a mark near the question number if he doesn't know the answer, so that he can come back to it.
❐ Check his work when he is finished.
❐ Change an answer on either true-false or multiple choice tests only if he has a very good reason to. Usually the first response is the most accurate.

What You Need to Know in Order to Learn

TO:	YOU'LL NEED TO
Acquire Information	Listen, and Read: skim, scan, study
Organize Information	Underline
	Take notes
	Outline
	List
	Question
Remember Information	Review
	Discuss
Apply Information	Take tests
	Write reports

If your child is particularly nervous about test taking, see Anxiety.

WHAT WILL A PROFESSIONAL DO?

Teaching study skills is not a major area for school psychologists. Usually, the involvement of a school psychologist would be needed only if she were developing a plan as part of an Individualized Education Plan for a child with a learning difficulty. Most likely, a special education teacher would consult with the regular teacher about improving study skills.

The school psychologist can, however, help you in communicating your child's needs and your concerns to the classroom teacher, and in assisting the teacher in developing a better study skills approach for the whole class, using methods similar to those described above.

If improved study-skills teaching doesn't seem to benefit your child over several months, and if his academics continue to be a strong concern, the school psychologist and special education teacher may be asked by a multidisciplinary child study team at your school (see Special Education, in Part I) to evaluate your child to determine if other factors (stress, lack of focus, a learning disability, or anxiety) are responsible for your child's difficulties. The nature of the evaluation in this case will depend on what those who know your child best are most concerned about.

See also:

❏ Anxiety
❏ Grades
❏ Homework
❏ Learning Disabilities
❏ Stress

Further Reading

Armstrong, T. *Awakening Your Child's Natural Genius.* New York: G.P. Putnam's Sons, 1994.

Bautista, V. *How To Teach Your Children.* Farmington Hills, MI: Bookhaus Publication, 1992.

Fuller, C. *Unlocking Your Child's Learning Potential.* Colorado Springs, CO: Naupress Publishing Group, 1994.

CHAPTER 39

Suicide

"I've noticed some of the poems my daughter is writing for her English class, and they are really morbid, talking about her not being here any more and everyone being sorry that she's gone. I know she's been upset lately over breaking up with her boyfriend, but I don't know whether to take this death talk seriously or not."

Difficult as it may be to think about, child and adolescent suicide is now the third leading cause of death for all youngsters; the second leading cause of death for teenagers. No one wants to think that their child, or their child's best friend, would take their own life, but estimates are that 30 to 50 percent of eighth- to twelfth-grade students have seriously thought about suicide, and 8 to 14 percent have attempted it. Statistics show that the teen death rate from suicide has tripled since 1955, with as many as 2500 teens taking their own lives each year.

Tragic as suicide is, there may be some comfort for parents in knowing you can dispel myths about suicide in your family by learning about suicide, talking openly and in a caring manner about it, knowing the warning signs, and frankly answering your child's questions.

WHAT WE KNOW NOW

Youth suicide is not limited to any one kind of child or personality, and it is not limited to adolescents, although suicides and suicidal behavior in younger children are rare. Among elementary children, there are fewer than 200 suicides a year. It's important, though, to know that suicidal behavior does occur even in the younger age groups.

There are no statistics kept for children younger than 5. But for these and children in the next age group, 6 to 11, suicidal behavior takes a similar, indirect form; the younger the child, the less likely he is to have a well-thought-out plan. Instead, they engage in extremely reckless or accident-prone behavior—climbing to very high places, for example, or purposely running in front of cars. It may be tempting for some parents to approve of "thrill-seeking" behavior in young children, but if it really endangers the child, it is not normal and should be looked into. While children normally have fantasies and worries about death, suicidal elementary-age children will have death on their minds much more than other children.

Overall, suicide is far more common among teenagers. When parents read the statistics about the tremendous increase over recent decades in teen suicide, the question that leaps to mind is "Why?" While there is no absolute answer to that question, there are plenty of clues.

In his book, *Suicide Intervention in the Schools* (Guilford Press, New York, 1989), Scott Poland cites a researcher who has identified as many as 28 factors that may play a role in teen suicides. Every suicidal youth's particular set of problems is unique to that child, but there are some patterns that emerge:

- Poland noted that family problems were cited by more than half of the respondents in one survey as a significant factor in youth suicide. This includes long-standing stress, pressure, drug and alcohol use within the family, divorce, and legal problems—all of which result in self-esteem problems for children. Many of these factors hinge on lack of communication: One study has shown that the average parent spends only seven minutes a week communicating with his or her teen. Many youths who complete suicide attempts had a parent who also committed suicide, and this relationship may be the result of children copying ways they see their parents dealing with stress.
- Precipitating events, sometimes revolving around school issues, can push a suicidal youth to make an attempt. Adolescent suicide is most often a reaction to a crisis event as opposed to adult suicide, which is more likely to happen after a long, slow, wearing away of the will to live. Precipitating events are such things as clashes with parents, the breakup of a relationship with a boyfriend or girlfriend, the death of a loved one, trouble with a sibling, loss of face at school with peers, trouble with a teacher, change of school or frequent moves, failing grades, and/or an injury or illness.
- Depression can be a major factor, but it is not always the determining factor for all teen suicides.

In addition, factors such as longstanding academic difficulties and/or social/emotional adjustment problems, conduct problems, impulsivity, substance use, and the availability of firearms have all contributed to the increases in teen suicide. Teens are probably more affected by media coverage of suicide than are other age groups, and they may also be affected by music, literature, and movies that glorify a mystic, romantic treatment of suicide. Two high-risk groups of adolescents are those struggling with sexual identity and those involved with gangs and violence.

Researchers have identified seven motives for suicide attempts among adolescents:

1 A cry for help with the kinds of family or other problems they feel incapable of solving—the most common motive.
2 Atonement for having done something they think is unpardonable.
3 Rejoining a lost loved one, either a person or pet they were close to or an idolized person they didn't even know, like a rock star.
4 Manipulation or a kind of blackmail to get better treatment. For example, the thinking may be, "If I threaten to hurt myself, they'll be nice to me."
5 Retaliation for real or imagined abandonment, either physical or emotional.
6 Self-homicide, or an intense rage at others that is directed at the self.
7 Psychosis or personality disorganization.

Suicidal teens have in common a strong feeling of isolation, rejection, and despair. Another common denominator that runs through many suicide cases, even when the primary motive may be one of the seven listed above, is a strong feeling of abandonment or rejection by someone important to the teen, leaving them in what they consider to be an intolerable situation. The suicidal teen becomes rigid in her thinking, unable to see any alternatives other than suicide. Her strongest feeling besides abandonment is that of hopelessness.

WHEN SHOULD I BE CONCERNED?

About 90 percent of teens who attempt suicide give either obvious or subtle warning signs that they are about to do so. While it may be upsetting to think of talking about suicidal thoughts with a youngster, that same talk is also a ray of hope. There is always conflict for youngsters who are thinking of suicide, and the warnings they give are the result of that conflict. Adults who listen to the warnings are acknowledging the ray of hope. Often, whether or not friends and family around suicidal youngsters pick up on these signs can mean the difference between life and death for them.

You should be concerned and contact the school psychologist immediately if you see any of these signs in your child or in your child's friends.

The five warning signs for teen suicide are:

1 A suicide threat or statement indicating a desire to die
2 A previous suicide attempt
3 Severe, prolonged depression
4 Marked changes in personality or behavior, as in a sudden change from extremely depressed to extremely happy; a sudden change in friends; extreme changes in eating and sleeping habits; decreased academic performance; becoming very agitated; running away from home or suddenly becoming irresponsible about such things as staying out late without telling parents, etc.
5 Making a will, giving away prized possessions, making final arrangements

While these may seem obvious, they can be missed, misinterpreted, or not taken seriously by others. Teens will sometimes give warnings of an impending attempt by writing poetry or essays about suicide or about their death, and English teachers are wise to alert the school psychologist if they see this kind of writing. Suicidal teens are also likely to talk to a friend before they make an attempt, so that it's important for your child to know what to do if a friend confides they are thinking about suicide. The rule of thumb any time you or your child hear talk of suicide from anyone is: NO ONE SHOULD KEEP A SECRET ABOUT SUICIDAL BEHAVIOR.

WHAT CAN I DO TO HELP?

If you believe your child is suicidal, you need to get professional help from a psychologist or counselor immediately. If the school is closed when you realize you need help, take your child to a hospital emergency room. The threat of suicide is too much for a parent to be dealing with on his or her own.

If your child has made only vague suicidal references, and you are not certain he is suicidal, it is okay to ask him directly if he has thought of ending his life. Talking about suicide will not put thoughts of suicide in his head. On the contrary, it may make him realize that you are aware of how he feels and are willing to help. Asking directly about his suicidal thoughts can also open the door for letting him know he is not alone, and that there is help for him.

WHAT WILL A PROFESSIONAL DO?

A school psychologist will become involved immediately if you or a teacher expresses concern. If it's a teacher who expresses concern to the school psychologist—for example, over a poem or essay your child has written—the psychologist will call you right away. This is always a difficult call for the psychologist to make, and an excruciating call for a parent to receive. But it's important that parents understand that both the teacher and the psychologist have your child's best interests at heart. In any case, the school psychologist is required to call the parent with this information.

When the school psychologist does evaluate your child, she will want to talk with him and with you for background, to determine how strong a suicide risk he is. It's extremely important for a parent to be open about these issues, as sensitive as they are. The psychologist will assess the risk, using the following breakdown of clues:

❏ *Situational clues:* Are there issues of divorce, family alcoholism, family violence, the death of a family member or close friend, extreme parental pressure to achieve, or the loss of a significant relationship?

❏ *Behavioral clues:* Has there been recent drug abuse, a decline in school performance; an inability to concentrate, sleep disturbances; withdrawal; isolation; sudden changes in behavior, especially in risk-taking; aggressive or acting-out behaviors; dropping out of activities (sports, clubs, away from friends); giving away important or cherished possessions; or previous suicide attempts?

❏ *Feeling clues:* Is there a fascination with death in songs and musicians who have committed suicide, or writing about death, or sadness, crying, depression, anger, and a hopeless, helpless attitude?

❏ *Child's statement clues:* Has he made direct statements about suicide, such as "I feel like killing myself," or "I don't see any point in living." Or has he made indirect statements such as "I can't take this anymore," or "You'd be better off without me."

Teen Suicide Myths

Here are some things you may hear about teen suicide but that are not true:

■ Those who talk about about suicide won't really do it. *Wrong.* 90 percent of teen suicides give clues ahead of time.

■ A person must be crazy to attempt suicide. *Wrong.* Very few are actually psychotic. Most are in emotional turmoil, but would not be judged crazy by a psychologist.

■ If a teen really wants to commit suicide, nothing can stop him. *Wrong.* Most are in turmoil and conflict because a part of them wants to live. With help, they can.

■ It's bad to talk about suicide; it might provoke a person to do it. *Wrong.* A suicidal person needs to talk about it and get their feelings out.

■ A person who is suicidal is always suicidal. *Wrong.* Many previously suicidal people live healthy lives later.

■ Suicidal tendencies are inherited; it runs in families. *Wrong.* Suicide is no one's destiny.

In addition, she will assess how immediate the risk is by asking directly if your child has made plans to kill himself. Teens who have voiced an intent to attempt suicide, who have a specific plan, and who have a method in mind that is immediately available to them are considered highly lethal. In this case, the psychologist will likely recommend immediate and strong action, such as going to the hospital emergency room with the possibility of hospital admission.

Teens with the intent to attempt suicide, but with a vague plan and low access to the chosen method, are considered less immediately lethal but no less in immediate need of professional counseling.

In addition to immediate outside counseling, a school psychologist may also request that a suicidal teen sign a "no suicide" contract agreeing not to harm themselves.

See also:

❐ Depression
❐ Divorce/Single Parents
❐ Self-Esteem
❐ Friends
❐ Grade Retention
❐ Stress

CHAPTER 40

Vision

"Mia has always loved reading. But since the beginning of fourth grade a month ago, she's less and less willing to spend time with her books. She says the words run together, but her last school eye test didn't show she needed glasses—what's the problem?"

Most of what we learn comes through watching others and copying what they do. In school, about 80 percent of learning requires normal, or nearly normal vision, both for close work such as reading and doing worksheets, and for faraway work, such as copying from the blackboard and general observation. Nothing is more central to how well a child learns than her vision, but it may be difficult to judge how well your child's vision is working for her. For example, some vision difficulties in school can be the result of changes in how educational material is presented. In Mia's case, reading became more difficult for her as the size of the print in her school books got smaller, as it typically does in fourth grade. For some children like her, if a thorough eye exam rules out other problems, time and practice will help their eyes adjust to the smaller print.

But for many other children, vision problems aren't so simply detected or remedied. For instance, children who have never had normal vision, and children whose vision has deteriorated slowly may not know they have vision problems, and they and the adults around them may assume that their school difficulties stem from other issues. Deciphering your child's behavior to figure out whether vision is the problem can be more challenging than it may seem, but understanding some terminology and what signs to look for will be key aids in figuring out when your child needs to be tested for a vision problem.

WHAT WE KNOW NOW

About 20 percent of the general population has some kind of visual defect, the vast majority of which are correctable with glasses.

School eye exams, which test how well your child can read letters on a wall chart 20 feet away, can give a general idea about your child's vision, but they don't detect problems such as those Mia had with close-up work—for example, with reading and writing. It's best to take your child to an optometrist or ophthalmologist for a thorough eye exam before your child enters school, and on a yearly basis thereafter to monitor the child's vision and to check for eye diseases like glaucoma—which are rare, but can happen in children. Of course, you should also take your child for an eye checkup if you see some of the vision symptoms on the list below.

Both of these specialists are trained in detecting vision problems and disease. Optometrists are also trained in behavioral optometry, in which they not only prescribe glasses when necessary, but they also use special eye exercises, called *vision therapy*, to address problems with focusing, depth perception, and eye coordination. Ophthamologists use corrective lenses to treat these problems. If you are uncertain which you would prefer to see, you can schedule a consultation with one of each to discuss their treatment approaches. In either case, understanding the terminology a specialist uses is helpful. Some terms eye specialists use frequently are:

❐ *Visual acuity:* This term refers to the clinical measurement of the sharpness and clarity of vision at a specified distance, usually presented as a fraction. Normal vision is 20/20, which means that a person sees at 20 feet what the normal eye sees at 20 feet. If your child's visual acuity is 20/100, she sees at 20 feet what the normal eye sees at 100 feet.

❐ *Low vision:* This term refers to children who have less than normal vision even with glasses. Testing for those with very low vision is often done at 10 feet rather than 20. As a result, on a vision report, a child with low vision may have acuity of 10/300, which means he sees at 10 feet what the normal eye sees at 300 feet. Children whose acuity measures 20/30 to 20/60 with glasses may not have problems with schoolwork at all, but those with acuity of less than 20/60 may need special help in the classroom. Those with vision of 20/200 or less are considered legally blind.

If your child needs glasses, he probably has what is called a *refractive error*, which is the failure of the eye to focus light rays properly on the retina. If the focal point is in front of the retina, he is nearsighted (myopic); if it is behind the retina, he is farsighted (hyperopic). On a vision report or glasses prescription, nearsightedness is indicated by a minus sign before the first number, and farsightedness by a plus sign.

Other common conditions are:

❐ *Astigmatism.* Occurs when the curve of the cornea is irregular, so that images are focused at several points rather than one.

❐ *Amblyopia/Strabismus.* Conditions, usually present from birth, in which one eye (amblyopia) or both eyes (strabismus) turn inward or outward. Surgery sometimes corrects these conditions, but it is not always appropriate. Get two medical opinions if surgery is recommended.

❐ *Retinopathy of prematurity.* Premature infants who were given high levels of oxygen at birth may have vision problems ranging from myopia to detached retinas. If this was the case for your child, even if he has no apparent eye problems, you should have a thorough eye exam for your child before he starts school. Then, it's a good idea to let the teacher or school psychologist know about your child's vision history when he begins school, so that if a vision problem turns up that has previously gone undetected, you can deal with it early.

WHEN SHOULD I BE CONCERNED?

As noted earlier, a child who has never had normal vision, or one whose vision has deteriorated slowly, may not know she can't see well. In those cases, you will probably see falling grades and general difficulty in school, along with:

❐ difficulty with or avoidance of copying words or sentences from the board

❐ avoiding reading or else holding books very close (closer than the distance from her elbow to her knuckles), losing her place while she's reading, sitting very close to the television (although in some cases this is just a bad habit)

☐ rubbing her eyes a lot, shutting or covering one eye, or tilting her head to read
☐ blinking more than normal when he's doing close work
☐ squinting or frowning at distant objects

Physically, a child may complain that his eyes itch, burn, or feel scratchy. His eyes may appear red-rimmed, swollen, inflamed, or watery (although this could also be caused by allergies.) Some children will complain of dizziness, headaches, or nausea after doing close eye-work, and some will say they can't see well or that they have blurred or double vision.

Other symptoms that are often associated with vision problems, but are not necessarily due to poor vision are:

☐ reversing letters (which is common up to about age 7)
☐ difficulty recognizing letters or words
☐ difficulty understanding what he reads

These are more likely to be the result of other kinds of learning problems (see Learning Disabilities), which you should discuss with the teacher.

WHAT CAN I DO TO HELP?

Every child should have a thorough eye exam before coming to school. Then, your best next step is to recognize the symptoms listed above and to have another eye exam by an optometrist or opthamologist once a year—more frequently, if you or your child notice a change in her vision or if she has had an eye disease.

Schedule your child's eye exam early in the day, particularly for elementary-age children. After school, they may be tired and less likely to be cooperative or able to sit still in the exam chair. For children younger than 12, ask your school psychologist or your pediatrician to recommend an optometrist or an ophthamologist who is used to working with children, or check the list at the end of this chapter for organizations that may be able to make a recommendation for you.

You can help your child adjust to getting glasses even before she gets them by monitoring your own attitude. For example, stay away from comments like, "I was afraid of that," when the doctor suggests glasses, and from saying things like, "I hope you don't need glasses," on the way to the checkup. You can set the tone with a positive attitude about how great it will be for your child to see well.

If, in spite of your positive tone, your child is still not thrilled about her glasses, you can help her to feel some control over the situation by letting her choose the frames and a croakie (a cord that attaches to the arms of the glasses), so she's less likely to lose them. (See also Self-Esteem.) Give the school nurse a copy of your child's eye report, and check in with her teacher ahead of time so the teacher can be ready with compliments when the child first wears her glasses to school. Be prepared, too, to talk with your child about other children who may make unflattering comments about her glasses (see also Bullies and Victims), but don't feel that you need to bring up this issue unless it actually happens to your child.

To bolster your younger child's spirits, play games that show how well she can see now. For example, hold up cards or pictures across a room for her to read or see, both with and without her glasses. She "wins" when she can see (with her glasses!). For older children, you might discuss with the doctor the possibility of contact lenses, but be very cautious about this idea with younger children, because of safety and hygiene issues.

The folowing organizations provide information regarding vision and visual impairment:

American Council for the Blind
1211 Connecticut Avenue, NW, Suite 506
Washington, DC 20036-2775
(202) 833-1251

American Foundation for the Blind
15 West 16th Street
New York, NY 10011
(212) 620-2000

American Printing House for the Blind
1839 Frankfort Avenue
Louisville, KY 40206
(502) 895-2405

National Federation for the Blind
1800 Johnson Street
Baltimore, MD 21230
(401) 659-9314

Texas Commission for the Blind
P.O. Box 180806

Austin, TX 78718
(512) 459-2500

Every state also has a chapter of the American Optometric Association and the Medical Society Opthalmology

WHAT WILL A PROFESSIONAL DO?

A school psychologist cannot give medical advice but can help with your child's social and psychological adjustment to glasses or to an uncorrectable vision problem. Her role is to serve as a consultant as you make decisions about your child's eye care, and to act as a liason between school services and professionals outside the school system. If your child is having a particularly rocky time adjusting to glasses, you might also talk to the school psychologist about having him vent some of his feelings about it with her.

See also:

❏ Bullies and Victims
❏ Learning Disabilities
❏ Self-Esteem

Further Reading

Cook, David L., *When Your Child Struggles: The Myth of 20/20 Vision; What Every Parent Needs to Know.* Atlanta: Vision Press, 1992.

Levinson, H. & Sanders, A. *Turning Around the Upside Down Kids: Helping Dyslexic Kids Overcome This Disorder.* New York: M. Evans & Company, Inc., 1992.

A P P E N D I X   A

Motivators: Privileges to Give and Take Away

In a certain sense, our children almost always do exactly what we tell them to do. It's just that we don't always realize what it is we have told them to do. For example, every time the toddler's mom gives in to her screaming child, she "tells" him that screaming is a great way to get what you want. Every time the 10-year-old's mom or dad rationalizes their child's lack of academic motivation, the child gets the message that school doesn't matter that much.

Experience and research have shown that rewarding academic or personal behavior you want to see in your child is usually more effective than simply punishing your child for behavior you don't want. Rewarding the right behavior also tells your child clearly what it is you want her to do. But you can't expect perfect results by sprinkling rewards around willy-nilly. A planned approach to handing out rewards will help you and your child reach school behavior goals you have set together.

When you plan a reward system, be sure to:

- Keep in mind that sometimes the smallest things are the most effective. Rewards don't

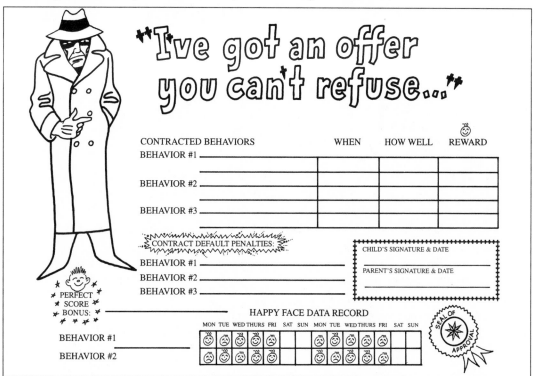

need to be—and shouldn't be, if you want to keep a steady supply—particularly big, expensive, or time-consuming for you.

■ Find out what kind of reward motivates your child. You can do this by brainstorming with your child about things she likes, things she wants, or events she wants to attend. You can also look over the Rewards and Privileges list that follows, for ideas.

■ Make an agreement with your child that a particular behavior will result in her receiving a particular reward. Be extremely clear about the behavior you expect. For example, the behavior may be that she complete all her homework and hand it in each day.

■ Think about whether you want to add a penalty clause to the agreement (a demerit of some kind rather than a reward for each day she misses her homework), or a bonus system (an extra reward for five days in a row of completed homework).

■ Write down the agreement. See the sample form below for a few ideas.

■ Have a time limit for your agreement. Meeting the terms of a specific agreement for weeks can be tedious and counterproductive for many people, whether child or adult. Be prepared to change your agreement as your situation and your child's needs change. And don't lose sight of the point: to motivate your child to eventually perform the behavior without the reward. For example, she should eventually do her homework because she gets better grades, or because it makes her feel more confident in school.

■ Use what is called a "token economy" when you plan a reward system. For example, when your child completes her homework, she can check off a square on a chart. A certain number of checks will earn her a particular amount of play money, or tokens, and she can

"buy" treats or other rewards with the play money. A token economy lets you expand the scope of your reward system according to your child's needs. For example, your child could "spend" play money for a small, immediate reward, or she could choose to save it up toward a larger goal.

■ Make your rewards, or tokens redeemable for rewards, immediately available. The more time between the expected behavior and the reward, the less motivating the reward.

If all of this sounds like a lot to do, remember that planning a system of rewards to change your child's behavior for the better is most likely easier in the long run than fighting with your child every day about homework or other issues.

The following lists show some ideas for rewards you could try. Some may be just right for your child, some may be rewards you've used, and some may be too far off the mark to consider. Choose what works for you and use the rest to spark your thinking about what might work for your child.

GIVING REWARDS

Food Rewards

■ a favorite dessert
■ the chance to "order" a special dinner at home
■ a trip to a fast-food restaurant for an after-school snack.
■ an after-school picnic—outdoors if weather permits; on a blanket spread on the living-room floor, if not.
■ a trip to a farmer's market or flea market
■ an afternoon of cookie making . . . and eating
■ having a friend over to make cookies

- having a small extra, such as sprinkles on an ice cream cone

"Thing" Rewards

- for younger children, a "grab bag" with small, inexpensive toys, notepads, stickers, or activity books
- for older children, a grab bag with hair bands, belts or socks, or gift certificate for a local pizza parlor or movie theater
- can earn tokens toward larger rewards, such as a new sweater, cassette tapes, compact discs, etc.
- can earn privileges for using things, such as driving the family car for adolescents, or the right to ride a bike or skateboard
- joke toys such as handshake buzzers and plastic snakes

Time Rewards

- any kind of time spent alone with a parent: going for a hike, going swimming, playing a board game, working on a hobby together
- 10 or 15 minutes added to bedtime
- a dress-up, make-up session with mom
- an extra half-hour of television time
- an extra half-hour of video game time
- can use tokens to work toward an overnight fishing or camping trip
- can use tokens to work toward an event such

as a car race, a concert, the circus, a movie
- can choose a special video to rent

TAKING PRIVILEGES AWAY

While it's almost always more effective to reward good behavior, sometimes it's necessary to punish undesireable behavior, too. You can do that by setting up clear consequences for your child's behavior, and using the list above to come up with privileges or items to take away from your child. Be sure to follow these guidelines:

- Just as you need to proceed in small increments when handing out rewards, be sure you do the same in taking away privileges. Don't make your child's once-a-year visit to grandma and the cousins in another state depend on her end-of-semester math grade.
- Be sure consequences are as immediate and clear as are rewards
- Be sure you reward good behavior as much as you hand out restrictions for poor behavior

If you find you're restricting or removing privileges so often you're running out of things to take away from your child, it may be an indication your approach to changing his behavior is not working. Call your school psychologist for more ideas or a different approach.

Parent Resources: Organizations and Associations

Alliance for Parental Involvement in Education (AllPie)

This parent-to-parent organization provides information about family education options (public school, private school, and home education), and parent and student rights within those options. Services include a newsletter, a book and resources catalog, a referral service, pamphlets, workshops, and conferences.

P.O. Box 59
East Chatham, NY 12060-0059
(518)392-6900
Contacts: Seth Rockmuller and Katherine Houk

The Home and School Institute (HSI)

For more than two decades, HSI has developed practical self-help programs to unite the educational resources of the home, the school, and the community. HSI is currently presenting MegaSkills seminars nationally to train parent workshop leaders.

Special Projects Office
1500 Massachusets Ave., NW #42
Washington, DC 20005
(202)466-3633
Program Contact: Dorothy Rich

Institute for Responsive Education (IRE)

This national research and advocacy organization studies schools and helps them become more responsive to citizen and parent involvement concerns. IRE publishes the journal *Equity and Choice* and various reports and is principal contact for the new National Center on Families.

605 Commonwealth Avenue
Boston, MA 02215
(617)353-3309
Program Contact: Owen Heleen

International Reading Association

This organization works with parents, educators, and researchers to improve reading instruction and increase literacy. IRA also offers information to parents on how to develop lifelong reading habits with their children.

800 Barksdale Road
Newark, DE 19704-8139
(302)731-1600
Program Contact: Peter Mitchell, Executive Director

National Association for the Education of Young Children (NAEYC)

NAEYC offers many resources for educators on all aspects of child development and early childhood education, including parent involvement. A free catalog is available.

1834 Connecticut Avenue N.W.
Washington, DC 20009
(202)232-8777
Program Contact: Pat Spahr

National Association of Partners in Education

This organization helps individuals and

groups start and manage school volunteer programs and business-education partnerships.

209 Madison Street, Suite 401
Alexandria, VA 22314
(703)836-4880
Program Contact: Daniel W. Merenda,
Executive Director

National Black Child Development Institute

This organization provides direct services and conducts advocacy campaigns to improve the quality of life for black children and youth. Family and early childhood education are emphasized, and speakers and publications are available.

1023 15th St. NW #600
Washington, DC 20005
(202)387-1281
Program Contact: Sherry Deane

National Coalition for Parent Involvement in Education (NCPIE)

This organization, composed of more than 25 national education and community-life associations, is dedicated to developing effective family and school partnerships. To receive a free brochure, "Developing Family/School Partnerships: Guidelines for Schools and School Districts," other information about NCPIE, and additional parent involvement resources, send a self-addressed, stamped business-sized envelope to NCPIE.

P.O. Box 39
1201-16th Street N.W.
Washington, DC 20036

National Coalition of Title 1/Chapter 1 Parents (National Parent Center)

This organization provides a voice for Chapter 1 parents at the federal, regional, state, and local levels. The Coalition publishes a newsletter, provides training, and sponsors conferences.

Edmonds School Building
9th and D Streets N.E.
Washington, DC 20002
(202)547-9286
Program Contact: Robert Witherspoon

National Committee for Citizens in Education

This organization has many publications for parents and also provides free information and help for parents with school problems. Request a free bookmark with information on parent involvement in the middle school.

10840 Little Patuxent Parkway, Suite 301
Columbia, MD 21044
1-800-NETWORK

National Council of La Raza (NCLR)

This research and advocacy organization works on behalf of the U.S. Hispanic population and provides technical assistance to community-based organizations. NCLR's Project EXCEL is a national education demonstration project that includes tutoring services and parental education.

810-1st Street N.E., Suite 300
Washington, DC 20002-4205
(202)289-1380
Program Contact: Denise De La Rosa

National Information Center for Children and Youth with Handicaps (NICHCY)

This organization provides free information to assist parents, educators, caregivers, advocates, and others in helping children and youth with disabilities. NICHCY provides information on local, state, and national disability groups for parents and professionals and maintains databases with current information on disability topics. Publications include *News Digest* and *Parent Guides.*

P.O. Box 1492
Washington, DC 20013
1-800-999-5599

Parent-Teacher Associations

National, state, and local PTAs have many resources and materials that can be used at home and at school to support children's learning. For a free list of publications, send a self-addressed, business-sized envelope to:

Publications List, National PTA,
Department D
700 North Rush Street
Chicago, IL 60611-2571

Parents as Teachers National Center (PAT)

PAT encourages parents of children from birth to age 3 to think of themselves as their children's first and most influential teachers. It provides information and training to parents,

supports public policy initiatives, and offers parent educator certification.

9374 Olive Blvd.
St. Louis, MO 63132
(314)432-4330
Program Contact: Claire Eldredge

Parent Training and Information Centers, and Technical Assistance to Parent Projects

The Office of Special Education Programs supports a network of 60 parent Training and Information Centers (PTIs) in all 50 states and Puerto Rico to enable parents to participate more effectively with profesionals in meeting the educational needs of children with disabilities. Technical Assistance to Parents Projects (TAPP) provides technical assistance and coordination to the 60 PTIs and to developing minority programs in urban and rural locations.

95 Berkeley Street, Suite 104
Boston, MA 02116
(617)482-2915
Program Contact: Martha Ziegler

Books

Rich, D. *Teachers and Parents: An Adult-to-Adult Approach.* Washington, DC: National Education Association, 1987.

Rich D. *Schools and Families: Issues and Actions.* Washington, DC: National Education Association, 1987.

Swap, S. M. *Enchancing Parent Involvement in Schools.* New York: Teachers College Press, 1987.

Wikelund, K. R. *Schools and Communities Together: A Guide to Parent Involvement.* Portland, OR: Northwest Regional Educational Laboratory, 1990.

Parenting Books

Albert, L. *Coping with Kids and School.* NY: Ballantine Books, 1984.

Canter, L., & Hauser, L. *Homework Without Tears: A Parent's Guide for Motivating Children to Do Homework and to Succeed In School.* NY: Harper & Row, 1985.

Cutright, M. J. *The National PTA Talks to Parents: How To Get the Best Education for Your Child.* NY: Doubleday, 1989.

Eyre, L., & Eyre, R. *Teaching Children Responsibility.* NY: Ballantine Books, 1984.

Ferguson, S., & Mazin, L. *Parent Power.* NY: Clarkson N. Potter, Inc., 1989.

Greene, L. J. *Smarter Kids.* NY: Fawcett Crest, 1987.

Johnson, E. W. *Raising Children to Achieve: A Guide for Motivating Success in School and in Life.* NY: Walker Publishing, 1984.

Kuepper, J. *Homework Helper: A Guide for Parents Offering Assistance.* Education Media Corp, 1987.

Levine, F. M., & Anesko, K. M. *Winning the Homework War.* NY: Prentice-Hall, 1987.

Maeroff, G. I. *The School Smart Parent.* NY: Times Books, 1989.

Rich, D. *Megaskills: How Families Can Help Children Succeed In School and Beyond.* Boston: Houghton-Mifflin, 1988.

Solomon, A.M., & Grenoble, P.B. *Helping Your Child Get Top Grades.* Chicago: Contemporary Books, 1988.

Stainback, W., & Stainback, S. *How To Help Your Child Succeed In School.* NY: Meadowbrook, 1988.

Thiel, A., & Thiel, R., & Grenoble, P.B. *When Your Child Isn't Doing Well In School.* Chicago: Contemporary Books, 1988.

APPENDIX C

Helping Children Through Crises

At Home and at School

One of the most overwhelming differences between most of our childhoods and those of our children is simply the number of crises our children are exposed to at very young ages. They can watch on television as a war explodes in a country tens of thousands of miles away. They read about, see pictures of, or watch movies about scores of violent crimes. Saddest of all, many of our children will witness violence themselves, or know someone who has, before they are old enough to vote.

As a result, many schools have developed plans to help children and staff deal with crises that may come up at school. If you know the principles they are following in carrying out their plans, you can echo those at home. And if your school does not have a crisis intervention plan for the situations listed below, you might contact the school and ask that a plan be made.

WHEN THERE IS A STUDENT SUICIDE

- The suicide should be acknowledged and school activities should continue. Youngsters will have a chance to vent their feelings and talk with counselors or psychologists, rather than remain isolated at home.
- The faculty should be assisted first, then students. A group of adults who know how to talk with the students will be more helpful.
- The family of the suicide victim should be contacted to express condolences and to request the funeral during nonschool hours. It is constructive for students, particularly those who may have some problems themselves, to know that life goes on, even after a suicide.
- Memorials to the student who committed suicide should be downplayed. While acknowledging and talking about the suicide is important, experience has shown that de-emphasizing the dramatic, romantic, or mystical aspects of suicide helps prevent copy-cat suicides.
- For the same reason, media coverage of the suicide should avoid front-page pictures and stories, and should downplay simplistic explanations and avoid details of the method used. Prevention information and community resources for suicidal teens should be included.

DEALING WITH OTHER DEATHS

The school should:

- Announce the death over the intercom so that everyone gets the same information, then have psychologists or people trained in crisis intervention visit each classroom if possible, but especially those most closely affected.

- Provide opportunities for discussing emotions, going through the grief process, and funeral arrangements.
- Send a letter home to all the parents that gives information about the death and how parents can help their children.
- Provide grief groups on an ongoing basis as needed.

FACING AN OUTSIDE CRISIS: NATURAL DISASTERS AND WAR

Any crisis means that normal routine is disrupted. The schools actions should focus on:

- Putting fears in perspective and feeling personally safe. In the case of the aftermath of an earthquake, for example, one teacher talked with her class about how unlikely it was that the children would ever feel an earthquake stronger than the one just passed. Or during the Desert Storm war, a teacher had the children make a "human map," figuring out how wall map distances translated to distance on the playground, for example, and then having children stand where Iraq would be, and where their state would be. They also talked about long-range missiles and how far they could really go, and about how far Iraqi planes could—and couldn't—fly before they refueled.
- Normalizing life as much as possible by continuing with routines.
- Helping children feel a sense of control by taking action. Children could send letters or cookies to military personnel involved in war, or classes could volunteer to help clean up after a natural disaster.
- Involving children in planning how to cope. Talk with them and get their feelings and ideas.

WHAT TO EXPECT FROM CHILDREN WHO HAVE BEEN TOUCHED BY CRISIS

Generally, children involved in some kind of disaster are afraid that whatever happened will happen again. As a result, they tend to lose interest in school; they tend to regress in their behavior to previous developmental stages (no matter what age they are); and they are likely to have nightmares and other sleep disturbances.

Preschoolers are likely to begin:

- ❏ thumbsucking
- ❏ bedwetting
- ❏ clinging to parents
- ❏ being afraid of the dark and animals
- ❏ having sleep disturbances
- ❏ having speech problems
- ❏ losing their appetite
- ❏ regressing in toilet training

Children of ages 5–11 are likely to begin:

- ❏ to be irritable
- ❏ whining and clinging
- ❏ being aggressive
- ❏ acting more competitive with siblings
- ❏ having nightmares or night terrors
- ❏ avoiding school
- ❏ withdrawing from friends
- ❏ having trouble concentrating

Young adolescents, ages 11–14 are likely to begin:

- ❏ having sleep disturbances
- ❏ appetite disturbances
- ❏ rebelling at home
- ❏ having school problems
- ❏ complaining of stomachaches, headaches,

and the like

❏ socializing less with friends

Older adolescents, ages 14–18 are likely to begin:

❏ complaining of stomachaches, headaches, and the like

❏ having appetite or sleep problems

❏ feeling agitated or having decreased energy

❏ having less interest in the opposite sex

❏ behaving irresponsibly or like a delinquent

❏ having problems concentrating

Any time you feel out of your depth in dealing with your child's responses to a crisis, call the school psychologist.

In any case, your behavior at home will help your child cope with crises. Parents should respond to children with:

■ Assurances of safety, love, patience, tolerance, and increased availability

■ Permission for the child to have their own emotions, without projecting the parent's emotions onto the child

■ Understanding the most common childhood response to a crisis is regression

■ Honesty and facts given in age-appropriate terms.

■ Understanding that children will differ according to their age as to how much they understand this crisis and its relevance to their life

■ Structure, normal routines, and encouragement to play

■ Patience to answer honestly all the questions your child asks

■ Less television viewing than usual; more family play or other activities

APPENDIX D

Samples from Tests and Assessments

I n this section you will find descriptions of some of the most commonly used psychological and educational tests. Because we have condensed and summarized their descriptions, you should talk to your school psychologist or other school specialist to answer more detailed questions about these tests. They are listed in alphabetical order.

For each, we have given the name, publisher, type of test, the age range of the child for whom the test could be used (there are some exceptions to this), and a description of the major components of the test. Because the contents of the tests are copyrighted and otherwise protected by professional and ethical standards, examples we give are not of actual items, but they are very similar to those on the test.

BENDER VISUAL MOTOR GESTALT TEST (BENDER, BENDER-GESTALT)

❑ American Orthopsychiatric Association, 1938
❑ Measure of the child's developmental visual-motor ability (measure of skill development in copying geometric designs).
❑ Age Range: The Koppitz scoring system is developed for children from 5 years to 11 years; the test without the Koppitz scoring system has been used as an aid in the diagnosis of brain damage in adults.
❑ Major Components:
❑ The child is shown 9 geometric designs, one at a time, and asked to copy them on a plain sheet of paper. When scoring with the Koppitz system, the evaluator records the number of errors on each of the child's 9 separate geometric forms. Four kinds of errors are recorded:

Distortion of Shape—when the copy of the design is so misshapen or distorted that the general configuration is lost; *Perseveration*—when the child fails to stop after completing the required drawing; *Integration*—failure to juxtapose correctly parts of a design; and *Rotation*—when child rotates the design by more than 45 degrees or rotates the stimulus card, even though the drawing is correctly copied. The cumulative number of errors that the child makes is then compared to a normative group of same age peers to determine the child's developmental level on this task.

BLOOMER LEARNING TEST (BLT)

❑ Brador Publications Inc., 1980
❑ Provides a description of a student's strengths and weaknesses in various learning processes such as memory and problem solving;
❑ Suggests procedures educators can follow to help student's develop his or her potentials in light of their strengths and weaknesses.
❑ Individually or group administered
❑ Age Range: Grade 1 to Grade 11
❑ Major Components:

❏ *Profile Scores*—Indicate a pattern of strengths/weaknesses in basic learning processes such as visual and auditory short-term memory, serial and paired associate learning, recall and relearning, concept recognition and production, and problem solving.

❏ *Indicator Scores*—Describes some behavior patterns/habits that a student may engage in which are detrimental to learning in school. Such factors include: low tolerance of frustration, anxiety, ease of responding, tendency to become confused as the learning requirements become more complex, ability to focus/concentrate, and tendency toward impulsivity.

CHILD BEHAVIOR CHECKLIST (CBCL)

❏ University Associates in Psychiatry, 1991
❏ Behavior Checklist

A behavior rating scale designed to identify behavior problems in children. Three forms are available—one to be completed by teachers (called the *Teacher Report Form*), one by parents or other primary caretakers of the child (the *Child Behavior Checklist*), and one by the youth himself of herself (the *Youth Self-Report*). Respondents are asked to answer questions on the following scale: "very true/often true"; "somewhat" or "sometimes true"; or "not true." High scores are indicative of the child expressing more of the problem behaviors than his or her same sex and age peers.

❏ Age Range: 4 years through 16 years
❏ Major Components: Problem behaviors are broken down into the following scales:

❏ *Anxious*—Assesses the extent to which the child appears to be more anxious than his or her peers. Typical items in this section will be similar to: is reluctant to do activities without an adult; appears to be jumpy; or is overly reluctant to try new things.

❏ *Social Withdrawal*—Assesses the extent to which the child appears to be withdrawing from his or her peers. Typical items in this section will include: plays or does activities alone often; has an indifferent attitude about anything presented to him or her; or is closed around other children.

❏ *Depressed*—Assesses the extent to which the child's behavior problems appear to be manifested in depression. Typical items in this category will include: dislikes self; cries easily; or is overly critical of self.

❏ *Unpopular*—Assesses the extent to which the student exhibits behaviors that result or could result in his or her peers ostracizing him or her. Typical items include: is immature; destroys his or her own or others' belongings or toys; prefers to be with peers younger than himself or herself; or lies.

❏ *Uncommunicative*—Assesses the extent to which the child experiences difficulty in communicating with peers or adults. Typical questions in this category will ask if the child: refuses to talk; rarely laughs or smiles; or appears overly shy.

❏ *Somatic Complaints*—Assesses the extent to which the student appears to be overly concerned or obsessed with minor aches and pains. Typical questions in this category will ask if the child: bumps into things a lot; feels dizzy often; feels sick a lot.

❏ *Self-Destructive*—Assesses the extent to which the child's maladaptive behavior tends to encompass self abuse or destruction of objects important to the child (i.e., a favorite toy, game, or book.) Typical questions in this category will ask if the child: hurts self; looks dirty; or breaks his or her own things when angry.

❐ *Obsessive Compulsive*—Assesses the extent to which the child's behavior problems appear to have either obsessive and/or compulsive features. Typical questions in this category ask if the child: becomes overly upset when his or her belongings are touched or moved; repeats odd phrases at times; or expresses strange thoughts.

❐ *Thought Disorder*—Assesses the extent to which the child's behavior has characteristics of irrational thoughts. Typical questions in this category will ask if the child: tends to hoard strange items; follows irrational beliefs; has many fears.

❐ *Inattentive*—Assesses the extent to which the child'sbehavior problems appear to be the result of inability to attend or pay attention. Typical questions in this category will ask if the child: acts immature for his or her age; daydreams often; or rarely completes projects started.

❐ *Delinquent*—Assesses the extent to which the child's behavior problems appear to be the result of antisocial, aggressive, and/or violent origin. Typical questions in this category will ask if the child: threatens or bullies peers; exhibits disregard for authority figures; or appears to lack remorse for actions that hurt others.

❐ *Nervous/Overactive*—Assesses the extent to which the child's behavior problems are the result of nervousness or anxiety. Typical questions in this will ask if the child: appears "jumpy"; hands in messy school work; or tends to have nervous mannerisms.

❐ *Hyperactive*—Assesses the extent to which the child's problem behaviors appear to be the result of hyperactivity. Typical questions in this category will ask if the child: experiences difficulty concentrating for long periods of time; will often start new activities before old ones

are completed; or bumps into things often.

❐ *Aggressive*—Assesses the extent to which the child's behavior problems appear to be the result of aggression or anger. Typical questions in this category will ask if the child: is nasty to others; associates with the "wrong crowd"; or curses.

❐ *Other Problems*—Assesses the extent to which the child's behavior problem may be the result of health, addiction or other problems. Typical questions in this category will ask if the child: has a weight problem; appears to have difficulty hearing in class; or tends to doze off in class.

CONNERS RATING SCALES (CRS)

❐ Multi-Health Systems, Inc., 1990
❐ Behavioral Rating Scale
❐ Evaluates the reported problem behaviors of the student
❐ Both parent and teacher forms are available in long and short editions.
❐ Age Range: 3 years to 17 years

I. *Teacher Rating Scales*

❐ Editions: Conner's Teacher Rating Scales (CTRS)-An item rating scale used to identify specific child behavior problems and dimensions of psychopathology. This measure has been widely used to identify child hyperactivity/hyperkinetic behavior. The Teacher's Scale is completed by the student's teacher(s). Each item is rated with one of four responses (not at all, just a little, pretty much, very much). Responses are respectively coded as 0, 1, 2, or 3. The Conner's is available in both a short and long form.
❐ Major Components:

❐ *Hyperactivity*—Assesses the extent to which

the teacher determines the child to perform behaviors which are usually indicative of an underlying diagnosis of hyperkinesis. Typical questions on this scale would include: Doesn't pay attention in class, constantly out of his or her seat, distracting to other students.

❏ *Conduct Problem*—Assesses the extent to which the student's behavior is indicative of defiance or aggression. Typical questions in this section will ask: Throws items in the class, talks back to teacher, refuses to follow directions.

❏ *Emotional Overindulgence*—Assesses the extent to which the student's behavior is indicative of depression, immaturity, or overly sensitive emotions. Items in this section will ask such questions as: Needs constant attention, pouts often, prone to cry if doesn't get his or her way.

❏ *Anxious-Passive*—Assesses the extent to which the student's behavior is indicative of severe passivity or anxiety. Items in this section will ask such questions as: Easily pressured by peers, doesn't participate in class, overly timid.

❏ *Asocial*—Assesses the extent to which the student's behavior is indicative of isolation or poor peer relations. Items in this section will ask such questions as: Student appears to have few friends, appears to have difficulty relating to his or her peers.

❏ *Daydream Attention Problem*—Assesses the extent to which the student's behavior is indicative of inattention or attention span problems. Items in this section will ask questions such as: Looks out window during lessons? appears to be "in his or her own world"?

II. *Parent Rating Scales*

❏ Conner's Parent Rating Scales (CPRS)—Completed by the student's parent(s) or primary caretaker(s). A behavior rating scale designed to yield multiple dimensions of child behavior problems and psychopathology. The Conner's has been widely used to identify hyperactivity/hyperkinetic behavior. The parent answers questions with the following scale: "Not at All", "Just a Little", "Pretty Much", or "Very Much."

❏ Major Components:

❏ *Conduct Problem*—See Conner's Teacher Rating Scale "Conduct Problem" information.

❏ *Learning Problem*—Assesses the extent to which the parent observes their child to be struggling with learning or school-based tasks such as homework. Typical questions on this scale will ask the parent: Slow to learn new tasks?; Leaves things unfinished?; or Difficulty in concentrating for long periods of time?

❏ *Psychosomatic*—Assesses the extent to which the parent observes the child to be overly obsessed with body aches and pains and appears agitated. Typical questions in this scale will ask parents to rate their children along the following lines: Complains of frequent headaches; complains of frequent sore throats; or uses physical complaints to stay home from school frequently.

❏ *Impulsive-Hyperactive*—See CTRS description for "Hyperactive."

❏ *Anxiety*—See CTRS for "Anxious Passive."

❏ *Hyperactivity Index*—See CTRS for "Hyperactivity."

DIFFERENTIAL ABILITY SCALES (DAS)

❏ The Psychological Corporation, 1990
❏ Intelligence
❏ Also contains an achievement component for school-age children
❏ Individually administered
❏ Age Range: 2 years 6 months to 17 years 11 months

❐ The DAS is broken down into two main divisions:

❐ *The Pre-School Level*—for children between the ages of 2 years 6 months and 3 years 5 months at the lower level; for children between the ages of 3 years 6 months and 7 years 11 months at the upper level.
❐ *The School-Age Level*—for children between the ages of 5 years and 17 years 11 months.

The Achievement tests can only be used with students in the school-age range.

Major Components:

COGNITIVE BATTERY

Lower Preschool Level:

General Conceptual Ability-Measures the child's verbal, reasoning, perceptual, and memory abilities. Typical questions will ask the child to point to or manipulate toylike objects when instructed by the examiner, match blocks or copy block patterns made by the examiner, match pictures linked by a common elementary concept, and correctly name pictures of objects.

Upper Preschool Level:

General Conceptual Ability—Represents the overall level of intellectual functioning.
Verbal Ability-Assesses the student's level of intelligence by assessing verbal skills. Typical question: ask the child to point to or manipulate toylike objects when instructed by the examiner and to correctly name pictures of objects.
Nonverbal Ability—Assesses the student's level of intelligence using tasks that do not require a verbal response. Typical tasks in this section would require the

child to match pictures linked by a common elementary concept, to reproduce designs made by the examiner with colored blocks, and to correctly copy line drawings.

School-Age Level:

General Conceptual Ability—Represents the student's overall level of intellectual functioning.
Verbal Ability Cluster—Assesses the student's level of intelligence by assessing verbal skills, reasoning, and general knowledge. Typical questions will require the student to define words that are presented orally (such as *immense*) and to explain how sets of three words are related (such as *English, math,* and *history*).
Nonverbal Reasoning Ability Cluster—Assesses the student's level of intelligence by assessing reasoning and nonverbal problem solving skills. These tasks are completed with a paper and pencil, and require the student to correctly complete an incomplete matrix of abstract figures and to correctly complete a series of abstract figures by providing a missing figure which fits into the relationship of the existing figures.
Spatial Ability Cluster—Assesses the student's level of intelligence by assessing tasks tapping visual memory skills and hand-eye coordination. Typical questions will require the student to reproduce from memory an abstract line drawing that is presented for 5 seconds and to construct a design by putting together flat squares or solid cubes with black and yellow patterns on each side.

Additional subtests give diagnostic information about the student's short-term memory ability and speed of information processing. The student at this time will be required to repeat a sequence of digits presented orally, to quickly mark the circle in a row that contains the most figures or the highest numbers, and to recall as many objects as possible after being presented with a picture card for a specified amount of time.

ACHIEVEMENT BATTERY:

Measure the student's basic skills in literacy and numeracy. Typical questions will require the student to solve computational problems presented on a worksheet, write words dictated by the examiner, and read aloud a series of words presented on a card.

GRAY ORAL READING TEST— THIRD EDITION (GORT—3)

❏ Pro-Ed, 1990
❏ Achievement in oral reading skills
❏ Individually administered
❏ Age Range: 7 years 0 months through 18 years 11 months
❏ Major Components:
❏ *Oral Reading Quotient*—Assesses the student's overall ability to read orally. This measure is determined by combining the Passage Score and Comprehension Score. Students are asked to read aloud passages before being questioned about the story by the evaluator. A typical passage at the lower levels may resemble:

"Our dog Ben likes to play with a ball. Ben will run across the yard to catch the ball. Then he wants you to throw it again for him. He could play ball all day. He even sleeps with his ball at night."

❏ *Rate Scores*—Assesses the student's ability to read passages with speed. The student is asked to read a passage aloud and scores are determined by recording the length of time the student needs to complete the passage.
❏ *Accuracy Scores*—Assesses the student's ability to read passages accurately. The student is asked to read a passage aloud and scores are determined by recording the number of mistakes which the student makes while reading.
❏ *Passage Score*—A combination of the Rate and Accuracy Scores. Determines the student's ability to read a passage quickly and accurately.
❏ *Comprehension Score*—Assesses the student's oral reading comprehension level. Typical questions will have the child respond to multiple choice questions following each story presented. The evaluator reads aloud the stem and response choices of the question, while the student selects the response choice that best completes the ideas expressed. The questions may come in the literal, inferential, critical, or affective forms. For the above story, typical questions may be:

The dog in the story is named

    Bill
    Benji
    Ben
    Bonnie

The dog in the story likes to

    chase cars
    chase cats
    chase children
    chase balls

What does Ben like to sleep with?

    a bone
    people
    a doll
    a ball

What does not go in the story?

    Ben likes to play with the ball
    Ben gets in trouble for chewing the
    ball.
    Ben likes to play with people.
    Ben is a playful dog.

Why do you think that Ben plays ball?

    It is fun.
    His master makes him.
    There are no cats to chase.
    It is good exercise.

HUMAN FIGURE DRAWING (DRAW-A-PERSON)

❏ Projective measure of the child's personality and/or development as compared to same age peers.
❏ Age Range: Appropriate for children, adolescents, and adults.
❏ Major Components:

A blank sheet of paper and a pencil with an eraser are given to the child and the child is instructed to "Draw a picture of a whole person." After finishing with the first drawing, the child is asked to draw a second drawing of the opposite sex. The purpose of the drawings can come in one of two avenues. The first application compares the child to same-age peers to determine if the child is developmentally drawing on an appropriate age level. In essence, this method is a measure of the child's maturation. The second aspect to interpretation attempts to: allow nonverbal children to express themselves with the psychologist in graphic form; gain an understanding of a child's inner conflicts, fears, interactions with family members, and perceptions of others; and generate hypotheses

and serve as a springboard for further evaluation. Interpretation of the developmental level of the child's drawing is the result of checking for a number of features to be present in the drawings (i.e., head, torso, etc.). Interpretation of psychological features inherent in the drawing rests on the qualitative analysis of the drawing by the psychologist. In this case, figure size, placement of the figure on the paper, theme of the drawing, special features added to the drawing, emphasis on certain parts of the body, as well as omissions of body features are all analyzed to generate ideas/hypotheses about the psychological functioning of the child.

JUNIOR-SENIOR HIGH SCHOOL PERSONALITY QUESTIONNAIRE (JR. SR. HSPQ)

❏ Institute for Personality and Ability Testing, 1968
❏ Personality Questionnaire
❏ The student answers 142 multiple-choice questions to give insight into the student's personality.
❏ Age Range: Junior and Senior High School Age Students
❏ Major Components:

❏ Factor A: *Warmth*—Describes the degree of interpersonal warmth or detachment that the student appears to have. Students scoring high in this category can be described as outgoing, kindly, or easy-going while those scoring low in the category can be described as reserved, cool, or aloof.
❏ Factor B: *Intelligence*—Describes the general intellectual level that the students perceives himself or herself to have. Student's scoring high in this category can be described as abstract thinkers or bright while those scoring

low in this category can be described as concrete thinkers or less intelligent.

❏ Factor C: *Emotional Stability*—Reflects the level of emotional control and stability, as opposed to uncontrolled, disorganized, general emotionality in the student. Those scoring high in this category can be described as mature or calm while student's scoring low in this category will be described as easily annoyed or emotionally less stable.

❏ Factor D: *Excitability*—Reflects the level of impulsivity or excitability of the student. Those scoring high in this category can be described as excitable, easily distracted, or impatient while students scoring low in this category can be described as phlegmatic, undemonstrative, or inactive.

❏ Factor E: *Dominance*—Reflects the degree that the student is dominant or submissive. Students rating high in this section will be described as assertive, aggressive, stubborn, or competitive while those scoring low in this category will be described as humble, mild, easily led, or accommodating.

❏ Factor F: *Cheerfulness*—Reflects the overall mood of the student. Those scoring high in this category can be described as cheerful, enthusiastic, impulsive, or expressive while students rating low may be described as sober, restrained, prudent, or serious.

❏ Factor G: *Conformity*—Depicts the level of the student's regard for group moral standards. Those scoring high in this category may be described as conforming, conscientious, persistent, moralistic, staid, or rule-bound while students scoring low in this category can be considered expedient, self indulgent, or to disregard rules.

❏ Factor H: *Boldness*—Depicts the degree of sociability, daring, or tactfulness that the student may possess. Those scoring high in this

category may be considered bold, venturesome, or uninhibited while students scoring low in this category may be described as shy, timid, hesitant, or intimidated.

❏ Factor I: *Sensitivity*-Assesses the degree to which the individual is tough-minded or tender-minded. Students scoring high in this category may be considered to be sensitive, overprotected, intuitive, or refined while those rating low may be considered to be self-reliant, no-nonsense, rough, or realistic.

❏ Factor J: *Withdrawal*—Depicts the level of interpersonal interaction that the individual is most comfortable with. Students rating high in this category can be described as withdrawn, guarded, individualistic, or restrained while those scoring low in this section may be described as vigorous, zestful, given to action, or going readily with the group.

❏ Factor Q1: *Apprehension*—Depicts the level of the individual's self confidence, fear, or internal conflict. A student scoring high in this dimension can be considered apprehensive, self-blaming, guilt-prone, insecure, or worrying while those scoring low may be determined to be self-assured, secure, guilt-free, untroubled, or self-satisfied.

❏ Factor Q2: *Self-Sufficiency*—Describes the level of the student's confidence, resourcefulness, or independence. Those scoring high in this category may be called self-sufficient or resourceful while students scoring low in this section may be determined to be group-orientated, a joiner, or socially group-dependent.

❏ Factor Q3: *Self-Discipline*—Describes the overall level of the student's self-control or constraint. Those scoring high in this category may be determined to be self-disciplined, controlled, socially precise, or exercising willpower while students rating low in this section can be called undisciplined, lax, careless of social rules, uncontrolled, or following own urges.

❐ Factor Q4: *Tension*—Describes the general level or frustration or sensitivity that the student possesses. Individuals scoring high in this category may be considered tense, frustrated, or overwrought while students rating low may be considered relaxed, tranquil, composed, or unfrustrated.

A typical question on this test may ask: I consider myself to be a loner. A) yes (often); B) sometimes; C) no (never)

KAUFMAN ASSESSMENT BATTERY FOR CHILDREN (KABC)

❐ American Guidance Service, 1983
❐ Intelligence and achievement
❐ Individually administered
❐ Age Range: 2 years 6 months to 12 years 6 months
❐ Major Components:

❐ *Mental Processing Composite*—Yields a global estimate of the child's intellectual functioning. Composed of the Sequential and Simultaneous Processing Scales.

❐ *Sequential Processing Scale*—Assesses the child's level of intellectual functioning by focusing on the child's ability to solve problems in which questions are ordered serially or temporally (i.e., copy a sequence of hand movements performed by the examiner.) Typical questions in this category will require the student to:

❐ copy a sequence of taps made by the evaluator with the fist, palm, or side of hand;
❐ repeat a series of digits read by the evaluator,
❐ point to silhouettes of common objects in the order named by the evaluator.

❐ *Simultaneous Processing Scale*—Assesses the child's level of intellectual functioning by focusing on the child's ability to integrate many stimuli to solve problems by using a gestaltlike or holistic approach. Typical questions in this section will require the child to:

❐ identify a picture that the evaluator rotates behind a narrow slit, exposing only a part of the picture;
❐ recall one or two faces that have been briefly presented by selecting the correct face(s), in a different pose, from a group photograph;
❐ complete an inkblot drawing and to name or describe it;
❐ assemble rubber triangles to match an abstract design;
❐ select the picture or design that completes a 2 by 2 visual analogy;
❐ remember where pictures were arranged on a page;
❐ organize photographs that illustrate an event and place them in proper chronology.

❐ *Achievement Scale*—Assesses the child's knowledge of facts, language concepts, and school-related skills. Typical questions in this section will require the student to:

❐ name objects from photographs; to name famous persons, fictional characters, or places from pictures (i.e., Snow White, Marilyn Monroe, Mount Rushmore);
❐ name numbers, to count, to compute, and to understand mathematical concepts;
❐ name a concrete or abstract concept when given several of its characteristics (i.e., for cat—It meows, has whiskers, and chases mice);
❐ name letters and to read words orally;

❏ act out commands given in sentences they read (i.e., *stand up.*)

❏ *Nonverbal Scale*—Included to assess the mental processing of hearing impaired, speech- and language-disordered, and non-English speaking children ages 4 years to 12 years 6 months. Made up of those subtests that may be administered in pantomime and responded to motorically.

KAUFMAN TEST OF EDUCATIONAL ACHIEVEMENT— BRIEF FORM (K-TEA)

❏ American Guidance Service, 1985
❏ Achievement
❏ Individually Administered
❏ Age Range: 6 years 0 months to 18 years 11 months
❏ Major Components:

❏ *Battery Composite*—Composed of the Mathematics, Reading, and Spelling subtests. Assesses the student's overall skills in reading, mathematics, and spelling.

❏ *Reading*—Assesses the student's ability to decode printed words and in reading comprehension. Typical questions in this section will require the student to identify individual letters; correctly pronounce words such as *and, carnation,* or *glacier*; and respond orally or by gesture to written commands such as giggle, touch a wall, describe a sibling, and act oppositional.

❏ *Mathematics*—Assesses the student's basic arithmetic concepts, ability to apply mathematics principles to lifelike situations, numerical reasoning, and simple and advanced computational skills. Typical questions in this subtest will ask the student to correctly complete problems such as $7 - 5 = ?$; $500 \times 5 = ?$;

Sally, Ann, and Mary were given twelve dollars by their grandmother for helping her rake leaves. How much money did each girl get if they split it evenly?; and to answer questions by reading various graphs.

❏ *Spelling*—Assesses spelling ability by having the student correctly write down words dictated by the evaluator. Typical words would include: *man, block, rectangle,* and *achievement.*

KEY MATH REVISED

❏ American Guidance Service, 1988
❏ Achievement
❏ Individually administered
❏ Age Range: Used primarily in pre-school through grade six, although there is no upper limit for use.
❏ Major Components:

❏ *Total Test Performance*—Gives an overall assessment of the student's performance/achievement in mathematics.

❏ *Basic Concepts*—Assesses the student's achievement in the areas of numeration, fractions, and geometry and symbols. Typical questions in this category will require the child to identify written numerals; count the number of objects in a picture; correctly complete sets; identify fractions; identify shapes such as rectangles; identify the meaning of math signs and abbreviations(i.e., =, +, oz.); identify relationships between lines (i.e., parallel); and round numbers.

❏ *Operations Area*—Assesses the students achievement in the areas of addition, subtraction, multiplication, division, and mental computations. Typical questions in this section include: Three students left a group of five students. How many students are left?; This plate has two cookies on it. If I were to put two more cookies on the plate, how many would you have?; and written computations.

❑ *Applications Area*—Assesses the student's achievement in areas such as measurement, time, money, estimation, interpretation of data, and problem solving. Typical questions in this ares may include: reading and problem solving with calendars and clocks; problem solving and reading of measurement instruments such as yardsticks; comparing coin values; estimating change from purchases; gaining information from graphs; and solving word problems.

KINETIC FAMILY DRAWING (KFD)

❑ Projective assessment hypotheses about the student's personality as well as the student's feelings and perceptions of family interactions at the time of the drawing.
❑ Age Range: Appropriate for both children as well as adolescents.
❑ Major Components:

The KFD is administered by giving the child a sheet of paper and a pencil with an eraser. The student is instructed to "draw a picture of everyone in your family, including you, doing something—some kind of action." The examiner records verbalized statements as well as other behavioral observations for qualitative analysis as well as analyzes the drawing. The drawing may be analyzed along the following dimensions: characteristics of each figure present, omissions of body parts, omissions of family members, additions of people who may not be "family" in the picture, actions performed in the picture, other objects present in the picture, family interactional styles, placement of family members on the page, and symbols present in the drawings.

MCCARTHY SCALES OF CHILDREN'S ABILITIES (MCCARTHY)

❑ The Psychological Corporation, 1972
❑ Intelligence
❑ Evaluates strengths and weaknesses in developmental ability areas
❑ Individually administered
❑ Age Range: 2 years 6 months to 8 years 6 months
❑ Major Components:

❑ *General Cognitive Scale*—Composite of Verbal, Perceptual-Performance, and Quantitative scales. Assesses the child's overall level of intellectual functioning.
❑ *Verbal Scale*—Assesses the child's ability to express himself or herself verbally, and also to assess the maturity of his or her verbal concepts. Items in this scale tap such mental processes as short- and long-term memory, divergent thinking, and deductive reasoning. Typical questions in this sections would ask the child to:

❑ recall pictured and named objects after they were presented for a brief time period, to point to 5 common objects and to name 4 additional objects shown to them on cards, to define words (i.e., What does shirt mean?),
❑ repeat words and sentences in their correct order,
❑ recall the highlights of a paragraph read by the examiner,
❑ name words that fall into each of 4 different categories within a time limit (i.e., Let's see how many different things to play with you can think of before I say *stop.*)
❑ provide opposites of key words in statements spoken by the evaluator (i.e., Milk is cold, but coffee is ===.)

❑ *Perceptual Performance Scale*—Consists of gamelike tasks which do not require a verbal response from the child. Assesses the child's reasoning ability, ability to imitate, classify objects, and organize materials visually through manipulation of materials. Typical questions in this section will require the child to:

❑ copy block structures built by the examiner;

❑ assemble cut-up puzzlelike pictures of common animals and foods;

❑ copy sequences of notes tapped by the examiner on a xylophone; demonstrate his or her knowledge of right and left;

❑ copy geometric designs;

❑ draw a picture of a child of the same sex;

❑ classify blocks on the basis of size, color, and shape.

❑ *Quantitative Scale*—Measures the child's facility with numbers and his or her understanding of quantitative words. Assesses the child's number aptitude. Typical questions in this section will require the child to:

❑ answer questions involving number information or basic arithmetical computation (i.e., How many hands do you have?; If you buy a toy for 85 cents, how much change should you get from a dollar bill?);

❑ repeat a series of digits in the order presented by the evaluator, and in reverse order;

❑ count and sort blocks into equal groups.

❑ *Memory Scale*—Assesses the child's short-term memory. Typical questions in this section will require the child to:—

❑ recall named and visually presented objects,

❑ imitate the examiner's performance on a 4 note xylophone,

❑ repeat words and sentences,

❑ recall the highlights of paragraphs read by the evaluator,

❑ repeat sequences of digits both forward and backward.

❑ *Motor scale*—Assesses the child's coordination as he/she performs a variety of gross and fine motor tasks. Typical tasks in this section would require the child to:

❑ walk backwards, stand on one foot, bounce a rubber ball, catch a beanbag, throw a beanbag through a hole in a target, copy simple movements, copy geometrical designs, and draw a picture of a same-sex child.

PERSONALITY INVENTORY FOR CHILDREN (PIC)

❑ Western Psychological Services, 1982

❑ Behavior rating scale completed by the child's parent or other primary caregiver. PIC is used as an objective, multidimensional measure of behavior, affect, ability, and family function. PIC questions are answered in a true/false format. PIC is available in a 131-item form, a 280-item form, and a 420-item form.

❑ Age Range: preschool ages through adolescence

❑ Major Components:

❑ PROFILE SCALES-/*Achievement*—Measures the extent to which the child's parent feels that he or she has limited academic ability; poor achievement; and/or poor adjustment characterized by impulsivity, limited concentration, and over- or under-assertiveness with peers. Typical questions in this category to rate are:

■ My child appears to be smarter than his or her peers

- My child has or had difficulty learning to read
- My child rarely picks up a book to read.

❐ *Intellectual Screening Scale*—Used to identify children whose difficulties may be related to impaired intellectual functioning, or specific cognitive deficits. Typical questions in this section to rate are:

- My child doesn't seem to pick up on things quickly;
- My child seems to take considerably longer than other children to complete homework assignments.

❐ *Developmental Scale*—Assesses the extent to which the child appears to have retarded development in motor coordination, poor school performance, and a lack of any special skills or abilities. Other factors in this scale reflect limited motivation to achieve in school, clumsiness and weakness, limited reading skills, and deficient pragmatic skills (i.e., counting change.) Typical questions in this category to rate are:

- My child falls down or bumps into things often
- My child participates in many clubs, sports, or activities
- My child has no hobbies

❐ *Somatic Concern Scale*—Used to assess various health-related variables: frequency and seriousness of somatic complaints and illness, adjustments to illness, appetite and eating habits, sleep patterns, energy and strength, headaches and stomachaches, as well as physical basis for symptoms. Typical questions to rate are:

- My child often complains of aches and pains

- My child throws up often.

❐ *Depression Scale*—Used to assess the extent to which the child's behavior problems appear to be the result of depression. Typical questions in this section to rate are

- My child never laughs
- My child tends to cry for no apparent reason

❐ *Family Relations Scale*—Assists in determining the role that family and parental factors play in the development of the child's behavior problems. Typical questions in this section to rate are:

- Our family rarely spends time together
- The child's parents rarely disagree on child rearing practices

❐ *Delinquency Scale*—Used as a diagnostic aid in the identification of delinquent children. Typical questions in this category to rate are

- My child has been in trouble for threatening adults
- My child rarely will listen to adults.

❐ *Withdrawal Scale*—Used to measure the degree to which the child's behavior is indicative of withdrawal from social contact. Typical questions to rate are:

- My child doesn't like to meet new people
- My child prefers to play alone

❐ *Anxiety Scale*—Used to measure various manifestations of anxiety in the child's behavior. Typical questions to rate are:

- The idea of starting new projects worries my child
- My child reacts very negatively to change.

❐ *Psychosis Scale*—Used to discriminate children

with psychotic symptoms from other disturbed children. Typical questions to rate are:

- My child has mannerisms that other kids think are strange
- My child has many irrational beliefs.

❏ *Hyperactive Scale*—Used to separate children with behavior characteristic of clinically diagnosed hyperactive children from other children. Typical questions to rate are:

- My child has difficulty sitting still through dinner
- My child has few friends

❏ *Social Skills Scale*—Used to identify children with possible problem with social skills. Typical questions to rate are:

- My child is rarely looked on as a leader with his or her peers
- My child is very charismatic

❏ FACTOR SCALES—*Undisciplined/Poor Self-Control*—Reflects hostility/emotional lability, impulsivity, and antisocial behavior. Composed of primarily the Adjustment, Delinquency, and Hyperactivity Scales.
❏ *Social Incompetence*—Reflects children with behaviors indicative of social withdrawal and depressive/somatic symptoms. Composed of the Adjustment, Depression, Withdrawal/ Anxiety, Psychosis, and Social Skills Scales.
❏ *Internalization/Somatic Symptoms*—Reflects children with depressive/somatic symptoms. Composed of the Somatic Concern, Depression, and Anxiety Scales.
❏ *Cognitive Development*—Designed to determine children with possible developmental delays, cognitive/attentional deficits, academic delay, and/or language/motor deficits. Composed of the Achievement, Intellectual Screening, Development, and Psychosis Scales.

PIERS-HARRIS CHILDREN'S SELF-CONCEPT SCALE (PIERS-HARRIS)

❏ Western Psychological Services, 1983
❏ Self-concept measure of children's feeling about themselves.
❏ Useful for screening for low self-concept.
❏ Provides scores which indicate high or low self concept in relation to their peers.
❏ A yes/no questionnaire filled out by the child.
❏ Age Range: Ages 8–18
❏ Major Components:

Six factors rate the student's self concepts in the following areas: Behavior, Intellectual and School Status, Physical Appearance and Attributes, Anxiety, Popularity, and Happiness and Satisfaction. A high score represents a high self-concept in the stated area while a low score reflects a low self-concept in the area. Typical questions to rate are: I am a leader. Yes/No; or I feel comfortable in a bathing suit. Yes/No.

ROBERTS APPERCEPTION TEST FOR CHILDREN (RAT-C)

❏ Western Psychological Services, 1982
❏ A thematic approach to the personality assessment of children.
❏ Used to assess children's perceptions of interpersonal situations, including their thoughts, concerns, conflicts, and coping styles.
❏ Age Range: 6 years through 15 years
❏ Major Components:

The RAT-C is made up of 27 pictured cards depicting parental disagreement, parental affection, aggression situations, and school and peer relationships. The child is required to create a story about the picture, including what led up to the depicted scene and how the story ends.

The RATC yields 5 Clinical Scales which represent the child's feelings about the self or the environment. They include:

❏ *Anxiety* (a measure of guilt, remorse, apprehension, self doubt, and the themes of illness and death)
❏ *Aggression* (a measure of physical or verbal expressions of anger)
❏ *Depression* (designed to measure themes of sadness, despair, and/or physical symptoms related to depression)
❏ *Rejection* (measures themes involving separation and feelings of being left out, jealousy, and discrimination)
❏ *Unresolved*

This technique also yields Adaptive Scales yielding information about the child's Reliance on Others, Support to Others, Support of the Child/Self-Sufficiency/Maturity, Limit Setting by Authority Figures, Problem Identification, and Resolution of Problems Presented Within the Stories. In addition to adaptive and clinical scales, critical indicators such as atypical responses, maladaptive outcomes, and card rejections or refusals are also included in the scoring system. An Interpersonal Matrix (interactions with significant others), Ego Functioning Index, Aggression Index (the child's ability to deal with situations needing some kind of aggressive response), and Levels of Projection Scale (cognitive and ego development) can also be obtained.

RORSCHACH INKBLOT TECHNIQUE

❏ Verlag HansHuber Publishers, 1921, 1948
❏ Projective personality assessment device.
❏ The student is asked to look at a series of 10 inkblots and tell the evaluator what the blot looks like or reminds them of.
❏ Age Range: Can be used with any child old enough to produce verbal responses, but generally used with ages 5 through adult.
❏ Major Components:

The manner in which the child responds to this test represents how the child sees and responds to other experiences they have. That is, interpreting the inkblot is a problem-solving task, and children try to solve it using the same cognitive, perceptual, and personality traits they would use when faced with decisions they have to make in school or outside life every day. If we can understand those psychological traits used most often to make the kinds of decisions described above, then we can know more about the disposition, attitude, and emotions the child uses; all of which can help explain why the child has behaved the way she has, and can help predict how she might act in certain situations.

In addition, results can give insight into possible adjustment difficulties, dispositions, emotional and attitudinal states, how people feel about important figures in their lives, self-image, or individual problem solving approach. The Rorschach can also be used as a guide to identify the development of psychological problems such as schizophrenia, depression, anxiety-withdrawal, and conduct disorder.

SELF-DESCRIPTION QUESTIONNAIRE (SDQ)

❏ The Psychological Corporation, 1988
❏ Measure of the student's self-concept in a number of areas.
❏ The student rates questions on the degree to which it pertains to themselves (i.e., false,

mostly false, sometimes false/sometimes true, mostly true, true).

❏ Can be administered individually or in groups

❏ Age Range: The SDQ I is for children in Grades 4 through 6 (ages 8 through 12); SDQ II is normed for children in early adolescence; SDQ III is normed for students in late adolescence.

❏ Major Components:

Provides a measure of the student's self concept in general (General-Self Scale), as well as in the following areas: Physical Ability, Physical Appearance, Peer Relations, Parent Relations, Reading, Mathematics, and General-School.

Typical questions will ask the student:

❏ I enjoy doing math problems in school
❏ I hate the way I look
❏ I am usually one of the first kids chosen for teams

SENTENCE COMPLETION TECHNIQUES (INCOMPLETE SENTENCE BLANKS)

❏ Personality and Attitude Assessment
❏ Age Range: Appropriate for children, adolescents, and adults
❏ Major Components:

The Incomplete Sentence Blanks consists of a number of incomplete sentence stems which an individual completes either orally or in writing. Responses to these sentence stems are voluntary and are limited only to the range of attitudes and feelings that they elicit from within the individual. The evaluator qualitatively analyzes the responses to determine attitudes, personality styles and dynamics, and overall psychological adjustment. Using this method, the evaluator gathers clinical impressions about the personality characteristics of a subject, integrating them with other information generated through interviews, other projective instruments, and behavioral observations.

Typical examples include: When I am around other kids I feel——————; School is——————; or When people argue with me I feel——————.

STANFORD BINET INTELLIGENCE SCALE-FOURTH EDITION (SB:FE)

❏ Riverside Publishing Company, 1986
❏ Intelligence
❏ Individually administered
❏ Age Range: 2 years 0 months to 23 years 11 months
❏ Major Components:

❏ *Test Composite*—Represents overall level of intellectual functioning

❏ *Verbal Reasoning*—Assesses the student's level of intelligence by assessing verbal skills, vocabulary, and verbal comprehension. Typical questions in this section include (at younger age levels): Verbally identifying pictures, explaining why pictures presented are absurd (i.e, a man driving while wearing a blindfold), and explaining why something is done (i.e, "Why is it important to look both ways before crossing the street?"). Typical questions at older levels include: asking for word definitions, explaining why more complex actions are done, and explaining why three verbally presented items are alike and why the fourth is different (i.e., gull, crow, owl—not penguin. . . . first three fly; last doesn't).

❏ *Abstract/Visual Reasoning*—Assesses the student's level of intelligence using nonverbal problem solving and reasoning questions.

Questions in this section resemble puzzles and require students to complete such tasks as assembling solid and striped blocks in a fashion to correctly copy a pictorial design presented to them, copy designs, solve matrix problems, and correctly visualize how pieces of folded paper with designs cut into them with scissors would look if opened.

❏ *Quantitative Reasoning*—Assesses the student's level of intellectual functioning using math skills, computations, and reasoning skills. Typical questions in this section would ask a participant to count, answer mathematical word problems presented orally, correctly complete a given series of numbers (i.e., 4, 9, 16, 25, 36,———————), and build a valid mathematical equation using a presented sequence of numbers and math symbols (i.e., 2, 2, 8, 4, ×, +, = correctly builds the equation $2 \times 2 + 4 = 8$).

❏ *Short-Term Memory*—Assesses the child's intellectual functioning using tasks that require the ability to store information in the immediate situation and then retrieve it within a few seconds. Typical questions in this section would require the student to remember the correct sequence of beads presented in a picture and subsequently build a correct copy of the picture from memory using actual beads, to repeat verbatim a series of verbally presented numbers, and to remember the correct sequence of a series of pictures.

TEST OF NONVERBAL INTELLIGENCE (TONI-2)

❏ Pro-Ed, 1990
❏ Intelligence (in the area of problem solving)

Requires no verbal response. No speaking, reading, or writing is required; therefore, this test is useful with those unable to read or write or who have impaired language abilities. This measure is considered to be useful in screening the intellectual functioning of students in instances when it is unwise or not feasible to use a verbal measure.

❏ Individually administered; can be group administered
❏ Age Range: 5 years 0 months through 85 years 11 months
❏ Major Components:

TONI is language-free and administered in pantomime. All TONI items require test-takers to solve problems by identifying relationships among abstract figures. The student must examine the differences and similarities among the figures in the set and in the response alternatives, identify the rule that is operating among the figures, and, on the basis of that rule, select the correct response. At this time, the student is required to point to the one response among several alternatives that best fits a missing part in a pattern or matrix. The symbols depicted in the TONI include one or more characteristics of shape, position, direction or rotation, contiguity, shading, size or length, movement, and pattern within the figure.

TONI Quotients—Represent the student's overall level of intellectual functioning as assessed by this measure. (Similar to the IQ on other intelligence tests.)

TEST OF WRITTEN LANGUAGE— REVISED (TOWL-2)

❏ Pro-Ed, 1988
❏ Achievement—used to identify students with writing difficulties, to determine strengths/weaknesses of individual students, and to evaluate student progress
❏ Individually (usually) or group administered

□ Age Range: 7 years 6 months to 17 years 11 months
□ Major Components:

1 *Overall Written Language*—assesses the overall writing ability of the student
2 *Contrived Writing*—Assesses the student's ability to write under structured conditions. Assesses areas such as:

□ vocabulary
□ spelling
□ punctuation/capitalization
□ grammar
□ ability to rewrite illogical sentences in a logical fashion (i.e., change "I like to walk my fish after dinner" to "I like to walk my dog . . . ")

3 *Spontaneous Writing*—assesses the student's ability to write a story using a picture as a "story starter" or prompt; the student's writing is judged incorporating areas such as spelling, grammar, vocabulary, punctuation, capitalization and complexity of the story

THEMATIC APPERCEPTION TEST (TAT)

□ Harvard University Press, 1943, 1971
□ Projective measure of the student's personality.
□ Used to attempt to discover ideas about a person's personality functioning—how they view, feel about, and react to situations that they have encountered or might face in life.
□ Individually Administered
□ Age Range: applicable for children, adolescents, or adults
□ Major Components:

The TAT is composed of 31 cards with drawings on them that primarily show people in implied actions or human interactions. These cards can be organized to create sets particularly for male and female children, adolescents, and adults. In general, approximately 10 cards are presented to a person. Each individual's spontaneously verbalized stories to the cards are recorded word for word as they are given, with scoring and interpretation based on the content, structure, and tone of these stories. An inquiry or a series of clarifying questions is completed after each TAT story to generate additional data which may facilitate a more complete analysis or understanding of the child.

WECHSLER INDIVIDUAL ACHIEVEMENT TEST (WIAT)

□ The Psychological Corporation, 1992
□ Achievement
□ Individually Administered
□ Age Range: 5 years 0 months through 19 years 11 months
□ Major Components:

□ *Total Composite*—Assesses the student's overall level of academic achievement encompassing the Reading, Math, Language, and Writing Composites.
□ *Reading Composite*—Assesses the student's overall achievement in reading. Typical questions in this section will ask the student to point or respond to printed words and pictures in response to evaluator's questions; to read a series of printed passages and correctly respond orally to the evaluator's queries; and to make inferences about read passages.
□ *Mathematics Composite*—Assesses the student's overall achievement in mathematics. Typical questions in this section will ask the student to

correctly answer questions after reading charts and graphs; answer questions requiring math reasoning in every day activities; and to solve written problems with paper and pencil.

❏ *Language Composite*—Assesses the student's ability in the areas of listening comprehension and oral expression. Typical questions in this section ask the student to correctly identify pictures that correspond to orally presented words, answer correctly questions about orally presented stories accompanied by pictures, express words, describe pictured scenes, give directions and explain steps to everyday processes—such as baking a cake.

❏ *Writing Composite*—Assesses the student's writing skills. The student is given a picture to write a story about, while the evaluator assesses such skills as development and organization of ideas, capitalization, and punctuation.

WECHSLER INTELLIGENCE SCALE FOR CHILDREN—THIRD EDITION (WISC-III)

❏ The Psychological Corporation, 1991
❏ Intelligence
❏ Individually administered
❏ Age Range: 6 years 0 months to 16 years 11 months
❏ Major Components:

❏ *Full-Scale IQ*—Assesses the student's overall level of intellectual functioning
❏ *Verbal IQ*—Assesses the student's level of functioning in areas with a scholastic base and/or generally acquired information. Questions require a verbal response from the student. Components of this section include:

❏ assessing factual knowledge such as "Which fast food franchise is represented by a symbol of a colonel?";

❏ assessing the student's ability to understand specific customs/mores such as "Why is it important to wear boots after a large snowfall?";

❏ asking the student to identify similarities in superficially unrelated stimuli such as "In what ways are a scale and a ruler alike?" (i.e., they both measure something);

❏ assessing the student's ability to solve verbally presented arithmetic problems such as "Bill had 12 candies. He gives 2 to Mary and 3 to Jack. How many candies does he have left?";

❏ assessing the student's ability to define words such as "What is a pig? "What does *concentrate* mean?";

❏ assessing immediate recall of orally presented digits

❏ *Performance IQ*—Assesses the students intelligence using a variety of mostly manipulative or puzzlelike tests requiring no verbal response by the child. Components of this section determine:

❏ ability to identify missing parts of pictures (i.e., a picture of a mouse missing whiskers),

❏ ability to sequence a set of comics-like cards to produce a logically correct story,

❏ ability to manipulate a set of striped/solid blocks to copy a visually presented design,

❏ ability to put together puzzles to produce complete objects,

❏ ability to associate certain symbols with others and to copy them on paper with time constraints,

❏ ability to trace a path through progressively more difficult mazes.

WECHSLER PRESCHOOL AND PRIMARY SCALE OF INTELLIGENCE–REVISED (WPPSI–R)

❐ The Psychological Corporation, 1989
❐ Intelligence
❐ Individually Administered
❐ Age Range: 2 years 11 months to 7 years 3 months
❐ Major Components:

❐ *Full-Scale IQ*—Assesses the child's overall level of intellectual ability
❐ *Verbal IQ*—Assesses the child's intellectual ability in terms of verbal skills. Such questions require a spoken response, and typical questions in this section would ask the child to:

- answer questions about events or objects in the environment (i.e., What are cars made of?),
- express his or her understanding of reasons for actions and the consequences of events (i.e., Why do we wear clothes?),
- demonstrate basic counting and simple arithmetic skills (i.e., counting blocks/How many are three balls plus one ball?),
- name a pictured object or provide verbal definitions for orally presented words (i.e., What does *triple* mean?),
- demonstrate an understanding of how items are similar by either pointing to an object that is similar to those previously pictured or by completing a verbally presented sentence that reflects a similarity (i.e., You eat a hamburger and you also eat a————); or to explain how two verbally presented ojects or events are alike (i.e., How are a cake and a pie alike?),
- repeat verbatim a sentence read aloud by the examiner (i.e. Jan would like a new doll and a book.)

❐ *Performance IQ*: Assesses the child's intelligence using reasoning and problem solving tasks that do not require a verbal response. Typical questions in this section would require the child to:

- correctly put together pieces of puzzle,
- look at a simple design and to point to one exactly like it from an array of four designs,
- draw a geometric figure from a printed model,
- reproduce patterns with flat 2-colored blocks within a time limit when shown a picture of a design,
- solve paper and pencil mazes of increasing difficulty under time constraints,
- identify missing parts of pictures of common objects or events (i.e., a book with no words on the pages),
- correctly match pegs of different colors in holes within a time constraint.

WIDE-RANGE ACHIEVEMENT TEST-THIRD EDITION (WRAT-3)

Jastak Publishing, 1993
❐ Achievement—Used to measure the codes necessary to learn the basic skills of reading, spelling, and arithmetic.
❐ Individually administered
❐ Age Range: 5 years to 75 years
❐ Major Components:

❐ *Reading*—Assesses the student's skills in letter recognition, letter naming, and pronunciation of words in isolation. Typical questions in this section will ask the student to name letters of the alphabet and to read words such as and, some, and epidemic.

❐ *Spelling*—Assesses the student's skills in copying marks onto paper, writing one's name, and writing single words from dictation. Examples of dictated words include: or, square, and lamination.

❐ *Arithmetic*—Assesses the student's skills in counting, reading numerals, solving orally presented problems, and performing written computation of arithmetic problems. Examples of arithmetic problems include: How many are 5 pennies and 2 pennies?; 10 + 12 = ?; 127 × 53 = ?).

WOODCOCK JOHNSON TESTS OF COGNITIVE ABILITY—REVISED (WJ-R COG)

❐ DLM Teaching Resources, 1989
❐ Used to measure cognitive ability, scholastic aptitudes, and achievement.
❐ Individually administered
❐ Age Range: 2 years–79 years
❐ Major Components:

❐ *Broad Cognitive Ability*—assesses the overall level of the child's cognitive ability
❐ *Cognitive Factors*—assesses underlying skills important for scholastic achievement including memory, processing speed, auditory & visual processing, general knowledge & comprehension, and reasoning ability. The student may be asked to draw inferences from given material, recognize rotations/reversals of visually presented figures, find hidden figures in pictures, work as quickly as possible under distracting conditions, store information in the immediate situation and then retrieve it within a few seconds, and to recall previously learned information.

❐ *Differential Abilities*—assesses scholastic aptitudes. Includes such areas as oral language, reading, math, written language, and general knowledge.

WOODCOCK JOHNSON TESTS OF ACHIEVEMENT— REVISED (WJ-R ACH)

❐ DLM Teaching Resources, 1989
❐ Academic Achievement
❐ Individually administered
❐ Age Range: 2 years–79 years
❐ Major Components:

❐ *Reading*—assesses the student's reading and comprehension skills
❐ *Math*—assesses the student's ability to comprehend quantitative concepts/relationships and to manipulate numerical symbols
❐ *Written Language*—assesses the student's basic writing skills in areas such as written expression, punctuation, spelling, word usage, and handwriting
❐ *Broad Knowledge*—assesses the student's knowledge in content areas such as science, social studies, and the humanities (i.e., literature, the arts)
❐ *Oral Language Skills*—assesses the student's oral language abilities
❐ *Skills*—assesses student's abilities to identify letters and words, assesses abilities on dictation tests
❐ *Intra-Achievement Discrepancy*—a comparison of each of the above components with the others to determine a pattern of the student's individual strengths/weaknesses

Sources for **Solve Your Child's**
School-Related Problems are all publications of:

The National Association of School Psychologists
4340 East West Highway, #402
Bethesda, MD 20814
(301)657-0270

Christenson, S. L. and Conoley, J. C. editors. *Home-School Collaboration: Enhancing Children's Academic and Social Competence.* 1992.

Graden, J., Zins, J. and Curtis, M. editors. *Alternative Educational Delivery Systems: Enhancing Educational Options for All Students.* 1988.

*Miller, Y. and Cherry, J. *Kids On The Move: Meeting Their Needs.* 1992.

*NASP. *Helping Children Grow Up In The 90's: A Resource Book for Parents and Teachers.* 1992.

*NASP. *Should My Child Repeat A Grade?* 1992. Brochure.

*NASP. *Student Grade Retention: A Resource Manual for Parents and Educators.* 1991.

Stoner, G., Shinn, M.R., and Walker, H. M. editors. *Interventions for Achievement and Behavior Problems.* 1991.

Thomas, A. and Grimes, J. editors. *Best Practices in School Psychology, II.* 1990.

Thomas, A. and Grimes, J. editors. *Children's Needs: Psychological Perspectives.* 1987.

Wise, P. S. *Better Parent Conferences.* 1986.

*These titles are specifically written for parents and teachers.

INDEX

Note: Page numbers in **boldface** refer to illustrations; page numbers followed by t refer to tables.

Learned helplessness. *See* Dependency.
Learning
  skills for, 230t
  stages of, 225–26
Learning disabilities, 143–48
  evaluation of, 147
  help with, 145–48
  reasons for, 143–44
  school entry and, 25–26, 117 .
  symptoms of, 144–45
Least restrictive environment, 22
Linguistics, 187
Listening, active, 51
Lying, 149–54
  help for, 150–54
  kinds of, 149–51
  signs of, 150

M

Mapping stories, 140, **142**
Math anxiety, 193
McCarthy Scales of Children's Abilities, 261–62
Megavitamin therapy, 39
Merenda, Daniel W., 245
Mitchell, Peter, 244
Motivation, 155–59
  help with, 157–58
  problems with, 156
  reasons for, 155–56
  rewards for, 241–43
Motor tics, 167, 168–69t
Mourning, 248–49
Moving, 160–66
  adjustment to, 160–61
  checklist for, 164–65
  help with, 162–66
  problems with, 162
  stress with, 162

N

NAEYC. *See* National Association for the Education of Young Children.
Nail biting, 167, 168–69t
  case study on, 182

National Association for the Education of Young Children (NAEYC), 244
National Association of Partners in Education, 244–45
National Association of School Psychologists, 272
National Black Child Development Institute, 245
National Coalition for Parent Involvement in Education (NCPIE), 245
National Coalition of Parents, 245
National Committee for Citizens in Education, 245
National Council of La Raza (NCLR), 245
National Federation for the Blind, 239
National Information Center for Children and Youth with Handicaps (NICCYH), 245–46
National Parent Center, 245
Natural disasters, 249–50
NCLR. *See* National Council of La Raza.
NCPIE. *See* National Coalition for Parent Involvement in Education.
Nervous habits, 167–72, 168–69t. *See also* Anxiety *and* Stress.
  case studies of, 170, 172
  causes of, 168
  evaluation of, 168–69
  help for, 169–72
Neurofeedback, 39
NICCYH. *See* National Information Center for Children and Youth with Handicaps.
Norm-referenced tests, 29
No to drugs, 100
Nunn, R.G., 169
Nurse's role, 6

O

Ocular-motor training, 39
Optometrics, 39
Organizational skills, 173–79
  help with, 175–79
  for homework, 140
  problems with, 174–75
Orthomolecular therapy, 39